Working *the*
Gray Zone

ALSO BY CHARLES G. OAKES

Mentoring for an Audience of One
Foundations of Practical Gerontology
The Walking Patient and the Health Care Crisis

Working *the* Gray Zone

A Call for Proactive Ministry by and with Older Adults

CHARLES G. OAKES

PROVIDENCE HOUSE PUBLISHERS
Franklin, Tennessee

Printed in the United States of America

04   03   02   01   00   1   2   3   4   5

Library of Congress Catalog Card Number: 00-109517

ISBN: 1-57736-208-X

Cover photograph by Gary Bozeman

Cover design by Gary Bozeman and Elaine Kernea Wilson

All scripture quotations, unless otherwise indicated, are taken from the New American Standard Bible. Copyright © 1960, 1962, 1963, 1968, 1971, 1972, 1973, 1975, 1977 by The Lockman Foundation.

PROVIDENCE HOUSE PUBLISHERS
238 Seaboard Lane • Franklin, Tennessee 37067
800-321-5692
www.providencehouse.com

To John, Sally, and Allison,
whose faithful care and encouragement
promoted meaning and purpose in the lives of
seven parents, uncles, and aunts—all nearing
or well beyond ninety years of age—
until the day they, like Jacob, blessed their offspring,
pulled the blanket over their heads,
and went home to their Father.

CONTENTS

FOREWORD

FROM THE STANDPOINT OF THE SOCIAL SCIENCES THAT NORMALLY INFORM STUDIES OF AGING, THE NEWS ABOUT GROWING OLD IS "ALL BAD." *BIOLOGICAL AGING* IS INEVITABLY VIEWED AS DECLINE. HERE THE attention is upon nearness to death in relation to the life span. *Psychological aging* refers to the adaptive capacity of an individual viewed in terms of behavior. Here decline is said to be "incremental," suggesting that there are plateaus that interrupt the overall decline. *Social aging* deals with the habits and roles of individuals in relation to the expectations of various social groups.

These and other constructs from the sciences are extremely useful. Such constructs were helpful in relating to my parents during the years preceding their death, which were marked by weakness, injury, cancer, heart disease, and dementia. Thus it was because of a felt need to "honor my father and mother" that I took a university course in gerontology.

I learned a great deal that helped me function more adequately as a caregiver. For example, I learned the necessity of listening more carefully to older people. This was a very simple learning, but oh so fruitful. I also learned to allow more time for my eighty-some year-old parents to process information. Sometimes that information was drawn from reading the Psalms, but other times it had to do with interpreting effects of new prescriptions. Then too, familiarity with certain findings relative to social aging helped me respond more effectively to my mother's special needs. With dramatic results I was able to draw a small number of her closest friends from hundreds of miles away into a supportive telephone network during the last days of her life. These octogenarians continued the network in my support even after she passed from this world.

Even the basic information from the gerontology course referred to above would have been extremely helpful in my earlier years as pastor. Three of my appointments were to churches blessed with a high percentage of older members. I worked hard at relating to them. Nor did I shy away from spending time with them during the weeks and months leading to the day when eventually I stood with their families at a gravesite. Still, I longed to have had a more successful ministry with these beautiful Christians as they crossed the threshold into eternity. I was instinctively aware that my ministry was shot through with an undue expectation of decline.

Of course *entropy*, or decline, is a core feature of this world. In recent years though, some perceptive scientists and futurists have remarked upon the potential in the Christian message to reverse certain aspects of entropy. Any such a potential, if true, would certainly foster hope. That hope, if properly understood and incorporated into the Christian ministry, might well ameliorate the secular pessimism that is little diminished within the church.

Thus a reading of *Working the Gray Zone* by Charles G. Oakes came as a pleasant surprise. *Working the Gray Zone* is a confirmation of my growing conviction that the church has more resources at its disposal than most of us have been willing to incorporate into our ministry. To begin with, even though he is a social scientist by training, Oakes does not subscribe to the cynicism that finds roots in the scientific disciplines which inform his understanding of gerontology. Neither does he discount the findings of the social sciences. Rather, he proceeds by offering his view that the factors that foster hope are reserved for "righteous older believers." He boldly states: "Not all older people are righteous, and we do well not to idolize or idealize all older people." Given the milieu in which we live, this is indeed a radical statement. As I first reflected upon the above sentence, I thought: "Here is a gerontologist who at least takes the Christian message seriously." Still, I wondered whether Oakes could carry his proposed dichotomy to a successful conclusion. He had gained my attention, but I feared he would not devote the serious attention to those biblical and theological foundations necessary to support such a proposal.

Happily, Oakes devotes eight of his fourteen chapters to develop just such a foundation. These eight chapters comprise part 1, entitled "A Systematic Theology of Advancing Years." Briefly, they provide a satisfying underpinning for his argument that the elderly have a biblically founded role to play in bringing God's will to pass in every generation. "The old and their wisdom are," he states, "foundational for social stability and continuity." The legacy of the Christian of advancing years is to have "declared God's glory throughout the earth."

Oakes appeals to such passages as Ephesians 4:14-24 in support of his thesis that older Christians are to leave behind ineffective patterns of thought and action. Then they are to move positively against the prevailing entropy of this world by being continually renewed in the way they think so as to bring the "likeness of God" into the very environment of this world. So armed, the older Christian will be able to effect (through such processes as mentoring) life-renewing change in all areas of human relationships, but especially within the family. Of course, Oakes states, "There is no guarantee that one's age will be a measure of spiritual maturity, but the probability of finding it in the older is greater than finding it in the younger."

In part 2, Oakes' thrust is to describe a practical theology of church ministry with older adults based upon the principles outlined earlier. He quotes Oliver Wendell Holmes with approval: "Most people go to their graves with their best music still in them." The obvious suggestion is that a core challenge of church ministry is to bring, and sustain, *purpose* in and through the everyday life of individuals. Perhaps the most important passage in this part of *Working the Gray Zone* focuses on a theologically based vision for the church to minister with integrity by enabling "older adults to live out their God-given purposes." To accomplish this vision requires that the church provide appropriate information and assistance in accessing available financial and medical assistance along with appropriate architecture and space. The awakened church may require a "reengineered" set of attitudes and operations to enable its older members to find ways to contribute their wisdom, leadership, and capacity to mentor. Oakes envisions the possibility of older believers arriving at a moment in time when they can truthfully say:

"My needs are met. This is what I have been waiting for. My seventy (or eighty or more) years now have meaning; I have been granted a new defining moment."

The final part of *Working the Gray Zone* is a helpful catalogue of principles, practical suggestions, and paradigms for empowering, motivating and releasing seniors into an extensive variety of ministry activities both within and without the institutional church.

Just days ago I wrote a letter of intention to retire from the institution where I have been teaching for more than two decades. So it has been a kind of serendipity for me to have had the opportunity of reading *Working the Gray Zone*. I am sorry that I did not have access to it years earlier. Then I could have employed these principles in a number of settings along the way both as a pastor and as seminary professor. Perhaps a bit selfishly, I am joyful at the prospect of others having *Working the Gray Zone* as a resource. You see, they may have occasion to minister to me in the coming years as I work my way through the gray zone.

Harold W. Burgess
Wilmore, Kentucky
Fall, 2000

PREFACE & ACKNOWLEDGMENTS

THE BIBLE CARRIES A PROPHETIC MESSAGE ABOUT GROWING AND BEING OLD. ITS WRITERS, THEREFORE, WOULD NOT HAVE CARED WHETHER THE LONG-HELD SOCIOLOGICAL SIMPLICITIES AND cultural stereotypes were those of secular institutions that flipped a coin in choosing one convenient philosophy or another, or whether they found their basis in the institutional church. As it turns out, many of the contemporary church's views on aging and the elderly aren't altogether biblical anyway, but have been derived from secular philosophies, policies, and practices. This makes our task even harder. *Working the Gray Zone* is not merely an effort to straighten out bad doctrine, but to challenge and excise beliefs that don't belong in the Christian church at all. This is accomplished by presenting a timely and more comprehensive picture of where older adults—those of the Gray Zone—fit into God's economy. The last systematic theology of aging was written a quarter of a century ago, and Christians need to be reminded that a revitalized theology still exists.

The Bible, for the most part, is pretty forward-looking and promising in its handling of righteous older believers. Not all older people are righteous, and we do well not to idolize or idealize all older people. The Bible paints a profile of the elderly just as it does for other groups, and I have identified universal principles that are as applicable today as they were several thousand years ago. When placed in logical order, these principles cause two things to happen. First, they become what we call a systematic theology: a comprehensive compilation of relevant Scripture addressing some particular subject, in the present case a systematic theology of the older adult. This is the emphasis of part I.

The same principles also function as a microscope for examining and reassessing the modern church's practical applications of ethics, policies, and programs for those in the Gray Zone. These practical theologies are the subject of parts 2 and 3.

Part 2 deals with the institutional church's ministry in behalf of older members. If this practical theology is to be biblically accurate, then it must derive from the cohesive principles found in part 1. Unfortunately, the church's programs often leave out what should be included and include things that might better be left out. I come from a forty-year career as a gerontologist in the secular marketplace; I have been trained in the Scriptures for more than half a century and hope I can tell the difference between man's way and God's way. This certainly applies to policies and programs for older adults. The institutional church in many ways has become a reflection of the larger society in which it exists. Therefore, I have attempted to discern what is biblically authentic for the institutional church and its members so that we can eat the corn and spit out the gravel.

Part 3 also derives from part 1 and is a practical theology describing the capabilities of those in the Gray Zone who are uniquely equipped to minister in, to, and out from the church. Can we agree the church has been called as steward over what God has put on its platter? If so, then it must be committed to optimizing the capabilities of all its members. No one can talk about a viable interdependent body of Christ and still have idle, isolated members passively filling up the pews. The contrast to this is a church that sits on a veritable gold mine of yet-to-be-tapped resources among its older adults. Some of their skills, talents, and experiences can be used to enrich the church's programs. Many older adults have the precise skills and experience to remove the barriers preventing some of their peers from living purpose-driven lives. Others engage in challenging, innovative tasks quite sufficient to meet the adventure needs of any age group.

Several friends suggested I waited until I was in my late sixties to write this book, implying in concert with the book's theme that this was a Gray Zone autobiography. Nonsense! The vision for this book was born forty years ago when I was a graduate research associate for the first-ever nationwide study of the non-institutionalized elderly. That experience was a springboard to work thereafter as a gerontologist and behavioral scientist, and I have benefited from all those years in the field where the validity of the biblical principles shared here played out over and over again among older people. Truth was born in the findings of that study, but I nevertheless had a few insights of my own. I am careful to point out that over the past forty years I have became more of a forecaster than a prophet. Any deficiencies in this book, then, are more those of an inaccurate forecaster than of a false prophet!

The nationwide research that launched my career inquired of a remarkable generation of Americans. The principal investigators of the study were James W. Wiggins and Helmut Schoeck, and the study's findings were titled *Profile of the Aging, USA*. Teddy Roosevelt became the childhood hero of that generation during the Spanish American War of 1898. Many were still too young to fight in the First World War, but mourned for fathers, older brothers, and uncles killed in Europe. The same generation suffered, was debilitated from, and survived the Great Depression. They fought in the Second World War, and as an insulting afterthought, were recalled for the Korean Conflict—all before retirement. This was indeed a remarkable generation. It also was the first generation to have Medicare, which was enacted in 1966.

Profile of the Aging, USA, described people with fortitude, resiliency, resourcefulness, self-sufficiency, and self-sacrifice. They were positive about the future and most certainly not as desperate as policy makers of the day made them out to be. Religious people were not singled out for special attention in the study. Its subjects represented a cross section of America's elderly population. I read with fascination vignettes describing lifestyles of resourceful oldsters ranging into their late eighties. Modern gerontologists refer to these as the "frail elderly." Being a man of faith, I wonder if pre-Christian Israelites and early Christians would have been good models for a more positive picture than the population at large. Would oldsters with a strong biblical orientation have held to a higher standard? This leads us to chapter 1.

The following words by Dr. Wiggins were part of his welcome address to the presenters and conferees of the first South Carolina Statewide Conference on Aging in 1967:

You are not here . . . to meet present or prospective personal needs. I believe that you share in some way my own experience of some years ago. As I sat in church on Sunday morning, my mind wandered from the sermon to the pew in which I was sitting. Suddenly I was aware that an earlier generation had built that church, placed the pew—had given me a setting, with comfort, to which I had not contributed. Figuratively, I was still sitting in the lap of an older generation.

Acknowledgments are intended to recognize our figurative personal pews and the shoulders of the giants on which we stand. Professor James Wiggins and Herr Professor Helmut Schoeck, now both deceased, allowed me to participate in the first nationwide study of the non-institutionalized elderly, completed in the late 1950s. In their day, they swam against the tide of popular opinion regarding the elderly. Despite academe's rejection of their prognostications, particularly about the eventual costliness of the federal Medicare program based on a study of over fifty thousand research subjects, today, in retrospect, they should be considered laser-accurate prophets. From these, I learned that truth will not always be popular, but it can be prophetic.

Three other scholars, all of the University of California-Berkeley, deserve special mention for the impact they had on my life and for the principles that continue to be carried over into this book. I remember these scholars today as clearly as when I sat at their feet. Herbert Blumer, as giant a man as any linebacker, said: "Always establish the soundness of your adversary's premises before you debate him." Erving Goffman, who directed my master's thesis, encouraged me to personally experience the life of those whose behavior I wished to study. And Tomatsu Shibutani, whose warmth and encouragement ever will be remembered, said: "Truth is never compartmentalized or fragmented; it is a complex synthesis of many layers of fact, and only the noble will be driven to discover the intricate complex interweaving of man's nature." The counsel of these men helped guide the evolution of this book.

P A R T 1

A SYSTEMATIC THEOLOGY OF
ADVANCING YEARS

CHAPTER ONE

Journey through Time

IMAGINE THAT WE ARE STANDING ON A REVOLVING PLATFORM. ON THE SAME PLATFORM IS A TELESCOPE. WE ROTATE THE TELESCOPE TO DUE EAST, AND IT ENABLES US TO SEE GRAND AND WONDERFUL EVENTS THAT took place in the past. We rotate 180 degrees to the west and we see, as if following the setting sun, events forecasted for the future. The exercise provides our limited perceptions the ability to conceive an idea of divine purpose soaring through time. The philosophers describe what we have just done as "teleology," or the study of final causes. The events captured in time from the east help explain what we see all around us right now in the present, and we exclaim, "Aha! That sure makes sense." And what we see now helps make sense of future events shrouded in the myriad pastels of clouds reflecting a brilliant magenta sun.

A perspective of things past, present, and future helps in our understanding of a theology of advancing years. And so in this first chapter, I want to take a brush and paint with broad strokes a historical plan, leaving the more detailed strokes of the picture to later chapters. I begin with a view of the present, explain it by looking back in time, and lastly view where all this is taking us.

METAPHOR: LIVING IN THE PRESENT

The Israeli King David began his career as a lowly shepherd, and the poems and songs he composed while herding on the

Palestinian steppes have given us hundreds of metaphors with which to understand how he lived day-in and day-out, and how he thought and understood. Metaphor is a linguistic device that is a veiled comparison. Understanding the historical and cultural setting allows us to get behind the veil and accurately interpret what the writer had in mind. Two metaphors describe David's musings about the elderly. He praised the Father who, in behalf of those in the Gray Zone, satisfied their years with good things, so that their youth was renewed like the eagle (Ps. 103:3–5). In addition to the eagle, David also used the exalted horn to describe the elderly. Imagine yourself watching older adults, some in a shopping mall, another in the woodshop making toys for grandchildren, and still another helping a disabled friend, or sitting in the midst of family at a festive holiday table. As you watch, think "eagle" and "exalted horn."

The Eagle

The eagle says something about God's forward-looking wisdom and His plans for older saints. He is the Master of metaphor, after all, never wasting a word! The golden and imperial eagles were native to Palestine, held in high honor, and used in the Bible as prophetic symbols (see Ezek. 1:10; 10:14; Rev. 4:7). It long has been held that even the oldest of eagles, living well into their twenties, renewed their strength after molting and took on the appearance of a younger bird.[1] The psalmist describes "youth renewed like that of the eagle," no doubt recognizing then, as now, that the annual molt and replacement of feathers leads even the oldest of birds to take on the appearance of younger birds. The eagle aptly describes many older Christians who, well into their seventies and eighties, shed their depression, replace dull eyes with bright and excited ones, renew their hope, calling, and purposes in God, and accept new challenges with a spring in their step, using the accumulated knowledge of past years. The more modern gerontologists and geriatricians (physicians specializing in health care of the old) find out about the elderly, the more

> *The eagle aptly describes many older Christians who . . . renew their hope, calling, and purposes in God, and accept new challenges . . . using the accumulated knowledge of past years.*

impressed they are with the capacity of older people to rejuvenate under proper conditions. Therefore, the eagle as a metaphor is an apt comparison.

Eagles are majestic birds with keen eyesight. Solomon marveled at how they stayed aloft for hours and efficiently used the air currents as a source of energy (Prov. 30:19). Contemporary gerontologists tell us older people don't work harder; like eagles on the wind drafts, they just work smarter. Prophets spoke of eagles as symbols of God's judgment (Jer. 48:40; Ezek. 17:3, 7). We are reminded of elders of old standing at the gates of the city as well as those of today in church congregational and board meetings providing counsel to all who come to them. In the Book of Revelation, two wings of a great eagle represented God's intervention to deliver His People from persecution. Some of us remember parents and grandparents who prevailed before God for their children, cities, and nation. It should not surprise us that John, the oldest of the apostles, contrasts children and youth with fathers who have intimately known and walked with the Father from the beginning (1 John 2:13). The eagle, then, directs our attention to the elderly who are righteous, and this challenges us, our families, churches, and communities to revise stereotypes where they exist and use Scripture as the basis for ministering to older adults and giving them their rightful place as they in turn minister to us.

The prophet Isaiah, like David, contrasted youths (who grew weary and tired) and young men (who stumbled badly) with those who, with seasoned wisdom and efficiency of effort acquired from years of labor (by implication, the elderly), bound themselves tightly to the Father and from there mounted up with wings like eagles, to run and not get tired, to walk and not become weary (Isa. 40:29–31).

The Exalted Horn

During the time of harvest we think of the horn of plenty, standing for bounty, fruitfulness, a good harvest, and portending the time of annual Thanksgiving feasts. These images are found in David's metaphor of the exalted horn (which I have paraphrased below), perhaps written in praise of God when David was in his older years.

> You have exalted my horn like that of the wild ox, and I have
> therefore been anointed with fresh oil. My eye has looked exul-
> tantly upon my foes. Righteous men will flourish like the palm
> tree, growing like cedars in Lebanon. Planted in the house of
> the Lord, they will flourish in the courts of our God. They will
> still yield fruit in old age, be full of sap and very green, thereby
> declaring that the Lord is upright. (Ps. 92:10–15)

Zedekiah's horns symbolized power in prophetic action as they
did in Zechariah's vision (1 Kings 2:11; Zech. 1:18ff). The horn
metaphorically is used in poetic writings. God exalts the horn of
the righteous and cuts off the horn of the wicked (Ps. 75:10).[2] The
horn, then, paints a picture of righteous people of advancing age:
rejoicing, fruitful, resilient as a green bough in spring, espousing
prophetic truth, and protected from enemies.

Metaphor lays a foundation for understanding how the Bible
profiles older Christians—they have a ministry, a vision, a
prophecy, and an ordained, authoritative, and anointed role
either in or outside the institutional church. How does this come
about? What inspired David to say about older adults what he did
not seem to say about any other age group? To get a hint, we
rotate the telescope back in time toward the east and consider
the origins of the covenants.

A COVENANT-MAKING GOD

The historical intensity God exercised to bring mankind to
Himself cannot be seen any more clearly than in His covenantal
nature. This aspect of His nature is intrinsic to all sound
theology, is presented as a prophetic word to the modern church,
and is not lost in our study of the old.

God established those with whom He would covenant and He
unilaterally wrote the conditions of the covenant. By their nature,
covenants bind agreeing parties into a unit. God chose the
insignificant tribal society of Israel, and through covenant it
became a nation—a chosen people whose purpose as a nation was
to accept and proclaim to all peoples the *Shema* (Deut. 6:4–5).
Israel was born a nation of prophetic people. As long as the
Israelites kept the covenant, they received the blessings ordained

by God. Gentiles were not included in God's covenant with the Jews; they were "not a people," and Peter makes this distinction in 1 Peter 2:10 when writing to the young Christian church: "For you once were not a people, but now you are the people of God."

God has demonstrated His faithfulness and loving kindness, despite mankind's repeated failure to abide by His covenants. He tailored covenants to woo man back to Himself. He began with the Adamic covenant in the garden (Gen. 2:16–17), to which we refer in chapter 2, followed by the Noahic covenant (Gen. 6:13–15, 18) as the means by which a righteous family was saved from a flood designed to destroy evil mankind. The Abrahamic covenant established God's commitment to bless all generations that followed Abraham (Gen. 12:1–3, 7; 13:14–17; 17:16), and the Mosaic covenant provided deliverance from slavery in Egypt and gave the Law and the Promised Land (Exod. 12:35–36; 19:5; 24:12). The Davidic covenant led to the building of a permanent house for the Lord under the rule of Solomon and established a lineage through which the Messiah would be born (2 Sam. 7; Luke 1:32, 34). Collectively these are referred to as the Old Covenant.

Finally, God instituted the New Covenant, as prophesied in the Old and expressed by the New Testament. This covenant is more inclusive and available to all peoples through Christ, the Messiah, in whom all covenants are summed up. In Christ, the covenant is with a chosen race, the church, the body of Christ, a holy nation and royal priesthood, and the bride of Christ.

Whereas the contents of covenants changed over time, their eternal purposes did not. God's intention was always to woo and bring to Himself a people who would declare His glory throughout the earth. Advocates of modernism and postmodernism may be repulsed by the implications of a covenant-making and covenant-keeping God, but God is not easily swayed by democratic majorities or clandestine subversive seminars declaring contrary ways to fellowship with Him. The study of covenants reveals another immutable element in God's eternal strategy, and that is the role He continually gives to the elderly.

The part played by the elderly in bringing God's sovereign will to pass cannot be easily dismissed. In every generation of mankind and under every covenant, the old and their wisdom are foundational for social stability and continuity. The history of those of advancing age is coterminous with God's history. Leaders have come, ruled well or badly, and passed on, but a hallmark of God's plan has been righteous men and women of old age.

It is not coincidental that God chose aged Abraham and Sarah as the vehicles through whom to bless all nations; or Noah who labored for one hundred and twenty years merely to make the ark; or Moses who began the forty-year journey into the wilderness when he was a mere lad of eighty; or weakened, shriveled, and infirmed Simeon and Anna to be the first outside Joseph's family to recognize and proclaim Jesus in the temple as the Salvation of the Lord and the one through whom the New Covenant was established; and John, then over one hundred years old, to be the revelator who saw Jesus in the heavens as the Lion of Judah and the slain Lamb of God, worthy to open the scroll, read the judgment of the universe, and usher in the *parousia* of all time. God's written plan, purpose, and history have, among their common threads, a special deliberate place for the hoary heads—those of advancing years. Not the young and strong but the old, wise, and seasoned. The covenants were introduced on seasoned shoulders, bent, perhaps, but deliberate and given to the long view.

The covenants were introduced on seasoned shoulders, bent, perhaps, but deliberate and given to the long view.

God has a vital place for those of His children who remain righteous in their later years. Ours is not a gerontology that concerns all old people. It concerns only the righteous in whom the sap continues to flow and the fruit continues as yield. Hence, the theology of advancing years becomes an object lesson for those of younger years who themselves will, through time, ascend to those exalted places in their own generation.

THE COSMOLOGY OF THE CHURCH

Biblical cosmology makes God's creation understandable. It answers questions about humankind, why we are here, and what the meaning of our lives are. Chapter 2 addresses the Creation and humankind's unique configuration in the image of God. Literally, humankind is born of God and is the vice regent in charge of overseeing all natural creation. Our role on earth continues unabated, limited only by our span of life. We are stewards of the creation throughout the length of days.

With man and woman in place, God expanded His purpose by establishing a family crafted after His own qualities, and chapter 3 describes the family as the earthbound model of "heaven on earth." From it grew the clan, tribe, and nation of Israel, whose purpose was to declare to all nations the primacy of the Lord as God. This was the pattern under all expressions of the Old Covenant. Israel's holy mission was a prophetic one.

Under the New Covenant, the church as the bride of Christ is formed. Two facts stand out concerning this: the ultimate vision of the church is to make known the glory of God throughout the earth, but the ultimate goal is that the church will reign with Christ:

> And they sang a new song, saying, "Worthy art Thou to take the book and to break its seals, for Thou wast slain, and didst purchase for God with Thy blood men from every tribe and tongue and people and nation. And Thou has made them to be a kingdom and priests to our God; and they will reign upon the earth." (Rev. 5:9–10)

No better description of the perennial purpose of the church in its cosmological sense is likely to be found than in Paul Billheimer's *Destined for the Throne*.[3] He outlines how the church, now in preparation for its role as the bride, will be consummated. In this age, the church is in rehearsal for reigning with Christ, which it does through prayer and praise.

Prayer and praise are the armament for engaging in spiritual warfare, bringing down strongholds, practicing the eternal verities associated with faith, miracles, and healing, spreading the Gospel, and making disciples from out of all nations. What we do on earth prior to the wedding feast of the Lamb with His bride prepares us for our eternal role of reigning with Him.

This remarkable fact casts all of life into a different mold, for now longevity is not the goal, but rather part of a process of practicing for the other side of eternity. Death is not the end, but a final transition prior to reigning with Christ. Sickness, disability, and the emotions of the end days, as we discuss in chapter 8, are not to be feared but rather are events to be embraced because they signal a time when personal focus more clearly perceives the things of spirit and eternity.

For the believer, heaven is not a consequence of the end of life. It is an inevitable and irrevocable promise over which the believer has no control. All believers go to heaven. Life, then, with all its blessings and vicissitudes, is a time of rehearsal for something much greater than the best of blessings that have occurred on earth. The future is more than a time of relief and reprieve from suffering whose purposes we have failed to comprehend while here. Because of this, we can appreciate the forward looking, eternity-oriented, and purposeful intercession of Abraham for Isaac, Ishmael, and Lot; Job for his sons and their households; Moses for Israel that they might find a righteous shepherd; Samuel for Israel; Paul for the church; and Jesus that all His children may be one. The mature saints of hoary head have been singled out throughout the ages to engage in this prayer and praise-laden rehearsal for reigning, not because natural weakness and infirmity leave them incapable of doing anything else, but because of sharpened vision borne of having laid aside the encumbrances often associated with strength, beauty, and youthfulness.

Now we understand the metaphor of the eagle and the exalted horn of plenty. They came into being because of a covenant-making God who had a plan that would be realized through the agency of older adults. Their righteousness, bearing fruit on heavily laden branches in their season, was evidence of God's past faithfulness and the promise of ruling with Christ in the days to come. Surely, among the old, the past may be a prologue, but the present is prophetic and holds a promise.

CHAPTER TWO

In the Image of God

THE LINK BETWEEN OUR CREATION AND OUR GROWING OLD MUST BE SEEN NOT IN TERMS OF OUR DIMINISHING STRENGTH, DECLINING YEARS, AND MORTALITY, BUT RATHER IN THE FACT THAT WE WERE created in the image of God and then forsook the privilege. God is always the point of departure for the study of human nature. To make our longevity the measure, certainly in the Christian context, diminishes men and women and our earthly experiences; the Creator is the measure of all things.

CREATED IN THE IMAGE OF GOD

Our creation and the fact that we were created in the image of God are valuable in determining when it was that the issues of growing and being old became important. In regard to both of these, our relationship with God is one of intimacy that is conveyed first in the account of physical creation (by the Master Potter) and then our creation in the image of God (the Father of all spirits).

David hinted at the degree of intimacy in Psalms 37:4, by using a term common to all cultures of the day, which we translate "delight." It is a deeply sensuous term, depicting a warm, almost seductive embrace between lover and beloved. Words do not easily connote what the depth of God's motive and design was when He gave expression to the ultimate object of His creation, but David's effort comes close.

The necessity of sharing this brief note on intimacy is that all the rules changed when we, of our own free will, destroyed intimacy by our disobedience. To distinguish between the physical creation of man and the creation of man in the image of God lays the foundation for the forthcoming discussion on loss of intimacy, after which age and aging become prominent issues.

The Creation

The Hebrew words *create* and *make* often appear together and are of profound significance in that they only have God as their subject. Only God can make or create in the sense of Genesis 1:25–27: "Let us make man in our image, after our likeness. . . . So God created man in his own image."[1]

The starting point for consideration of the doctrine of creation is Heb. 11:3: "By faith we understand that the worlds were prepared by the word of God, so that what is seen was not made out of things which are visible." The biblical doctrine of creation is based on divine revelation and understood only from the standpoint of faith.

The Genesis account was not intended to be a scientific treatise. The work of creation was hidden from man and can be perceived only by faith. Reference to this doctrine is widespread in both the Old and New Testaments, among the prophets, Psalms, Job, Nehemiah, Acts, Romans, Hebrews, and Revelation.[2]

The Genesis account was not intended to be a scientific treatise. The work of creation was hidden from man and can be perceived only by faith.

Modern man, however, has a problem with accepting practically anything by faith. And to do so in regard to the present discussion may cause him some personal discomfort or trouble among his peers. Faith, after all, is pretty countercultural. The Enlightenment gave rise to an arrogant and self-sufficient man—it made his opinions as worthy as any other man's. The Renaissance later focused his attention on the birth of modern science and its emphasis on naturalism and rationalism: "to see and measure is to believe."

It is one thing to have the faith of Hebrews 11:3 concerning the creation of the physical universe, which we can't really pin down as accurately as we want. It is quite another thing to have faith about the biblical account of our creation, since we look at him or her in the mirror every morning. Who and what he or she is always is in question depending on what pop-psychology books we read and how much we accept for ourselves the values originating in the Enlightenment and the Renaissance.

The last decade of the twentieth century witnessed major debate at the national level in America on whether the creation account of humankind's origins should be taught in the public schools along with Darwinian evolution, or whether the latter should prevail, inasmuch as it had received the approval of much of the scientific establishment. The credibility of the creation account was not even the central focus of the debate since, at least for the Christian, creation could be accepted only by faith. Most important were the attacks being made on the credibility of evolution itself. At the heart of the attacks was the challenge that evolution as a belief system required faith by its adherents. Simply put, evolution just didn't measure up to the stringent demands required of formal theory construction in the scientific method. In other words, it was not a theory that could be tested and supported through replication.

If the orthodox Christian was able and willing in accordance with Scripture to dismiss secular naturalistic explanations and to accept by faith the creation of the physical universe, was he or she also able to accept by faith the creation of human beings in the image of God? To pit the naturalist's view against the biblical view regarding the origin of the physical universe is not too threatening, since most of the advocates for a non-biblical position are outside the walls of the institutional church.

But what do we do with the biblical account of our creation in the image of God? This issue is not distant from us. This is right where we live. It is basic and essential to what we call foundational truth. How we come down on one side or the other of this belief is critical and has considerale consequence for our entire subject.

And so, I ask you and the institutional church: do you really believe that we were created in the image of God, and if you do, just what do you mean and what are the implications? Most important for this book is the question, "What are the implications for growing and being old if we are created in the image of God?"

A human is primarily an economically controlled creature if one accepts Karl Marx, a sexually repressed human animal if Sigmund Freud is correct, an amoral higher ape if Charles Darwin is given his due. And one's beliefs end up being relative anyway if he or she was educated in a public institution influenced by the philosophy of John Dewey. With cultural mentors such as these, who needs a faith based on Holy Writ?

I mention these twentieth-century giants, questionable as they may be in some but not all Christian circles, because the institutional church has unknowingly mixed much of this thought with Christian doctrine. And if there is any one pivotal concept where the Christian must choose one side of the fence or the other, it is the concept of the humans in the image of God.

Men and women are always in dynamic tension inasmuch as secular and biblical worldviews are forever in dynamic tension. A Christian is at least schizoid in the sense of having his or her feet planted in two different worlds.

Some readers may find the rest of this book uncomfortable because the implications of being created in the image of God can have devastating effects on how they look at life, aging, and old age. But that is precisely why this book was written.

The sequence of the creation events is important for our understanding of God's general purposes for humankind and for a balanced appreciation of our duration of days.

Creation ex nihilo

"What is seen was made out of things which do not appear" (Heb. 11:3) coupled with "In the beginning God created the heavens and the earth" (Gen. 1:1) indicates that worlds were not made out of preexistent materials, but solely by the divine Word. He spoke, it happened. Prior to the divine creative act, there was no other kind of existence.[3] The creation from nothing—*creatio ex nihilo*—is important because in the beginning matter was determined as not being eternal. It had a beginning and it did not precede God or exercise external control over Him.

It is critical to remember that our physical bodies are matter. Only God is infinite; He privileges our finite qualities for a season of His making. Those in the Gray Zone need be humbled by the idea that "from dust to dust" is God's prerogative!

The committed Christian who at seventy-five years of age runs a marathon or competes in a triathlon still is not exempt from dustness. Even if medical researchers, physical trainers, and nutritionists extend the average life span to 120 years, at the end dustness still awaits. Quite literally, we live physically only to the extent God wills it. It is this attitude toward life and death that has remarkable consequences for the believer who looks death in the face and confidently prepares to move to the "other side" without remorse or regret. This perspective puts matters of illness, declining days, and impending death in contrast to the perspective offered by secularists who do all they can to prolong the inevitable. This will be further discussed in parts 2 and 3.

Primary and Secondary Creation

Primary creation expressed by the formula *creatio ex nihilo* does not exhaust biblical teaching on creation. Humans and animals were not created out of nothing; they were formed of the dust of the ground (Gen. 2:7a, 19). This has been called "secondary creation," meaning materials already in existence were used. It's from this secondary creation that we get the phrase "from dust to dust."

A Living Soul

The process of making man had two parts. First, he was made of the dust of the ground; second, God breathed into his nostrils and he became a living soul (Gen. 2:7b). God did not do this for the animals who possess no soul (however much we may ascribe human soul- or personality-like qualities to our pets). Within the soul are to be found the unique qualities of man that mirror the image of God.

The original account of the creation distinguishes between the body and the soul. The body is from the dust of the earth, the soul is from God Himself, and this distinction is kept up throughout the Bible. Different substances. Different origins. The body shall return to dust, says the wise man, and the spirit shall return to God who gave it. Man is part of a grand plan that includes his physical deterioration and death. Following Billheimer's cosmology discussed in chapter 1, man immediately goes to reign with Christ after his physical death.

A Christian's tendency to overspiritualize his or her religious experience to the cavalier neglect of his or her physical body is cause for concern. God gave Adam and Eve dominion over all created things, and He did not exclude the responsibility of being good stewards over their physical bodies, which later would be called the temples of God and abodes for the Holy Spirit (1 Cor. 3:16–17). This runs counter to the quip: "Where two or more are gathered together, there you find coffee and doughnuts," or "the best of all expressions of Christian fellowship is an excessively caloric and high-cholesterol covered-dish supper."

The soul and its origin are given higher priority than the body. The Scriptures state that God formed the spirit of man within him (Zech. 12:1), breathed into the people on the earth, and gave spirits to them (Isa. 42:5). For this reason, God is called the "God of the spirits of all flesh" (Num. 16:22).[4] However, giving higher priority to the soul does not justify benign neglect of man's physical body.

Preparing for Creation of Man and His Mate

According to Moses' account, God's decision to take six days for the creation had the purpose of preparing the earth to be inhabited by man and his wife and for putting in place all they would have as their responsibility. The earth was not barren or unfurnished, not devoid of light or the movement of the sun and stars, not lacking in air, earth, water, living creatures, or fruit to feed the body. God prepared all things for those who were to become an industrious family.[5]

Ethical Beginnings

Genesis is more than an account of the creation. It is also the first of the five books of the Torah, the Law. So, the theology found here contains ethical statements—be fruitful and multiply, fill the earth and subdue it; rule over the fish of the sea and the birds of the sky, and over every living thing that moves on the earth (Gen. 1:27–29).

God's first words to Adam and Eve were commands: Be fruitful and multiply, fill and subdue the earth—rule! Those simple words contained the basic elements of family structure and function, community and intergenerational organization, cultural stability and continuity, and the vision and mission of the forthcoming church. The Christian doctrine of salvation and the specific purpose for each person stood upon the fact that God created the human race and that the world still belonged to its Creator.[6]

In summary, the creation process laid a foundation for all that was to follow. It prepared for humankind's subsistence, dominion over the earth and its living things, the responsibility for stewardship, and the helper who would stand by each person's side.

In the Image of God

The Bible does not indicate exactly what the image of God in humans is. One understanding is that it refers to qualities or attributes present in a person, such as human reason, will, or personality. Another view holds that in relationship with God, His person is mirrored back onto us when looking upon His face (as contrasted from the idea of image in the sense of a photograph). Others see image as action—doing what God has commanded, such as having dominion or authority over the whole earth and tending and caring for it.[7]

Image of God in the Creation

Reformed theologian Charles Hodge has analyzed several schools of thought concerning what "in the image of God" meant to early theologians. They debated whether it referred to the intellectual capacity and behavior of humans or our moral capacity and behavior.[8] He agrees with other Reformed theologians who take the middle ground that it consists of one's intellectual or rational capacity and moral conformity. Scriptures tend to make the original moral perfection of man and woman the most prominent element of God's likeness. But as the created children of God, humans also had a rational capacity, as witnessed in our ability to carry out the mandates of God, such as naming the species and beginning stewardship over plants and animals.

The moral image of God is expressed as four progressively related propositions that provide for an all-encompassing human being. (1) Human reason was subject to God. (2) Human will was subject to human reason. (3) Human affections and appetites were subject to human will. (4) The body was the obedient organ of the soul. Concerning the last, there was neither rebellion of the sensuous part of human nature against the rational, nor was there any disproportion between the sensuous and the rational needing to be controlled or balanced by additional outside gifts or influences.[9] Knowledge, righteousness, and holiness were elements of the image of God in which humankind was originally created.[10]

Whatever the validity of this assumption about Adam, it is more important that he knew God, which meant life eternal. As he came from the hands of His Maker, Adam's mind was imbued with this spiritual or divine knowledge, fully encompassing and standing alongside righteousness and holiness. He was made like God and was pronounced to be exceedingly good.

The man of original creation was radically different from those who followed him and derived their origin from him after his corruption. Adam's descendants received a defective hereditary gene pool—mutant spiritual and physical strands on the DNA spiral. Adam had the soundness of mind and freedom of will to choose the good, and no argument suffices to suggest his will was predicated on some original constitutional weakness. Whatever will he had was sufficient to take away whatever excuses he made to God who made man with the capacity either to sin or not to sin.[11] This introduces us to the first anthropological cataclysm in the history of mankind.

Loss of Original Intimacy

A critical interlude occurs when our relationship with God is diminished through sin. This has a profound significance for how we henceforth define man and woman. Prior to the fall, Adam and Eve were in static relationship with God. If ever the status quo was a desirable place to be, it was in the garden prior to the fall. Following the fall, humankind was forced to embark on an arduous journey to refind the Father, first as a member of a chosen race and then as a member of Christ's church.

There was no journey to find the Father prior to the fall. Life itself was tantamount to fellowship with the Father. Journeys have a destination and a goal, but Adam began living in the presence of the ultimate goal—the Father. But, alas, Adam closed the door to that fellowship, and he and his descendants from then on, like

Bunyan's pilgrim, commenced on a journey, always seeking, always wondering, "Will I find Father again?"

Adam was not time bound in regards to his original fellowship. Short of sin, he would have lived forever, and gerontology would have been a moot issue. After Adam, humankind was inextricably bound to time. Stewardship initially had to do with how humans oversaw the creation. After sin entered, stewardship over time was added to dominion over the earth. By some strange logic, the degree to which Adam exercised stewardship over time determined how efficiently he could exercise stewardship over the creation.

We cannot dismiss the importance of time and how we utilize it.

As time went on, men and women learned that the longer they lived, the more opportunity they had to translate acquired knowledge into wisdom for living. Wisdom translates into David's "youth renewed like the eagle's" and "being fruitful like the exalted horn."

The journey ties us to God's purposes for His people collectively and for each of us individually. Paul knew when he had finished the course set for him by God (2 Tim. 4:7). David was chosen by God to replace Saul, was anointed and ordained king, and then died when he had completed God's purposes for his life (Acts 13:21–22). As we move toward the predetermined end of our own days, we cannot dismiss the importance of time and how we utilize it.

Time is both enemy and friend. It is an enemy if misused; it is a friend when it becomes an instrument to accomplish the divine purpose placed in us by the Creator. This is the challenge for every man in Christ.

Stewardship over Time

The writer of Proverbs and Ecclesiastes recommends that we look to the ant as an example of industriousness. But he criticizes the "sloth who wastes his time," and demeans the person who lazily "sits in the sun with idle folded hands." These, says the preacher, lead to destruction. Stewardship over time entered when humans were sentenced to a finite number of days.

Mortality delimited both the space in which to rule over the earth and the time during which it could be done. Original sin sentenced us to a fate that stewardship through Christ seeks to rectify.

When Jesus laid down the conditions for following Him in Luke 14, He identified several natural influences, which, if not managed wisely, would encumber and prevent us from following Him as disciples. Among the resources we all have for being a disciple is time. Time, as a matter of longevity or advancing years, is in God's hands, but our final disposition is dependent on what we do with what is given to us. The same applies to how we manage our bodies as a resource. Failure to care for them increases the number of disabilities we experience and shortens our length of days.

The moral image of God, then, requires that we be prepared and unencumbered so that we are capable of responding to God's will for our lives.

The moral image of God sets up a sequence of cause and effect: it holds that the body is the obedient organ of the soul, which is subject to our affections. Those affections are subject to our will, which is subject to our reason. Reason derives from and is coterminous with our possession of the image of God. The moral image of God, then, requires that we be prepared and unencumbered so that we are capable of responding to God's will for our lives.

The righteous and holy person lives God's purposes. The unrighteous person does not. God initiates and imbues us with the desire and power to do what is necessary to declare His glory throughout the earth. We either reach out and accept the desire and power or put our hands to another task. The former is the legacy of the Christian of advancing years.

Image of God in the New Testament

New Testament teaching on the image of God builds on the Old Testament account. As examples, 1 Corinthians 11:7 and James 3:9 echo the earlier teaching asserting a continuation of humankind's position in the created order to reflect God's glory, despite our sinfulness. The New Testament, contrasted with the creation account of Genesis, focuses more on the person of Jesus Christ who is called the "image of God."[12]

"Christ as the image of God" derives from His unique eternal preexistence—the *Logos* from all eternity (John 1:1–18). He alone is able to faithfully and fully reflect the glory of the invisible God (see Heb. 1:1–3 and Phil. 2:6–11). Jesus is no mere paradigm or model of the Father. He is the objective manifestation of the essence of God, the visible expression of an invisible God, the ultimate Adam who stands at the head of a new humanity that draws its life from Him (1 Cor. 15:45). He is the unique image and prototype of all who owe their knowledge of God and life in God to Him (Rom. 8:29; 1 Cor. 15:49; 2 Cor. 3:18; 1 John 3:2).

Two passages, Colossians 3:10 and Ephesians 4:14–24, elaborate on the "image of God" as the "new man." The former says that believers have put on a new self that is in the process of being renewed through knowledge consistent with the image of the One who created us. A personalized journey or process with definable tasks is elaborated in the Ephesians passage, and the specificity is amazing: Stop being like children (v. 14). Grow up in all aspects in Him (v. 15). Quit walking in the futility of your minds (v. 17). Lay aside your old self (v. 22). Be renewed in the spirit of your mind (v. 23). Put on the new self, which has been created in righteousness and holiness of the truth in the likeness of God (v. 24). The implications are staggering.

These are not Sunday school recommendations. They are not designed merely to fill in blanks in some didactic class on discipleship. These are mandates. They describe in nonarbitrary terms a lifelong journey in God.

The new person is now said to be after or according to the image of God, and that image is said to consist of righteousness and holiness, which, when used in combination, mean moral excellence. For Paul, the presentation of Christ as the image of God was to be worked out fully and consistently through the increasing transformation of the people of Christ into that same image by the power of the indwelling Spirit. For how long should this continue? It should continue until nothing remained of the earthly image in those who finally in old age, with seasoned shoulders, exhibited the image of the heavenly man.[13]

F. F. Bruce, who was among the best of the apostle Paul's expositors, goes a step farther, saying that living in terms of the image of Christ is a function of the quality of relationships that occur within the body of Christ.[14] In order for the body to collectively exhibit the image of the heavenly man, then all members are required to edify, build up, support, encourage, and assist in bringing completeness to each other member to whom he or she is joined. At no point in the Gospel record or the doctrine of the

Body of Christ are members conceived as uninvolved. Is it any wonder that in both the Old and New Testaments the older, wiser, tested, and proven members were given the responsibility for guarding over the welfare of the members of the congregation? (See chapter 4 for a detailed discussion of this.)

There is no guarantee that one's age will be a measure of spiritual maturity, but the probability of finding it in the older is greater than finding it in the younger.

Living in terms of the image of Christ is a process. In discipline, we increase in knowledge that comes from the Father. The fruit of that knowledge, borne of further discipline and obedience, is holiness and righteousness (Heb. 12:9–11). These are qualities acquired from years of experience and the conversion of that experience into wisdom. There is no guarantee that one's age will be a measure of spiritual maturity, but the probability of finding it in the older is greater than finding it in the younger.

One Man's Purposeful Journey until the End

This chapter concludes with the story of a remarkable little man with a foreign accent whose journey in Christ continued until his last years. I tell it because it epitomizes the sense of purpose among those who believe that they must live out what God has given them to do until their dying days.

Otto was eighty-four when I first met him. He had moved from Wisconsin to be near his son, a consulting engineer and missionary who lived in the Southeast. Otto was a happy man who spoke of his faith to all who would listen and who loved to play the harmonica. He was happy except for one fact. Several years before he moved to be with his son, unthinking relatives had convinced Otto's very difficult and mentally disturbed wife to divorce him. It was unbearable for Otto to think that the day would come when he would have to stand before God a divorced man, his wedding vows broken against his wishes.

Otto prayed. His new friends prayed. He was always happy, always had a joke to tell or a tune to play on his harmonica, but when the subject came up, he would sob, "God, I can't come and stand in Your presence without my wife; it'd be too much a shame." Otto's younger relatives were unsympathetic; yet he never stopped praying and pleading. Otto was now eighty-seven.

God heard Otto's prayers and those of his friends, and like the rivers of water, He turned the hearts of men. A wedding was planned. A youthful groom could never have been happier and more rejoicing than Otto as he said the vows to his wife for a second time. The next year Otto fell, was injured, and died. But at eighty-eight, he had fulfilled the purpose God had given him many years before to be the husband of one wife until death parted them.

A postscript on Otto's story is found in his own conception of the image of God. For him, God's image in its completeness was best bestowed to a couple—the man with his wife—not each in their individual and independent states, but to them collectively. For Otto, divorce destroyed the totality of the imageness. To stand before the Father as a divorced man, without his wife alongside him, would have been an affront to the Creator whose intention was to transfer a portion of heaven to man and wife in their togetherness. To Otto, this is what "heaven on earth" meant.

CHAPTER THREE

Families Designed to Last

ADAM AND EVE WERE THE COEQUAL MEMBERS OF THE FIRST FAMILY—DIFFERENT IN DESIGN, FUNCTION, AND TEMPERAMENT, BUT IN THEIR TOGETHERNESS THEY COMPRISED THE IMAGE OF GOD. THEY complemented each other, and this design forecasted the manner in which God wanted humankind to extend the culture of the garden to the rest of the earth. In the original assignment of responsibilities, God laid the responsibility for headship on Adam—a task that Adam didn't request and many times may have regretted, but it was his because the Creator wanted it that way.

Modern science speculates on the left- and right-brain capabilities found in men and women. Popular books extend the analogy to planetary origins—men from Mars and women from Venus. Among the more bizarre popularizations, feminist and Mother Earth cults meet on one side of a forest, while male cults physically exhaust themselves on the opposite side of the same forest with incantations, painted faces, different degrees of undress, and primal screams. None of these, of course, describe the biblical pattern, but we can't help but feel that extreme feminism and primal screaming are modern day efforts to recapture something of God's original intentions, misguided as they may be.

For this reason, a more accurate characterization of the family is needed so that we finally arrive at a theology of aging consistent with what Scripture says about the family. Chapters 1 and 2 laid the foundation. First, man and woman were created in the image of God, and this gave the family its initial substance. The "imageness," like a primordial genetic code, made its way through every generation of mankind and looked forward to the time, as Paul eloquently explained in the letter to the church at Ephesus, where the relationship between husband and wife would mysteriously mirror the relationship between Christ and the church. In this sense, what took place in the Garden of Eden anticipated the bride of Christ, which concluded with the bride cosmologically reigning with Christ in heavenly places. Second, Christ is said to be the bodily fullness of the Godhead, and the fullness permeates the church with the intention that it grows to a perfect and mature body doing the work of Christ. Third, and here is an amazing truth, the divine DNA bestowed on man and woman in the garden continues on throughout history and returns as the perfect and pure bride at her wedding feast with the slain Lamb who has become the Lion of Judah and the ruling Lord of the universe.

And this is why it is important for us to understand God's purpose in having families built to last. What has occurred historically is purposeful, intentional, and reflective of His story of the perpetuation of His investment in the creation.

In the Garden, the design was not for male and female to be in isolation. Never was there an ethic of self-sufficiency, competition, and independence, but always an attitude and expression of interdependence and utter dependence on the Father, responsive to His design and purpose for their lives. In their original innocence, interdependence was a way of life for man and woman. After the fall, man was ashamed, hid, and blamed his wife, and from then on interdependence on each other and dependence on the Father were goals to be pursued. God's laws, some of which are addressed here, set man going in the right direction.

In their original innocence, interdependence was a way of life for man and woman.

For generations, social and behavioral scientists have considered the small group, including the family, to be the prototype for all levels of social organization. The small group has become the model on which larger groups and organizations build and assume varying degrees of complexity. Within the small group we learn of rules, roles, and relationships.

Any discussion of older people requires understanding God's plan for the family and how its composition and goals take them into account. Despite the antiquity of the cultures from which we draw hints at a theology of aging, we can never dismiss that God is anthropomorphic in His revelation. That is, He communicates in terms that are understandable to mankind despite time, events, and culture. His truth is universal. The task of the interpreter is to recapture timeless universal truths and apply them to the present.

THE OLD TESTAMENT FAMILY

Two historical facts reward our search for universal principles with which to build a theology of growing old. First, family roles remained about the same throughout the biblical period. Changing culture, inclusive of the shift from a nomadic life to village and city dwelling, did not affect family customs to any great extent. Mosaic Law abolished marrying one's sibling, as was true in nomadic culture, but most of the early family styles continued. Second, earlier culture was quite different from the culture of modern Western nations. It is important to understand the culture in order to determine the correct interpretation of Scripture for its time, but our task is to seek principles applicable to life today.[1] In other words, differences between pre-modern and modern family structures do not invalidate the value of what can be learned from the past.

For a number of years, Cornell University child development specialist Urie Bronfenbrenner extolled the value of the Israeli *kibbutzim* as an ideal communal environment in which to raise children and perpetuate Jewish culture following the return of Jews from all over the world to Palestine. Bronfenbrenner's contemporaries, Zimmerman and Cervantes, in their 1950s classic *Successful American Families*, described families with a minimum of deviant behavior and identified extended family structures and viable community relationships as causal factors. More recently, First Lady Hillary Clinton resurrected Bronfenbrenner's thesis in her *It Takes a Village* model of rearing children.

There are numerous examples of this model throughout America: the Amish and the Mennonites throughout the country; many Mormon families in Utah; many urban conclaves of

Mexicans, Thais, and Vietnamese in this generation; and Chinese, Poles, Japanese, and Eastern Europeans in earlier generations. These groups exhibited a pre-modern (by Western standards) family and community structure that provided stability and continuity of culture and minimized the chances of deviant behavior. Yes, there are historical pre-modern family structures that continue to exert their positive influence on one generation after another. Therefore, a resurrection of the biblical model for contemporary Christians should have value, if for no other reason than to give substance to what the New Testament body of Christ was meant to be for first-century believers.

. . . God's ideal for the family was a harmonious group, where love for God, each other, and neighbors was instilled in each member by learning and adhering to God's laws . . .

Families in biblical times often were much larger than they are today, especially if the head of the family had more than one wife. The extended family living in one home or compound could include the man and his wife or wives, concubines, female or male slaves, sons and unmarried daughters, aged parents, and grandparents. Others in the family could include servants and their children, and aliens and strangers who attached themselves for a time before moving to another location.

Regardless of size and diversity, God's ideal for the family was a harmonious group, where love for God, each other, and neighbors was instilled in each member by learning and adhering to God's laws in order to accomplish overall harmony and a common purpose. This helps us to appreciate the Old Testament requirement not to marry nonbelieving foreigners (Ex. 34:13–16; Deut. 7:3–4), and in the New Testament, not to be unequally yoked with unbelievers (2 Cor. 5:3).

It is from the individual family roles and the overall structure of the family that we begin to understand the significance of longevity, the acquired wisdom of older members of the community, and God's design for the ruling elder.

Family Stability and Cultural Continuity

Two propositions set the stage for our discussion. First, social stability is essential for social continuity. Second, continuity is essential for God's plan for spreading the message about Himself and His preeminence throughout the earth. Here structure—social stability—is essential to process—social continuity. If you are among those who are dismayed over the weakened and temporary nature of today's American family, including the breakdown of the Christian family, then read carefully about structure.

In the beginning, God determined that the father was the key person to provide stability for his own family and to assure the continuity of the "heavenly culture." Corporate continuity benefits from personal longevity. Each father's commitment to family stability laid the foundation for the future joys of grandparenthood. The anticipated joys were motivation for the quality of relationship the father provided his immediate children. In a word, the righteous and holy man of God had the long view in mind: he was carving out and living his own legacy in the present.

In the best of circumstances a father's diligence continues as he later nurtures his grandchildren. It is a blessed family that has grandparents who continue their investments in grandchildren and great-grandchildren. The Scriptures promise parents the coveted status of grandparent if they are righteous, fear God, and walk wisely in His ways.[2]

A task of every society is to teach each generation how to carry out the roles it will occupy at different points in life. This is called socialization. The child learns how to be an adult—wife, husband, mother, and father—by watching and learning from his parents. For a man, the rules for being a grandparent begin first by learning what it means to be a husband and father.

The Husband

The Hebrew word for husband means to dominate or rule, and to be a master. However, this meant that the father was responsible for the family's well-being and not that he was a dictatorial autocrat. Adam's stewardship over creation began with Eve and their children. True to God's command, Adam and Eve's joint effort was to have many children and, if God smiled (according to Jewish culture), they all would be sons, for sons inherited the father's assets and carried on the father's name (Jer. 20:15).

The Father

If we have a biblical understanding of "father," much in Scripture addressing the stability and continuity of the family, subsequent generations, and society as a whole will become clear. God is described as the father of Israel, and Jesus taught His disciples to pray "our Father" (Deut. 32:6, Matt. 6:9). He is the One who begat and protected them and He is the One they should revere and obey. The Fifth Commandment to honor one's parents was essentially a prescription for family order, and some suggest it was intended to accomplish in the family what the First and Second Commandments established for the nation of Israel in its relationship with Jehovah. What Jehovah had commanded all men and women to do in the first two commandments, He ordered children to do in the fifth.

If we have a biblical understanding of "father," much in Scripture addressing the stability and continuity of the family, subsequent generations, and society as a whole will become clear.

Small children seldom have an understanding of God, abstract as the concept and reality are, but children sit at the feet of father, where they learn from him, are loved by him, and are guided in right and wrong. And then the natural father bows his head and says: "Our Father," and the small child slowly begins to make a transfer from one he sees and hears to One whom he one day will also hear and revere.

By implication, the concept of father went beyond the immediate family to include all legitimate authority. Malachi 2:10 tells that God is the father of all people, the protector, father of the fatherless, and a judge of widows (Ps. 68:5). To honor one's parents harkens back to our original parent-God. For any earthbound creature to be called "father," then, is pretty heady stuff!

The family in Bible times was to function as a miniature replica of the earth-to-heaven relationship. As God's children, we address Him as "Father." As our father's child, we address him as "father." When the father becomes older—gray hair and all—we can appreciate Daniel's title of God as "the Ancient of Days." It is no wonder small children everywhere, enamored as they are with gray-haired grandparents, ask if their grandparents were alive when Jesus was alive.

The Hebrew *ab*, translated "father," has many uses. It can be a title of respect, as applied to older people, teachers, prophets, and advisors. Every usage of the term retains the essential connotation of deference, respect, obeisance, and, if we dare, of acquiescence in the face of a superior force.[3]

We fully appreciate God as the believer's Father. He knows all about His children, even numbering the hairs on their heads. He protects and rescues them, teaches them in the way they should go, and supplies their needs. All of this makes sense of the Fifth Commandment for children to honor and obey their parents.[4]

Father as Progenitor

"Father" was not restricted to one's biological father or, as above, our heavenly Father. It was an all-encompassing word, which meant a line of men from whom a given individual is descended, a clan, those with a special calling, a dynasty, or a nation.[5] The effect of this extended usage was that the deferential and respectful use of *ab* based one's identity on past allegiances, associations, and generations. It is as if the Israelite said of himself: I bow my knee to those of long ago who spawned me, to whom I owe my existence, and on whose shoulders I stand this day. In America, many place special importance on the founding fathers and the fathers of our nation. I will later address standing on the shoulders of giants.

God's choice of "father" as *ab* was intentional and perpetuated the significance of ancestors, assured the continuation of His purposes, and made sense of the connections among generations. Regardless of era, *ab* has remained timeless and universal as it was at the beginning. Each conception and birth and each child that is reared is done so under the umbrella of a God-created archetype, deeply imbedded in the soul and spirit of each person. God's intention that all of us carry His name remains intact. There may be friendly familiarity in "Pop," an implied buddy relationship with "Dad," or daughterly coziness with "Daddy." But "Father" tells of one who is stable and who endures, and the enduring quality transcends each generation and makes sense of the role of grandparent and other functionaries in Old Testament culture such as the mentor and elder, of which more is said in a subsequent chapter.

Father as Prophet, Priest, and King

A religious elaboration of the father's role includes three responsibilities—priest, prophet, and king. These are expressed differently throughout the Bible without loosing their significance. In its simplest form, the prophetic responsibility is to

educate all members of the family and prepare them for productivity and survival in the world at large. The priestly
responsibility represents God to the family, the family to God,
and requires the father to be a wise intercessor and discerning
spiritual leader. The kingly role is that of an administrator, who
oversees the economic welfare of the family, delegates responsibility to others, and otherwise leads the family in peaceful
cooperation to achieve important family goals.

No doubt existed that the Jewish father was the spiritual
leader of the family. He literally functioned as the family priest
(Gen. 12:7–8; Job 1:5), leading the family in observing religious
rites (such as the Passover in Ex. 12:3), sacrificing on their
behalf, representing Jehovah to the members of the family, and
interceding for them. At the time the tabernacle in the wilderness was established, it was the priests and not fathers who
functioned at the altar, but the father nevertheless continued as
the religious leader in the home (Ex. 26–27; Eph. 6:4). It is well
for moderns to remember, that *to his family, the father, and not the
priest in the past or the pastor now, was and is* ab!

The father, with the help of the mother, taught the essentials
of the written law and admonished the children to obey it (Deut.
6:7–9). In this prophetic role, both parents ascertained the child's
particular leanings and guided him in the realization of his gifts
(Prov. 22:6). In contemporary society, determination of the child's
bent or leaning is more open to possibilities than in traditional
society where the son's occupational future was pretty well determined by what the father himself did to earn a living. The
modern, more socially mobile, and occupationally open marketplace puts greater responsibility on Christian parents to discern
a child's natural and early social and psychological leanings if
they wish to meet the mandate of Proverbs 22:6. In a later
section, I will discuss the "social trust fund" which assisted traditional parents in making these decisions.

The father's administrative or kingly role identified both
what he should and should not do. He disciplined the children as
necessary—not sparing the rod, but Paul admonished fathers not
to drive them to wrath, which was equally understood by the Old
Testament father (Eph. 6:4).

The family was the essential economic unit, with the father
receiving assistance from his wife when she was free to help, and

from the children, particularly the sons, as they grew in strength and eventually began working full time in the family business. The Talmud specified four specific duties of the father toward his son: to circumcise or have him circumcised, to pass on an inheritance to the first-born son, to find him a wife, and to teach him a trade. The first of these is a priestly function, the next two are administrative or kingly responsibilities, and the last is prophetic or educational.

The community considered the man who failed to provide for his family a derelict, and others had little hesitation in mocking and shunning him (Prov. 6:6–11; 19:7). This carried over to the New Testament, and Paul warned that "If any provide not for his own . . . he has denied the faith, and is worse than an infidel" (1 Tim 5:8). The administrative role also required that the father and husband defend his family's rights before the judges, and, unfortunately, those who were fatherless or widows lacked protective representation in court and often were denied justice (Deut. 13–19; 16:18). The forthcoming description of the kinsman-redeemer provides partial remedy in the absence of a husband and father.

Grandparents were a key factor in successful child-rearing, and it was more the exception than the rule that grandparents were not available.

The Old Testament Jewish family was patriarchal in its rule, but it did not approach the abusive totalitarian practices of Israel's heathen neighbors. Similar to what has been said of Abraham Lincoln, it can be said the Jewish father was "a man of steel and velvet," a fine balance between firmness, decisiveness, and discipline with gentleness and consideration of individual differences. According to J. I. Packer and his colleagues, a mature father thought of his children as human beings, taking account of their feelings and abilities, and as one scholar of the time said, the good father should "push them away with the left hand and draw them near with the right hand."[6] This delicate balance between firmness and affection was the desired ideal of a Jewish father.

These details describe the many details each generation passed on to successive generations. Contrary to modern families, the responsibility of rearing children seldom fell to a single person. Rather, the process was something assisted by both the extended family and the larger community. Grandparents were a

key factor in successful childrearing, and it was more the exception than the rule that grandparents were not available.

The New Testament parables perpetuated the idea of an
involved larger community. The woman who found the lost coin
called her neighbors to celebrate its discovery. All the shepherds
joined in celebration when the lone shepherd returned with the
lost lamb. Many neighbors, perhaps with some reluctance
because of the late hour, provided food for the man who received
an unexpected visitor from afar late at night. And, finally, the
whole village was summoned by a father to feast and rejoice when
his prodigal son returned home. Examples such as these forecast
the way the body of Christ is to support, encourage, and assist
one another.

Mother: Helper, Partner, and Comforter

The mother's role emerges from qualities inherent in her
creation. When these are yielded to God, they are designed to
last in perpetuity. They also give stability to the family and assure
the continuity of the family and the community beyond. A right
relationship with God, based on a quiet and gentle spirit, is the
foundation for experiencing godly womanhood.

God created woman from the substance of man; she followed
man in creation; she was fitted to the man so that, together, they
became a completed work. Her distinctive qualities were tailor-
made to enhance irreplaceable family and social roles.[7] God
fashioned the woman to be a nurturer and to bear and rear children through their early stages of growth. He fashioned her to be
a manager capable of work outside the home, and He equipped
her to be a minister of good deeds and to train other women.[8]

God's creation of man was purposefully incomplete. He created
woman to complement and complete all that He invested in man.
The opposite also is true; man completes what is missing in woman.
In the synergy of the sexes, the full image of God is made manifest.

In the Old Testament family, the wife's primary goal in life
was to bear children for her husband and to propagate a race of
people whose responsibility was to make known that Jehovah was
the one and only God and Lord. Her purpose, like that of her
husband, had God's eternal view in mind. The spokesman for
Rebecca said to her, "May you, our sister, become thousands of
ten thousands, and may your descendants possess the gate of

those who hate them" (Gen. 24:60). The typical Jewish family hoped the wife would, like a fruitful vine, fill the house with many children (Ps. 128:3).

The mother supplemented the father's prophetic role by training the children during their formative years. When the sons were able to join their fathers at the family place of work, the mother turned her attention to the daughters, teaching them to become successful wives and mothers.[9] A woman's performance of her tasks determined the family's success or failure because her roles were so intricately related with those of her husband. "An excellent wife is the crown of her husband, but she who shames him is as rottenness in his bones" (Prov. 12:4).

In the synergy of the sexes, the full image of God is made manifest.

The Old Testament extended family provided for the mother's continuing role as counselor for her daughters and daughters-in-law, as well as seasoned teacher and comforter to the grandchildren. Like that of her husband, her importance for assuring continuity of the culture did not end with childbirth or the graduation of her children to adulthood.

The virtues of the Jewish woman were extolled in Proverbs 31 and have become a model for generations of wives and mothers. Because of her faithfulness to duty and design, she flourished in all she did. Proverbs 31:25 sums up her purpose for the long term: "Strength and dignity are her clothing, and she smiles at the *future*," literally at her latter days, in which she places confidence (italics added). She anticipated continuing partnership with her husband, in whom she had pleasure, in the advancing years.

The Complete Picture

The details accumulated and available to us from the larger body of Scripture obviously should be of more benefit to us today than to those of the past, since we have the advantage of having the "complete picture." In retrospect, we recognize the cumulative value of all these passages and their conclusion in a model of family structure that is best described by 2 Timothy 3:16 as profitable for teaching, reproof, correction, and training in righteousness.

Models are ideal types and not intended to be replicated, because we cannot recapture the past in its entirety; rather, they are standards against which we measure our contemporary efforts. The rigor with which Scripture describes the family produces a perspective on which whole social orders were built, and this should not surprise us. The New Testament church's understanding of family was of the Old Testament model, and there have been numerous examples throughout the past two thousand years where groups of Christians and non-Christians alike have sought to replicate the wisdom of ancient patterns.

Within the confines of the family, elders, mentors, and grandparents were shaped and then emerged, and from the family the clan, tribe, and nation took shape. In other words, the family as crafted by Father in the beginning and shaped by Him by directive and circumstance throughout time, has laid the basis for a theology of aging.

From Family to Nation

The recurring themes of social stability leading to social continuity also apply to the family's graduation from a unitary structure to groupings in the form of clans, tribes, and finally the nation of Israel. Every society must solve the problem of how family solidarity extends to larger groups.

God's covenant promise to Abraham and the descendants of his household, individually and collectively, was based on Abraham's faith. God blessed Abraham and then Isaac and Jacob with the view of blessing an entire nation whose force would be felt throughout the earth. But before there was a nation, the family had to be consolidated into natural groupings. When Jacob's extended family moved to Egypt, he was accompanied by at least sixty-six people who were his direct descendants (Gen. 46:26). Eleven of these were his sons (Joseph was already in Egypt). Of the leaders who went into Egypt with their families, God produced six hundred thousand men plus their families.

All persons outside primary families who were related by blood and who felt close affinity or connection based on common ancestry or blood relationship belonged to a clan. The Book of

Numbers gives a census of the leaders and the numbers of the twelve tribes according to these clans, which numbered in the hundreds (Num. 1–4, 26; Ezra 8:1–14).

Membership in the clan and tribe, while important for the special responsibilities reserved by them, still depended on social safety nets to maintain family strength when it was challenged. After all, the strength of the clan or tribe was dependent on the continuing strength and integrity of the family. One such safety net was the kinsman-redeemer.

The Kinsman-Redeemer

Standing at the interface of the nuclear family and the larger society was the kinsman-redeemer. Each male member of the clan had one person designated as the kinsman-redeemer who was expected to perform any of four tasks:

- If someone was required to sell his property to pay debts, the kinsman repurchased the property in order to keep the property within the clan. (Lev. 25:25; Ruth 4:1–6; Jer. 32:6–15)
- If someone was captured and enslaved or had sold himself into slavery, he had every right to expect his kinsman to redeem him and set him free. (Lev. 25:47–49)
- If a man died childless, the redeemer had the option of marrying the dead man's widow in order to rear a son to carry on the family line and to honor the deceased person. (Deut. 25:5–10)
- If someone were murdered, his redeemer would track down the killer and even the score. (Deut. 19:32)

The kinsman-redeemer helped to assure the stability and continuity of each man's family and was a safety net for clan, tribe, and nation. He was God's prescription for preserving groups in distress in order that they might carry out His purposes. The four functions listed here suggest the kinsman-redeemer was not a young man, but rather one who had accumulated significant resources and who was an older adult. The first three responsibilities required a substantial surplus of money, and the second of these indicated he had sufficient influence to persuade a slave owner to sell the redeemer's relative. In other words, the kinsman redeemer was likely to have been a male of resources and influence, and these were the symbols of accomplishment of a man of later years.

The kinsman-redeemer of Israel also became a type of the intimate relationship of God with His people (Isa. 41:14; 43:14; 44:24). God, the Father, is our next of kin who ransoms us from bondage, and in the New Testament, pays the price to set us free (Isa. 48:1–3). Paul reminded the believers at Corinth that God had bought them at a price so that they could glorify Him and thereby make His glory known (1 Cor. 6:19–20). These concepts carry over to the structure of the New Testament family and eventually to the contemporary institutional church.

A common mistake in biblical interpretation is to focus primarily on the spiritual application of a "type," such as the kinsman-redeemer, while overlooking the very real benefit that took place in practical application. This is unfortunate and somewhat deceptive. The genius of the Father has been to provide for the natural welfare of His children as well as to convey concepts linking them to Him in a spiritual sense. It is incumbent upon theologians—scholarly types and everyday ones such as ourselves—to translate theological truth into practical applications for the living, breathing, and searching church. The kinsman-redeemer lives in the form of real people today, and we suffer to the extent he or she is neglected by being relegated to only a spiritual type. Had it not been for Boaz, the biblical model for all human kinsman-redeemers, the very real lineage of King David and King Jesus through Ruth would not have occurred.

There likely is no example of family solidarity within the annals of mankind that surpasses in excellence God's handiwork in the ancient Hebrew family.

Beyond the clans were the twelve tribes of Israel. God's mandate to the primordial family extended through faithful fathers to the clan and thereby to the tribe and eventually the nation. God told Abraham to expect continuing unity of family, clan, and tribe in His reference to all nations: "And I will bless those who bless you, and the one who curses you I will curse. And in you all the families [nations] of the earth will be blessed" (Gen. 12:3).

There likely is no example of family solidarity within the annals of mankind that surpasses in excellence God's handiwork in the ancient Hebrew family. When it worked, it was a heaven on earth, including the times when the stability of the family was threatened.

The structure of ancient Hebrew families was enhanced by what cultural anthropologists refer to as the social trust fund, which served as partial solution to a number of forces that have eroded families throughout time, and of which the kinsman-redeemer was a participant. Discussed more fully below, the social trust fund is the presence of numerous relatives that are brought together upon the marriage of previously unrelated people. Sociologically, the fund represents the cumulative support of numerous relatives and their resources to the benefit of the young couple. A brief description of seven eroding forces pave the way for better appreciating the importance of the social trust fund and the manner in which older adults contributed to it.

Erosion of the Family

From biblical times to the present, social, economic, and religious pressures eroded families. Wherever family stability is threatened by any of the following elements, the culture is threatened. Where relevant I also give modern parallels.

Childlessness
So great was the social and religious pressure to have many children, and particularly sons, that couples in biblical times often thought the absence of children was a curse from God. Hanna's consternation is a good example. Short of her prayers and God's answer resulting in her eventual conception of Samuel, her life would have been miserable, despite Elkanah's assurance that he loved her with or without a child (Sam. 1–2). Some men wrongly divorced their wives in order to have children; others, like Abraham, wrongly produced a child through a servant girl or concubine. Conception by illicit means may have solved immediate problems, but it did not insulate the parties from long-term consequences (for example, witness the Arab/Israeli conflict and its worldwide impact on oil supplies).

A converse issue, enduring throughout history but most acute in the last twenty-five years, is the multifaceted impact of unwanted pregnancies both in and out of marriage. So divisive is the issue that it has ascended to the level of political and religious animosities among contending groups at the societal level, and it has profoundly impacted individuals and families.

Polygyny

When two or more women shared a common husband (polygany), trouble was inevitable. The Hebrew word for second wife was "rival wife," and bitterness and hostility often existed between multiple wives. Even when some accommodation was struck, there was the consequent problem of deciding whose son to consider the firstborn for purposes of distributing the inheritance (Deut. 21:15–17; Ex. 21:10).

Politics also played a role. Since preliterate societies, there have been rules that advocate, "marrying out or being killed out," meaning rival tribal leaders agreed to take a wife from each other's tribe. Intermarriage prevented attacks by a rival tribe. After the Exodus, most Hebrew marriages were monogamous, each husband having only one wife (Mark 10:2–9). Anthropologists also agree that the "marry out or be killed out" custom countered incest and its consequences, such as determination of inheritance and the confusion of role definitions.

Polygyny is now rare in western society, compared to its widespread practice by the Mormons in times past. To the dismay of many who mentor and counsel young couples, an insidious substitute in the form of pornography has assumed grave proportions among men—young and old—religiously committed and not. Pastors are finding that addiction to pornography has also captured many to whom they preach on Sunday mornings. Pornography is vicarious fornication, and by biblical standards it is as wrong as having physical relations outside of marriage. It is a vicarious form of polygyny in that, true to the idea of a second wife being a "rival wife," wives of guilty men frequently experience insecurity, anxiety, and depression in a way equal to what is expected if the husband was actually involved in adultery.

Husband's Death

The death of the husband throughout history has had far-reaching consequences for his family, and numerous remedies have sought to provide security for the widow. Levirate law provided protection by the kinsman-redeemer (Deut. 25:5–10). In the absence of a kinsman-redeemer from within one's own clan, the widow could marry into another clan (Ruth 1:9). The deuterocanonical Book of Tobit allowed a widow to return to her family of origin, or, if she was elderly, her son might care for her (Tob. 1:8). If she was financially secure, she might live alone (Jth. 8:7). When penniless and without male relatives to depend on, however, the widow faced great hardships (1 Kings 17:8–15; 2 Kings 4:1–7). In the absence of a son or other relatives in New Testament times, the church was called on to care for the widow (1 Tim. 5:16).

In modern western societies, there are numerous ways to protect against the threat of economic devastation brought about by the illness or death of the husband: retirement programs, health and life insurance, long-term care insurance, as well as the safety nets of Social Security, Medicaid, and Medicare. The protection of the family is a function of the husband and father's stewardship by laying up for the future out of current surpluses— a point I urge older overseers to impress upon their counselees or mentorees.

Rebellious Children

Moses ordered any child who dishonored or struck his parents to be put to death (Ex. 21:15, 17; Lev. 20:9). We have no record of this punishment being carried out, but the Bible describes instances when children did dishonor their parents.[10] Parents were certainly capable of provoking their children to rebellion. David's adultery with Bathsheba and the murder of her husband Uriah obviously had long-term consequences on David's children who, with the exception of Solomon, hardly distinguished themselves (2 Sam. 12:10).

Western societies have widespread problems among adolescents including violence, emotional disturbance, alcohol and drug use, underachievement, and rebellion against authority at all levels.

Sibling Rivalry

Proverbs 18:19 addresses children who argue with one another: "A brother offended is harder to be won than a strong city." The Bible shows numerous instances of rivalry, even to the point of murder.[11]

Adultery

The Hebrews considered adultery swiftly and harshly punishable. In contemporary society and in the contemporary church, such punishment and/or excommunication (particularly in Protestant churches) are left largely unenforced, although the long-term consequences remain.

The incidence of adultery and divorce has never been higher in modern society, and the rates among churched groups equal those among the non-churched. Ministers are not exempt from unfaithfulness, and the threat to the contemporary church has never been greater.

The Social Trust Fund

Every society develops mechanisms to provide for stability and continuity. In fact, the concept of culture refers to that which enjoys continuity over time. In time, social institutions become integrated and balanced with each other, one tending to augment or make up for the deficiencies found in another. The primary protection against family erosion in biblical times and in the present is the social trust fund, with its numerous supporting relatives. The kinsman-redeemer is one, but not the only, example of how the social trust fund works. Friends and parents typically are at the vanguard of the social trust fund. Its composition is both inter- and cross-generational.

Grandparents make up the intergenerational influence of the social trust fund. They were the repository of wisdom and understanding; through their grandchildren, they possessed a crown of glory, and they were fruitful.[12] The full force of the Fifth Commandment was seen when honor given to parents naturally extended to the grandparents and others in authority, turning all those of advancing age into mainstays of social solidarity and continuity. If ever there was a sociological safety net for the family it was the social trust fund.

The social trust fund started at the time of marriage and brought people of different generations together. Some of these folks would never have gotten to know each other if there hadn't been a marriage and a big celebration. Collective familial influences always produce strength for the nuclear family. Modern anthropologists consider the absence of the social trust fund as one of the major factors contributing to the breakup of the modern family.

The deliberate practice of the fund is less prominent in modern western families because of social mobility and independent decision making of younger adults, but it nevertheless continues as a major sociological and psychological strength for family stability wherever it exists. Social scientists have long advocated a cooperative approach to childrearing. The Israeli *kibbutz* excelled in it following the founding of the new nation of Israel. Some political leaders advocate that "it takes a village" to successfully rear a child and prepare him for adulthood. And, while it may come as a shock to some of our readers, the New Testament model is not silent on the responsibility of the body of Christ to exercise interfamilial support and nurturing. The most notable examples of stability in America are among the enclaves of ethnic minorities that share a culture, speak an indigenous language in the privacy of their homes, practice native religion and holidays, and (of considerable value) trade with each other within ethnic neighborhoods. Economists have determined that the collective wealth of some minority groups can be measured by the number of times a dollar is turned over within the minority community. The more times it turns over, the wealthier the community. Early Jewish and Asian immigrants to America are prime examples of this pattern.

Grandparents make up the intergenerational influence of the social trust fund.

The social trust fund consisted of resources on both sides of the nuclear family and could be mobilized in times of need or distress. A young couple usually contributed two sets of parents to the marriage and, perchance, four sets of grandparents, and then brothers, sisters, uncles, aunts, and cousins by the dozens. Happy is the young couple whose children are supported and surrounded by a large extended and committed, multigenerational social trust fund waiting in the wings to provide support, counsel, correction, and admonition at the proper time. We see evidence of the fund less in modern times, although, as noted above, immigrant families concentrated in neighborhoods make it the mainstay for survival and later social and economic success in a new country. Recollection of the fund's historical efficacy is especially strong among older relatives and friends who have been included in the

community of persons surrounding the families. It is reassuring to
know that a call for help mobilizes members to come to the aid of
a needy couple.

At the head of the social trust fund was the family council of
elders, pooling its collective wisdom to provide counsel, adjudi-
cating wrongs, and mobilizing resources to meet individual and
communal needs. No one could become a member of these coun-
cils short of having proved themselves in their own families and
the community—in work, leadership, moral uprightness, and
receiving favor by others. The council was a council of elders,
men of renown who had earned their reputations through years
of righteous living and accumulated wisdom. In short, the older
men stood between every family and the larger society, assuring
the continuity of the latter by guaranteeing the stability of the
former. The family provided the initial crucible from which came
men on whose seasoned shoulders depended the continuation of
God's plan for each succeeding generation.

THE NEW TESTAMENT FAMILY

The tie between family, clan, and tribe in the Old Testament
and remembrance of the founding patriarchs, shifts in the New
Testament to more of a focus on the household (*oikos, oikia*), and
to a lesser extent, on the family (*patria*). Family has to do with
lineage, or the historical origin of a household. Abraham was a
founding father (Gen. 12:3), and Joseph, the husband of Mary,
was of the lineage of David (Luke 2:4). Abraham, Isaac, and Jacob
were patriarchal founders but they take second place to God in
the New Testament, where Paul (Eph. 3:14–15) bowed his knees
before the Father, from whom every family—*patria*—in heaven
and on earth is named. Every family, *patria*, implies a father—
pater—and behind each family is the universal fatherhood of God
whence the whole scheme of ordered relationships is derived.[13]
Hence, in the New Testament *ab* retains its importance in God's
eternal scheme of things.

Household was frequently used as a synonym for family, and
was more a unit of society known throughout the Roman,
Hellenistic, and Jewish worlds of the first century. In this sense,
it refers to the father as head of a household that consisted of the

immediate family, then servants, slaves, employees, and others who voluntarily joined themselves to a household for purpose of mutual benefits.

The household was also a unit of salvation, and therefore was important to church growth. God's promise of salvation to households was so well established that it became a model for early evangelism.[14] In Jerusalem, church households were instructed as units, as Paul reminded the elders at Ephesus. There were rules specifying the duties of all household members, inclusive of the relationship between servants and masters, and the household became the early New Testament church.[15]

From among heads of households approved by church leaders, elders (such as overseers or bishops) and deacons were drawn (1 Tim. 3:2–7, 12). Howard Marshall suggests it is not surprising that the church should be thought of as the household of God, where the term is combined with that of the church or the household of faith.[16] He notes in this regard that believers were considered adopted sons and as stewards and servants (Rom. 8:15–17; 1 Pet. 4:10).

The historical shift from the Old Testament emphasis on family to New Testament emphasis on household did not diminish the value of either the social trust fund or family patriarchs. Jesus knew that customs, traditions, and family ties and loyalties could control people and prevent them from following Him (Luke 14:25). But the issue for Him was not a generational one, for Jesus Himself was defined in terms of them (Matt. 1; Luke 3), but, rather, a sociological one: What is it that controls and prevents one from following God?

A review of Old and New Testament family structure and function reveals a remarkable consistency over thousands of years. This alone would justify the formulation of a theology of advancing years. Of course, there is much more, but the family in itself has been established as the lynchpin holding all other elements of the theology together.

From Father to Elder

The biblical roles of priest, teacher, and administrator were tantamount to the father being pastor of the household and therefore pastor of the primitive house-based church.[17] The sacraments of baptism and the Lord's Supper were carried out in the house churches, with the father officiating.

In the Old Testament, elders were men of advancing age, and the same is suggested in the New Testament. It can also mean "men of old time." Throughout the Bible, seniority entitles people to respect, and a long life is seen as bringing experience and wisdom together.[18]

THE FIFTH COMMANDMENT

The social trust fund was the structural component for a process that was first laid down in the Fifth Commandment, for children to honor their parents and older generations in order to receive their wisdom and understanding. Refusing to honor parents promised children disinheritance from all that prior generations had learned, experienced, and accumulated spiritually and in natural resources (Ex. 29:12; Deut. 21:18–21).

The new covenant validated by Christ's blood also calls for children to honor their parents. This pleases God and opens the way for blessing to attend the life of the children. Children learn to honor their parents within the home, and by extension, to honor their family's heritage and ancestry.[19]

Honoring all generations creates appreciation for the passage of heritage and truth from the preceding generation. By implication, honoring includes having respect and due regard for the age of those from preceding generations. This is one of several long-term effects of the Fifth Commandment.

The purpose of the Ten Commandments was to teach the knowledge of sin—a schoolmaster first separating Israel from heathen nations and later leading men to Christ.[20] By extension, the Fifth Commandment results in honoring all older adults in any generation (Lev. 19:32), caring for dependent parents when in need (1 Tim. 5:4), being responsive to parents when they are old (Prov. 23:22), and learning and being responsive to all those in authority (1 Pet. 2:13–14). The Fifth Commandment crosses multiple generations and reaches out to influence economic, political, and other institutional areas of a society.

Calvin links the matter of honor—comprised of reverence, obedience, and gratitude—with the promise of a long life. The promise of longevity provides insight into the relevance of the Fifth Commandment to a theology of growing old.[21] God promises longevity to those who honor older people. In the Fifth Commandment, what generations of scholars have considered as a mandate to children is also a springboard for a theology of growing old.

God's promise of longevity in connection with honoring parents is also part of the divine strategy for all social structures. Calvin uses Paul's letter to Timothy as a point of departure, where elders are to receive double honor (1 Tim. 5:17). Here, he means that future elders first receive the honor given to any father. Then, when a father becomes an elder, he receives honor again.

The Fifth Commandment crosses multiple generations and reaches out to influence economic, political, and other institutional areas of a society.

Within the family, reverence, obedience, and gratitude can be learned with least strain on the child's habits of submission, Calvin wrote. The child becomes accustomed to this, and as he grows to adulthood, deference and respect are given to all kinds of legitimate authority including other adult members of the extended family, elders, and mentors. The titles of Father, God, and Lord all meet in One. All human titles are provided a small spark of God's refulgence so as to entitle them to honor, each in his own place, for all legitimate authority derives from God. This is the legacy of the Fifth Commandment.

Parents, generally, and the father, particularly, are the historical spiritual fulcrums providing stability and continuity to all of society. The father's importance begins with stewardship over his own family, and this becomes the training ground for eventual leadership in the clan, tribe, and the nation of Israel, and later his leadership in the church as an elder and mentor. The Fifth Commandment is more than a dictum pertaining to the relationship between children and their parents; it is an expansive model for every level of social organization.

CHAPTER FOUR

Mentors and Elders:
Continuity of Skill and Authority

FROM OLD AND NEW TESTAMENT FAMILIES, FATHERS WERE ELEVATED TO BECOME LEADERS IN THE COMMUNITY, NATION, AND CHURCH. MENTORS AND ELDERS BOTH RECEIVED DEFERENCE. NOT all fathers became elders in the formal sense in the larger community, but the father who functioned as priest to his family was, *de facto*, elder to that family. All parents were expected to distinguish themselves as mentors within their own primary and extended families and therefore contributed to the stability and continuity of nation and church.

Those who exhibited righteousness and holiness by continuing in the knowledge of God and responding to His grace established a bedrock foundation where successive generations could stand with confidence. Those foundation builders are mentors and elders.

MENTORS: CONTINUITY OF SKILL

Fathers in nomadic and agrarian societies benefited from the assistance given them by brothers, brothers-in-law, and other older men in the education of their sons. Shared values and the sharing of skills were staples of preindustrial societies. Sociologists and anthropologists have long recognized that social solidarity is a function of shared values. The social trust fund referenced in the prior chapter supports this version of the cohesive community. In such societies, every son and daughter has numerous persons in addition to parents from whom they can acquire skills and gain perspective on essential values and ways of negotiating their environments. Every child is given early access to the matrix of influences, relative to the needs of the moment. In the New Testament, the matrix included the body of Christ whose members were jointly fitted in a complementary way and recruited to edify, instruct, and encourage one another.

Craftsmen taught their own sons in preparation for the time when they would inherit the family business. But they also taught—mentored—others who came to them, because their bents may not have been the same as their fathers'.

The founding and settlement of cities did not stop master craftsmen from mentoring younger apprentices and journeymen. Copper-, silver-, and goldsmiths; potters; tentmakers; carpenters; and other craftsmen taught their own sons in preparation for the time when they would inherit the family business. But they also taught—mentored—others who came to them, because their natural bents may not have been the same as their fathers'. This pattern was evidenced in tribal society as early as the design and construction of the tabernacle in the wilderness. Exodus 35–39 describes the instructions given to Moses by Jehovah for construction of the tabernacle. Two craftsmen, Bezalel and Oholiab, were called to lead and teach others in all matters of weaving, sewing, dyeing, carving, and metalwork.

In city societies, craft guilds arose and mentoring took on a fine art form, as guild masters accepted apprentices from many families, teaching a trade as well as reinforcing the precepts of the Law and customs. This system lasted until the Industrial Revolution in Western societies, and continues in many developing nations to this day.

Prior to the New Testament and lasting well into the first century, herding societies provided considerable opportunity for older men to mentor younger shepherds. Kenneth E. Bailey, who lived in Near Eastern cultures for twenty years among unchanged indigenous communities in order to better understand the Lucan parables, shows that herding was not a socially isolated business as many have assumed, but a corporate one.

Few owners had enough sheep to warrant hiring the required number of shepherds to protect their flocks, so shepherds combined their masters' sheep into one large flock. At the end of the day, they would gather the sheep into a common fold and sit around the fire discussing the events of the day. Older men would continue to mentor novitiates during these times of fellowship and offer solutions to the problems that had arisen during the day.[1]

Notable Old Testament mentors included Jethro of Moses, Naomi of Ruth, Elijah of Elisha, Mordecai of Esther, and Samuel and the school of the prophets.[2] These mentors were all older persons, well into and nearing the ends of their careers. Jethro had mentored Moses in the skills of herding sheep, a trade Moses carried on for forty years in the Midian Wilderness. After Moses had brought the Israelites out of Egypt, Jethro returned from Midian to deliver to Moses his wife and family, and resumed mentoring the new leader in management skills resulting in the delegation of authority to representatives of the twelve tribes.

Naomi mentored Ruth in the fine art of seeking and securing a husband, and Naomi's numerous culture-based instructions lets us know mentoring was not a casual, but rather a deliberate, goal-oriented activity. Elisha yielded to harsh tutelage by Elijah who broke Elisha's will so that he could clearly hear none other than the voice of God, for such was the requirement for being a godly prophet. Elisha's faithfulness to the older man began as he "poured water into Elijah's hands," and this helped win him the right to be heir apparent to Elijah's mantle and to see his mentor rise into the heavens on the chariots of God. Forty years as a judge earned Samuel the right to have his name in the Book, but it was only after he was forced into retirement in old age that he founded and mentored young men as novitiates in the school of the prophets—an event whose impact on Israel and Christendom far surpassed Samuel's forty years of being a judge. All of these were people of advanced age carrying on the work of God and were prophetic fulfillment of the sort of people whose youth was renewed like that of the eagle (Ps. 103:3–5).

Among the well-known examples of mentors in the New Testament are Paul of Timothy, Titus, and Philemon; Barnabas of John Mark and of Paul (following Paul's sojourn in the wilderness to hear from the Lord); Priscilla and Aquilla of Apollos; and, of course, Jesus of the Twelve, but particularly Peter, James, and John.[3]

The art of mentoring has its namesake in the Greek mythical character, Mentor, who, perhaps thirty-five hundred years ago, was a household servant and trusted friend of his master who went off for ten years to tend to the affairs of state. During that time, Mentor accepted the responsibility of overseeing the upbringing of the master's son as a surrogate father. Contrary to the assumptions of many in the institutional church, mentoring is not primarily training in spiritual matters. If mentoring is to be biblical, then the first responsibility for training in religious things resides with the parents. This was both the Old and New Testament model, and it persisted until the Industrial Revolution in Europe and America. During that time, rural life gave way to migration to urban centers where work in factories replaced family farms, blacksmith shops, and tanneries, resulting in the breakup of the extended family as it was known until that time. The move to the cities and the increase of salaried day jobs deprived the members of the family of close contact with each other for many hours a day, and with this the traditional role of the mentor lessened.

With urbanization came the rise of the urban church. It institutionalized within itself the responsibility of religious education, which had historically been up to the extended family. Church school methods followed the Enlightenment's model of didactic transmission of information, and the highly interpersonal role of the mentor (and for that matter, also the social trust fund discussed in the last chapter) lessened.

The mentor often augmented early education by the parents by providing guidance in character development, acquiring and applying natural skills, designing and building a home, learning military, hunting, and trapping skills, searching out a suitable spouse, conducting an honorable biblical courtship, and establishing a God-centered family. The proverbial matchmaker, in addition to finding potential mates for young men and women, was also a mentor in matters of courtship.

It was not until the second half of the twentieth century that mentoring once again came into vogue, and then it was in

American industry, from which it spread into every institutional area of society. Only recently has mentoring once again begun to assume a major role in church and parachurch education. The variations on its basic theme seem unending, providing guidance in functional skills as well as spiritual ones.

Priscilla and Aquila may have mentored Apollos in the correct doctrinal issues of the apostles' teaching, but it seems Barnabas had a few lessons to teach Paul on how to present himself in a civil manner before the council in Jerusalem and how to act humbly in the presence of new believers who were less educated and intelligent than Paul himself.

Only recently has mentoring once again begun to assume a major role in church and parachurch education. The variations on its basic theme seem unending, providing guidance in functional skills as well as spiritual ones.

Living the Christian life encompasses more than studying the Bible, learning to pray, witnessing to the gospel, and attending church. It is wide-ranging, and mentorees benefit from the multitude of skills and resources found within the body of Christ.

Secular research shows that the average age difference between mentor and mentoree is fifteen years. It goes on to document that the ideal mentors for younger persons are those of older years with a rich background in worldly experience, acquired skills, character development, personal on-hand resources, numerous contacts, discretionary time, and financial reserves.

Old age does not automatically qualify one as a mentor. In addition to the mentor's spiritual qualities of knowing God and exercising righteousness and holiness, the mentor in both the Old and New Testament had to exhibit the same qualifications required of elders as described in the writings of Paul and Peter. They were good leaders in their homes, they received honor in the marketplace, they were people of propriety, and they had tangible skills. It is difficult to distinguish between the qualifications and requirements of elder and mentor, and some have referred to mentors as "elders without portfolios." The most distinguishing characteristic of the biblical mentor is that while he or she may not have had any official leadership position in the institutional church, his or her qualities were those of the biblical elder.

ELDERS: CONTINUITY OF AUTHORITY ————————————

In most civilizations, authority has been vested in those who by age or experience have been thought best qualified to rule. It is not surprising that leaders in many ancient communities have borne a title derived from a root meaning "old age." In this respect the Hebrew *elder* stands side by side with the Homeric *gerontes*, the Spartan *presbys*, the Roman *senatus,* and the Arab *sheikh.*[4] (Westerners will recognize the anglicized derivatives of the italicized terms: gerontology, presbytery, and senator; *sheikh* retains its original spelling in the Near East and in Western cultures.) When there is this kind of similarity of connotation across cultures when referring to a single concept, such as elder, we can accept it as an explicit and unquestionable linguistic basis relevant to a theology of advancing years.

Authority and Age: The Old Testament Elder

Jewish elders likely had their origin during the Egyptian captivity, and elders also existed among the Egyptians and among the Moabites and Midianites (Gen. 3:16, 50:7; Num. 22:7). In Egypt, Moses collaborated with the Hebrew elders in planning the biggest escape in human history. These were the heads of families, but Exodus 24:1 identifies a fixed number of seventy upon whom the Lord poured out His spirit in order that they should share the government of the people with Moses (Num. 11:25).

Every settled city likely had its own ruling body of elders whose duties followed the Deuteronomic Code. They served as judges in apprehending murderers, conducting inquests, and settling matrimonial disputes. In the cities of refuge, elders heard pleas for asylum. The national body of elders exercised influence under the monarchy in agitating for a king and finally endorsed Saul. Solomon, Ahab, Jezebel, Jehu, Hezekiah, and Josiah all recognized their position and influence. Ezekiel dealt with them during his captivity, and they appear during Ezra's time and in the Greek period.[5]

The authority of elders was so well established that to run counter to their counsel courted disaster, even for kings and their nations. Young Rehoboam, son of Solomon, sought counsel from the elders shortly after ascending to the throne and then turned and received counsel from his young friends, rejecting what the elders had said. He began his rule in rebellion against the elders, and the subsequent downward spiral of events resulted in civil war and a split between Israel and Judah (1 Kings 12:1–20).

Old age never has been a guarantee of wisdom, a point made by the writer of Ecclesiastes 4:13, when he expressed his personal preference for a wise young man rather than an old fool. Nevertheless, throughout the ancient Near East, the aged were held in honor for their experience and wisdom (Job 12:12, 32:7). Among the Hebrews, this was not merely because of outward appearance—gray hair or attainment of days—but rather because of the assumption that the old person had feared the Lord and kept His commandments (Lev. 19:32; Deut. 30:19–20). It was on this basis they became arbiters of God-appointed authority and accepted positions of authority and responsibility as elders.[6] In addition to ruling in each city (sitting at the gate to provide counsel, keeping inappropriate persons out, and performing judicial tasks), the elders were viewed as representatives of the nation and its people, and were responsible for legal, political, and military guidance, and supervision. Eventually, the elders became the upper class, forming a type of ruling aristocracy. The Jewish Sanhedrin was comprised of a council of seventy-one elders who had both religious and political authority among all Jewish people in Palestine, particularly in New Testament times. The rule by elders in the local synagogues became the model for the early Christian church where eldership implied seniority by reason of age.[7]

Leadership by a council of elders predated the synagogue and was familiar to Jews and readers of the Greek Old Testament. The council of elders was one of Israel's oldest and most fundamental institutions—as basic as the family, where fathers functioned as elders in their immediate and extended families, from which elders were recruited for rule within the clan, tribe, and nation. Israel's elders were the people's official representatives, and this gave rise to the title "elders of the people," or "elders of the congregation."[8]

The role of the elders within the first-century synagogue, often in conjunction with the priests, is considerable, as attested to by both biblical and non-biblical evidence. In first-century Alexandria, they expounded on the Scriptures on the Sabbath. In Jerusalem, teaching was performed primarily by the elders who were called scribes; they served as judges for the purpose of excommunication and punishments. The elders also determined who should keep order, preach, read the lessons, lead in prayers, and be an attendant.[9]

Judging from limited historical information, it appears pre-Christian elders belonged to a non-priestly nobility or were heads of important Judean families and were known to Jewish Christians. Joseph of Arimathea was one such elder (Matt. 27:57), and the entire Sanhedrin is referred to three times as the council of elders (Luke 22:66, Acts 5:21, 22:5).

Appointment as an elder both in the synagogue and in Christian circles was the work of one's teacher. The elder, as teacher, ordained his own pupils, often with the cooperation of two other elders, and usually with the laying on of hands. Thereby, the succession of teachers and judges and a tradition of teaching and legal interpretation was established and continued.[10]

"Although the strict sense of advanced age is eliminated from the meaning of elder when referring to a community leader, certain connotations such as maturity, experience, dignity, authority, and honor are retained. Thus the term *elder* conveys positive concepts of maturity, respect, and wisdom," and these are most likely found among those of advancing years.[11]

Christ is the one great teacher and rabbi, and His disciples referred to themselves as elders.

We do well to embellish the reference to advancing years. The Old Testament elders were preeminently men of counsel and wisdom. "Wisdom is with aged men, with long life is understanding" (Job 12:12), to which is added Ezekiel's prophecy that visions belong to the prophet, law to the priest, and counsel to the elders (Ezek. 7:26).

From what we can discern about the religious environment in which the New Testament church was born, it was Jewish in nature and it appears that the elder was the only official functional role that was transferred intact from under the Old Covenant to the New Covenant. The responsibilities of elders were far ranging and inclusive of the major institutions of the culture, which should help in speculating how the role of elder will be relevant for the discussions of parts 2 and 3.

New Testament Presbyters

Against the background of customs for teaching and judging in the synagogue, the Christian eldership was established, and the Jewish-Christian eldership promoted the diversity of New Testament ministry more often than is realized. Much of that tradition has been lost, but we must exercise caution in attributing the role of elder merely to tradition.[12] A more fundamental question for our purposes is whether the elder continues to play a role in modern times as a result of God's wisdom.

Christ is the one great teacher and rabbi, and His disciples referred to themselves as elders. The teaching they received was passed on and committed to others, who committed it to still others. Those to whom it was committed are likewise called elders, following the laying on of hands.[13]

The family was the crucible where every father was tested by the vicissitudes of leadership, and every family was the source of Israel's elders, first in behalf of the clan, then the twelve tribes, and finally the nation. The position of elder seems to be the only form of authority brought over from the Old Testament into the New, although the function took on new expression. Nevertheless, Peter, steeped in the Law and Jewish history, summarizes the role of the New Testament elder in a way reminiscent of what was expected of every pre-Christian father in leading the members of his own family, for it was from successfully led families that elders of communities were recruited:

> Therefore, I exhort the elders among you, as your fellow elder . . . shepherd the flock of God among you, exercising oversight not under compulsion, but voluntarily, according to the will of God, and not for sordid gain, but with eagerness; nor yet as lording it over those allotted to your charge, but proving to be examples to the flock. . . . You younger men, likewise, be subject to your elders. (1 Pet. 5:1–5)

Paul, like Peter, recognized the wisdom of recruiting elders from successfully led families and from among men who had established themselves in their community.

> It is a trustworthy statement: if any man aspires to the office of overseer [elder], it is a fine work he desires *to do*. An overseer, then, must be above reproach, the husband of one wife, temperate, prudent, respectable, hospitable, able to teach, not addicted to wine or pugnacious, but gentle, uncontentious, free from the love of money. He *must be* one who manages his own household well, keeping his children under control with all dignity (but if a man does not know how to manage his own household, how will he take care of the church of God?); *and* not a new convert, lest he become conceited and fall into the condemnation incurred by the Devil. And he must have a good reputation with those outside *the church*, so that he may not fall into reproach and the snare of the Devil. (1 Tim. 3:1–7) (italics in original)

Apart from the fact that the instructions by Peter and Paul were to the New Testament church, the standards for eldership cited by them derived from the Old Testament model and the extrabiblical writings of ancient fathers. The point here is that throughout the history of God's people, a standard of leadership has been raised by the Father and divinely transmitted by the Holy Spirit to the writers of Scripture. Further, we easily infer from the instructions of Paul to Timothy that unless a church had appointed and ordained elders, it was not a church in accordance with New Testament criteria.

The standard determining who could become an elder is not only substantive as to content; it also is demographic in quality, focusing as it does in the majority of instances on those of older and advancing years.

By the second century, the sacraments came under the supervision of the ordained ministry, but this was historically based and not biblically prescribed, and the personal prerogative never belonged to the ordained ministry. In fact, since the middle of the twentieth century, there has been a resurgence of fathers of families, along with elders, assuming responsibility for the sacraments, particularly in nonaffiliated churches, irrespective of size, and even in mainline denominations that have been influenced by the charismatic renewal.

Mentors and elders throughout ancient history and in the history of the church are mechanisms conceived and ordained by God to provide stability at different levels of social structure. This assures the continuity of the nation of Israel to proclaim the coming Messiah and the church's ability to proclaim the gospel of the kingdom. Mentors and elders are recruited from those who possess maturity, experience, dignity, wisdom, authority, and honor—traits found primarily in older believers and those of advancing age whose lives have personified the knowledge of God. Paul left little question that when he gave instructions regarding the choice of elders, he had those of gray hair in mind, adding that caution was required to not choose young men who might, because of youthfulness and lack of experience, come under the influence of the Devil.

The careful reader should be asking more questions at this point rather than having been provided with answers. Until 300 A.D. when Constantine politicized the church and made it a state church, elders continued to function in the New Testament church. Church historians recognize that mistakes were made by institutionalizing the formal structure of the church in such a manner as to concentrate authority within the ordained ministry. Some may propose that there are many alternatives to the role of elder in the modern church and community, making the biblical prescriptions no longer necessary. If this is true, would we pick public school teachers, law enforcement officers, social workers, the courts, public day care centers, or youth organizations to serve as elders? Many would say no. Well, others add, we still have the institutional church; it offers somewhat of a continuation of the historical responsibilities of elders. Many traditional mainline denominations consider only the senior pastor as the elder, and he or she can hardly oversee (in any biblical sense) congregations of several hundred or more. Other churches do away with biblical elders altogether and replace them with boards of directors or trustees who seldom function as elders as

In the absence of biblical elderships, there has developed an institutional church void of what God seemed to think was a good idea for several thousand years.

described here. In the absence of biblical elderships, there has developed an institutional church void of what God seemed to think was a good idea for several thousand years. In fact, it was such a good idea that wiser, older, seasoned people of gray hair were the pinnacles of authority in every known culture of the pre-modern past.

In the late 1990s, I traveled to a Pacific Rim country on behalf of our health care consulting company, and one of the services we were marketing was the design and implementation of long-term care programs that involved the development of cooperative consortia among community organizations. A signature element in what we did then, and had been doing for several decades, was to mobilize local organizations in support of the family—particularly the older authority figures of the community. Frequently we heard comments such as, "This is the Chinese model. We revere our old, regardless of their state of health. We defer to their authority even in their weakened state. What you propose will be accepted here; isn't this the way it is done in the United States?"

CHAPTER FIVE

Parents: Continuity of Values and Character

OUR VALUES HAVE DEEP HISTORICAL ROOTS IN PHILOSOPHICAL AND SCRIPTURAL PRINCIPLES THAT ARE IMBEDDED IN THE PAST—SOMETIMES SO FAR IN THE PAST THAT WE HAVE LOST TRACK OF THEIR ORIGINS. The term "culture" refers to the knowledge, beliefs, and behaviors that last from generation to generation. Culture is stability and continuity, something I have referred to many times in earlier chapters. Each generation has the responsibility of passing on to each succeeding generation the content of culture. In every society from preliterate and pre-industrial to the present, parents are expected by their communities to teach their children how to implement values into daily life.

Parents are the most significant sources from which foundational values emerge for yet another generation. Values explain what drives us and why we act the way we do. Character, on the other hand, can best be described as a stylistic sort of thing.

Character qualities determine how we act. Our commitment to other Christians, as an example, predicts that we will have concern for others. This has to do with values. My character, on the other hand, says my commitment will have a certain style, involving long suffering, tolerance, and patience. Many have referred to the passage in Galatians 5:22–23 as the foundational list of character qualities—love, joy, peace, patience, kindness, goodness, faithfulness, gentleness, and self-control. Some, such as R. C. Sproul, have identified these nine character qualities as descriptive of holiness, which then makes sense of the teaching in

Hebrews 12. Here, natural fathers are said to discipline us for a season as may seem good to them, but the Father of all fathers disciplines us so that we may share His holiness. These are bedrock issues for the Christian, and they also are the substance of what parents first and foremost are required to pass on to their children.

With age, parents' values become sharpened and focused; with age they are increasingly expressed with seasoned grace. Time is beneficial for the effect it has on both values and character, for although there is no guarantee that either will possess virtue, there is a guarantee that we will more clearly see a person's authentic self—whether good or bad.

CONTINUITY OF VALUES

Paul taught values in the form of Christian doctrine, but he said to Timothy, "Follow my example," referring to consistency and persistency of effort—admirable character traits. Fathers of the Old and New Testament Scriptures served priestly, prophetic, and administrative functions. God's plan for fathers in the beginning has remained His plan for all time. First-century church elders were appointed from among the more qualified fathers of households to every church (Acts 14:23; Titus 1:5), and Paul considered it a "trustworthy statement: if any man aspires to the office of overseer, it is a fine work he desires to do"(1 Tim 3:1). The adjective "any" removes any limits to the number of fathers who could aspire to become elders, and it also recognizes there were many men of sound values and outstanding character who were otherwise qualified to be elders. The biblical record of the first-century house church leaves little doubt that to qualify as being a church, there had to be a biblically qualified elder. Some have speculated that in the several months following the day of Pentecost, as many as five hundred house churches were established and therefore five hundred elders were recruited from heads of families.

As was pointed out in chapter 4, the apostles, prophets, evangelists, pastors, and teachers of Ephesians 4 were likely elders or had met the qualifications of elders before assuming these ministry gifts. They may also have functioned as elders simultaneous with their responsibilities as one of the "five fold" ministry. The injunction nevertheless was to appoint elders.

Not all fathers of households would be chosen as elders in the church, and this would especially be true in those house churches that included more than two or more families. We must be careful not to assume that failure to be an elder was an indictment of one's failure to be a godly father—full of values and of excellent character. In part 3, the leadership opportunities for elders are expanded greatly and represent more effective stewardship of abundant resources in the local church. All older men were admonished to continue in the very qualities required of elders: to be temperate, dignified, sensible, and sound in faith, love, and perseverance (Titus 2:2). These are matters of character from which no good Jew or Christian was exempted. What the older man did not do within the institutional church, he would do in his family, on the job, and in a variety of other activities. As a member of the Jewish community, he was tied to others by the Law and synagogue; as a member of the body of Christ, he was jointly fitted by God to other believers to edify, support, and love them (1 Cor. 12, Rom. 12). Throughout history, we know more about the few heroes who were loved, revered, and followed by their families and their neighbors than we do about the thousands. The children of the Book have grown in number and become a veritable force throughout the earth. They do the work of the church without portfolios.

The New Testament ministers trained and brought the members to maturity so that they could do the work of the church.

Sociologically, the community's social institutions always have served as a safety net and backed up what God first prescribed families to do under the authority of parents. The priest and scribe reaffirmed and augmented the finer points of the Law first introduced and taught by the father. The New Testament ministers trained and brought the members to maturity so that they could do the work of the church.

Each higher level of social support reinforces the family. Then, in order, schools, synagogues and churches, and legal institutions regulate, govern, apprehend, convict, incarcerate, excommunicate, or execute incorrigible members. All societies have worked this way, irrespective of time and complexity. But the primary responsibility rested with the parents. The father's success, to which Scripture attests, was attributed to his godly wife whose behavior in the community as wife and mother became the glory of her husband (Prov. 31:10:31).

Distributing True Riches

Parents accumulated a store of resources over a lifetime of faithfulness that was measured out to offspring at just the right time. From the storehouse of experience, values, and character came such things as last words, blessings, and others.

Last Words

The last words of a dying person are accepted, both sociolog-ically and forensically, to be true. There is an accepted gravity and honesty to the last testament—a dying person is thought not to lie. Prior to his death, David called Solomon to his side and gave final instructions regarding his son's succession to the throne (1 Kings 2:1–11). David's last words to Israel were like-wise recorded as a final charge to the people he had ruled faithfully (2 Sam. 23:1–7). In the same manner, Joshua's farewell speech to Israel was both a warning against idolatry and a testi-mony to his and his family's faithfulness to God (Josh. 24:1–8).

The Blessing

Among the most significant acts of those advancing years is the blessing, particularly when accompanied by the biblical sacra-ment of laying hands on the one being blessed. The father in the Old Testament and both parents in the New Testament were the spiritual conduits through whom God worked in both a general and specific sense in behalf of each member of the family.

The act of declaring or asking for God's favor and goodness upon others not only has the desired effect of the good words themselves; it also has the power to bring them to pass. In the Old and New Testament, important persons continued the ancient sacrament of blessing those with less power or influence. The patriarchs pronounced blessings on their children, often near their own deaths. Abraham blessed Isaac; Isaac blessed Jacob; Jacob first gave a special blessing to Joseph's two sons and then blessed his own sons, after which he died.[1]

Leaders often blessed those they were about to leave. These included Moses, Joshua, and Jesus. In the beginning, God blessed by giving life, riches, fruitfulness, and plenty to those whom He created. The creation of man and woman in the image of God authorized each parent to continue in the Father's ways.[2]

The Old Testament word *braka* generally denoted a bestowal of good, usually conceived as material good.[3] The blessing often consisted of a combination of words or a formula, as in Moses' blessing for all the sons of Israel (Deut. 33). When expressed by man, the blessing was a wish or prayer for a blessing that was to come in the future. In the sense of Genesis 28:4, the blessing becomes an instrument of sociological continuity.

The Lord's blessing rests on those who are faithful to Him: "A blessing if ye obey the commandments of the Lord your God, which I command you this day . . ."(Deut. 11:27). God's blessing brings righteousness, life, prosperity, and salvation.[4] It is portrayed as a gentle rain or the dew: "I will make them and the places round about my hill a blessing, and I will cause the showers to come down in his season; there shall be showers of blessing" (Ezek. 34:26). For brothers who walk in unity (literally blood brothers in the Old Testament and implied brothers in the faith in the New), the Lord commands a blessing: "[It is] as the dew of Hermon, and as the dew that descended upon the mountains of Zion: for there the Lord commanded the blessing, even life for ever more."[5]

The contemporary concept of older adults serving as the spiritual conduit—from God to the family and on behalf of the family to God—beautifully portrays the family as heaven's vice-regent on earth. At the Sabbath celebration, the father (*ab*) stands at the head of the table, hands raised in adoration and praise, and invokes Jehovah's blessings from the Pentateuch on the family. Then, one by one, he circles the table, and with his hands on the heads of his wife and each of his children, he blesses them, in a general or specific way. In modern Jewish homes, the practice is still considered an important vehicle for communicating a sense of identity, meaning, love, and acceptance. In many orthodox homes, a weekly blessing is given to the children. Upon lighting the candles, the blessings begin. At times of special meals, kissing, hugging, laying on of hands, and asking God to provide a special future for the child are common practices in contemporary orthodox homes.[6] This same intensity of giving the blessing has increased among many Protestant homes of varied denominations since the 1960s, and it is universally a part of Messianic Jewish (Christian) congregational and family life.

Family counselors Gary Smalley and John Trent recognize the blessing as a critical element in preventing emotional disorders among children and healing old wounds between adult children and their aging parents. But the biblical value of the blessing is to be found first and foremost as an act mediating between man and God, and modern Christians are encouraged to continue in this spirit.

In the New Testament, blessing is denoted by *eulogia*, addressing God with a celebration or with praises, acknowledging His goodness with a desire for His glory, and carries a desire for material and spiritual benefits.[7]

Words of Wisdom

The old have the rare and valuable privilege of passing the wisdom of earlier generations to others (Ps. 78:1–4). Proverbs 12 is rich in such gems that come from a length of days. In God's discourse on His choice of Abraham, He specifically required the patriarch to command his own family to keep the way of the Lord (Gen. 18:17–19). But the old who were righteous were specifically set aside to declare the Lord's uprightness and righteousness (Ps. 92:10–15).

The Eulogy

In modern man's urgency to seize the day—*carpe diem*—and aggressively shape the future, the eulogy is the careful effort of thoughtful people who appreciate perspective and history and who recognize that the future invariably stands on the shoulders of giants.

Saul, despite his personal emotional problems, provided the occasion for David to become a general who killed his ten thousands, and Saul was also the crucible in which David received lessons on courtly rule. Above all, Saul was the threshing floor on which David learned the most important of all lessons, to live under legitimate authority. David could not dismiss these lessons, and was quick to take advantage of opportunities to pass the lessons on to future generations. He therefore sang a lament for Saul and Jonathan following their death on the battlefield, and ordered the lament to become a song immemorial for Israel (2 Sam. 1:19–27). Memorials are the essence of eulogies. In similar fashion, upon the death of King Josiah, the prophet Jeremiah sang a lament that was remembered in perpetuity (2 Chron. 35:23–25; Lam. 4:20).

Laying on of Hands

The blessing is bestowed when one person lays his hands on the head or shoulders of the one being blessed. This act has significance apart from the blessing itself. In the Old Testament, the priests laid their hands on the scapegoat to transfer to it the sins of the people; Jacob placed his hands upon Joseph's children to convey a blessing; and Moses conferred a portion of his wisdom and spirit upon Joshua.[8] It was no accident that older persons in authority used laying on of hands as a means of transferring, conveying, and conferring. The hands were an extension of the person who was a conduit, performing the work of God.

In the New Testament, Jesus and the apostles laid hands upon the sick and they were healed; true believers in Christ had authority to lay hands on the sick for healing; and Jesus laid hands upon children to bless them.[9]

Laying on of hands is a means by which believers receive blessings of strength, healing, and faith, and then pass those blessings on to others. In the New Testament, receiving the Holy Spirit was imparted by the laying on of hands (Acts 8:18–19, 9:17, 19:6). Confirmation through the laying on of hands is the means whereby members of the church are settled, strengthened, and established in the faith, after they have been taught the doctrines, ordinances, and sacraments of the church (Acts 15:32). Ordination for service is conferred upon believers to invest them with ministerial responsibilities and authority (Acts 13:1–3). Alexander Strauch proposes that, similar to the Old Testament succession of eldership, New Testament elders laid hands on those who had been chosen for eldership after meeting the requirements for service.[10] Finally, an anointed spoken word of prophecy pertaining to the gifts and ministries of believers, accompanied by the laying on of hands, imparts the creative Spirit of God.[11]

The Prodigal's Father

Probably the most poignant image of the blessing being conferred with the laying on of hands is found in Rembrandt's painting *The Return of the Prodigal Son*, which is beautifully described by Henri J. M. Nouwen in a book by the same name.[12]

The aging father and family patriarch had given the younger son, in response to his immature and impetuous insistence, his portion of the inheritance before his time. The father allowed the son to leave home; God also allows us to leave home. His love demands this of Himself, so that when we do return, as so many other prodigals, we do so with a will that is redirected toward the Father.

In the painting, the son is on his knees before the father. The father, old, bent, and almost blind, has placed one hand on the son's back, the other on his shoulder. The first hand is fragile, open, delicate, gentle, accepting, and merciful. These qualities, as interpreted by Nouwen, convey one part of the blessing. It is the female or mother quality of God.

The father's other hand on the repenting son's shoulder is strong, muscular, intense, and restraining, and these qualities represent the blessing of forgiveness and generosity. The prodigal's father has become like the heavenly Father. Perhaps when he was a youth, the father had also traveled the road of the prodigal. Or perhaps he had once stood proud, pharisaical, and judgmental like the older brother. But he understood, as do many men and women of advancing age, experience, and wisdom, that to become like the Father they must experience the Father's forgiveness, generosity, and acceptance in moments of impropriety. And in those moments, the blessing was conferred on them.

Last words, blessings, words of wisdom, eulogies, or the laying on of hands: these are the works of older adults. In each is the distilled experience of a lifetime . . .

Last words, blessings, words of wisdom, eulogies, or the laying on of hands: these are the works of older adults. In each is the distilled experience of a lifetime—the accumulation of all God has deposited in a man or woman—the skills, wisdom, hurts, various vicissitudes, and rewards of life. Each older parent has become the repository of his or her slice of the broad spectrum of culture and its values. In any of these five acts of graciousness, he or she transmits that portion, no matter how small or large, onto the next generation. These are moments of gravity, and they need to be weighed carefully, savored, and allowed to rest on the palate like good wine. They will not pass this way again. Those of gray hair possess value and are the conveyors of value. It is as God intended for all time.

Continuity of Character

The Old Testament deliberately portrays the older person as having a dignity that, by comparison, is not emphasized as much in the New Testament. The Old Testament established most of the social models whose essence was not lost to the first-century Christian. The parent full of quality was seasoned, steeped in experience, tried in the crucible, and buffeted by and reeling from the blows of adversaries. David wrote of these in the Psalms. Having tasted the blessings of God, yet not forgetting lean and fallow years, these godly folk of the Word are a memorial to having become seasoned or mellow.

Kindness and Goodness

Paul, in his list of the fruit of the Spirit in Galatians 5, uses a Greek word whose root, *crestos*, was used to describe old wine: mellow. The fruit referred to as *kindness* was sometimes translated *goodness* (Gal. 5:22). Kindness (*chrestotes*) is what Christ's yoke was called; it does not irk or gall (Matt. 11:30). Goodness (*agathosune*) is a peculiar biblical word, defined as "virtue equipped at every point" (Rom. 15:14; Eph. 5:9, 2 Thess. 1:11). Christ showed *agathosune* when He cleansed the temple and drove out the bazaar vendors, and He showed *chrestotes* when He was kind to the sinning woman who anointed His feet. The best of aged wine is kind in both flavor and aroma, and strong or substantial in body. Old parents tempered by the fires are good and kind. It is a character thing.

Unlike new wine, there is no bite or vinegary flavor. Old wine requires time to arrive at mellow maturity. It is this kind of character quality that saints of advancing age are known to have exhibited in the Old Testament, and Paul reminds us that this quality is not to be lost. It is an integral evidence of the Spirit within us. By analogy, Jesus implies recognition of the rich heritage of older family members and their blessing on the marriage when he performed the first miracle at Cana by reserving the best wine for last.

The issue of character development as a process of maturation is not to be dismissed lightly in a theology of advancing years. Three other character qualities are discussed here to illustrate how discipling brings the older believer to share the holiness of God and the peaceful fruit of righteousness (Heb. 12:10–11).

Love

Paul's brief comparison of his youthful days with those after he had grown up (1 Cor. 13:11) implies two different kinds of love. As a child, he demonstrated the immature, sensual, and selfish love called *eros*; as an adult he demonstrated *agape* to which the thirteenth chapter was devoted. Paul's familiarity with Greek history and its literature had exposed him to Hellenistic heavenly *eros*, the kind of love that was acquisitive, self-aggrandizing, and controlling. All children know *eros*. It is lifestyle for them as they seek to acquire and control. It is insatiable. Paul also knew that *eros* (although the word does not appear in the Greek New Testament) could impregnate and take over religious behavior, and the church at Corinth most certainly exemplified this. They sought the spiritual gifts for their own sakes rather than seeking the Gift-Giver, and they vied for position in the church rather than bowing at the feet of its Head. The city and church in Corinth were known for their *eros*. The culture of the city was infiltrating the church, and this was Paul's reason for writing.

In contrast, *agape* is an expression of God in us; it is a love that comes from a contented life free of striving, manipulation, and controlling others. *Agape* is the love found in a person who knows and finds contentment in his or her place. Jealousy and envy have no place in *agape*. It is the love of a person of advancing years who, like David, could declare:

> O Lord, my heart is not proud, nor my eyes haughty; nor do I involve myself in great matters, or in things too difficult for me. Surely I have composed and quieted my soul; like a weaned child rests against his mother, my soul is like a weaned child within me. (Ps. 131:1–2)

Paul echoed this same attitude in his testimony to the church at Corinth on a later occasion, explaining that he knew his purpose, place, and audience, and therefore he would not extend his ministry beyond that assignment (2 Cor. 10:12–15).

Advancing age can bring contentment of duty and place. It is, as V. Raymond Edmund called it, the "discipline of declining days," when competition, compulsive behavior, and daring are left to others.[13] With striving gone, *agape* is free to come forth as a fruit of the Spirit in the life of the older obedient child of God who walks confidently in the place given him or her by the Father. Fortunate is the younger person whose elder, mentor, or parent knows this as a way of life and passes this element of character on to the next generation.

Peace

Serenity. Contentment. Under the discipline of an all-benevolent Lord. These are the connotations of the secular Greek term *eirene*. In his younger days, a man might struggle and kick against the hardships of life until, by the mercies and grace of God, he yields to the discipline of the Lord. He turns his back on bitterness, resentment, and unforgiveness, and accepts the ever-increasing government of God in his life (Heb. 12:15; Isa. 6:7). This is no mere acquiescence. Having learned peace in his younger days, the octogenarian then becomes a "maker of peace" (Matt. 5:9).

Persistence

How does one reach beyond chronological age to become "advanced?" How are kindness, love, and peace achieved in a lifetime so that they can be passed on to children, younger elders, or the church? Persistence. For the mentor, elder, grandparent, matriarch, or patriarch, these are the things of legends. The writer of 1 Maccabees expressed persistence using the term *makrothumia*, which describes how the Romans had become masters of the world (1 Macc. 8:4). This concept forbade making peace with the enemy, even in defeat. Persistence was a conquering patience that outlasted those who scoffed, ridiculed, rejected, obstructed, threatened, or sought to control. Many are the illicit detours along any successful warrior's journey, but persistence emerges and takes shape on the way. Persistence is its own self-fulfilling prophecy. The strength of persistence builds and accumulates in the process of practicing it.

The man or woman born of the Holy Spirit must pay a hefty price over the years. Character cannot be learned by attending a class or a lecture, by listening to sermons or cassette tapes, or by attending a weekend conference. The seeds of character, as the potential fruit of the Spirit (Gal. 5:22–23), accompany the coming of the Holy Spirit at the time of new birth (John 3:5–8). Short of paying the price, fruit will remain permanently potential, encased in a shell of *eros*. For the persistent child of God, there is a price to be paid by having been refined, winnowed, pruned, and circumcised (Rev. 2–3).

Paying the Price to Overcome

The process of pressure

Younger persons sometimes discuss the tales of older persons who have experienced war, economic depression, untimely death of children, disability, occupational setbacks, scars, betrayal by friends, character assassination, backbiting, and slander. When these tales are found in a person with soft eyes and who walks with a limp, their value should increase. The Bible is replete with examples of these very experiences among the saints. Hebrews 11 catalogues the challenges faced by the champions of faith. Paul provides a litany of personal setbacks in 2 Corinthians 4 and 6. Paul, Peter, and James all recount the challenging processes leading to *agape*-producing endurance.[14] The price of salvation measures with clinical detail the horrendous death of Jesus on the cross, and first-century tradition identifies the manner in which each of the apostles was executed. The honor of wearing the hoary head comes with the same price each generation must pay if it wishes to stand on the shoulders of giants. This too is part of the theology of advancing years. The following metaphors aptly describe the process.

Messiah comes as a refining fire, measuring just the right amount of heat to drive off the dross while still preserving the elasticity of pure metal (Mal. 3:3). He comes to the winnowing floor, flailing the fork mercilessly as He thrashes the chaff of personal defenses and superficial protections from the grain that is destined to be fresh bread that salves a hurt heart or a hungry soul (Luke 3:17). The finest grapes come from the exceptional branches the vineyard keeper has repeatedly pruned to produce grapes for the finest vintage wine (John 15:1–2). The Word of God, sharper than a two-edged sword, divides the soul, spirit, joints, and marrow; discerns the thoughts and intents of the heart (Heb. 4:12); and circumcises the heart to prepare a person after God's own heart (Col. 2:11). Such a heart is vulnerable, transparent, tender, defenseless, and altogether public. These are coins of the kingdom, the price paid by the one who, in the face of temporary, inadequate, and sometimes weakening faith, rejects it and goes on to persist. These coins do not come easily, conveniently, or early in life.

The honor of wearing the hoary head comes with the same price each generation must pay if it wishes to stand on the shoulders of giants.

The metaphor of fine old vintage wine has similarities to the process by which the finest extra virgin olive oil was made in Bible times. Like grapes, olive pulp has to be separated from the oil, and the more the pulp is pressed, torn, and progressively filtered out from the oil, the clearer and gentler the oil becomes. The finest oil is referred to as virgin and beyond that, extra virgin. The analogy is wonderfully described in James A. Michener's *The Source* where he describes medieval Crusaders just prior to their being attacked and massacred.

> Beloved children of Christ, we have come to the day when we shall meet God Almighty face to face, and if there are among those who ask, "Why has this tragedy overtaken us?," I cannot explain, but centuries ago that great man St. Augustine, surveying a similar period, spoke thus to all who are perplexed: "For the world is like an olive press, and men are constantly under pressure. If you are the dregs of the oil you are carried away through the sewer, but if you are true oil you remain in the vessel. But to be under pressure is inescapable. Observe the dregs, observe the oil, and choose, for pressure takes place [throughout] the world: war, siege, famine, the worries of state. We all know men who grumble under these pressures and complain, but they speak as the dregs of oil which later run away in the sewer. Their color is black, for they are cowards. They lack splendor. But there is another sort of man who welcomes splendor. He is under the same pressure, but he does not complain. For, it is the friction [that] polishes him. It is the pressure which refines and makes him noble."[15]

The converse of the analogy of pouring off the dregs, whether from the wine vat or the olive press, is found in the description of the region of Moab in Jeremiah 48:11 NIV.

> Moab has been at rest from youth, like wine left on its dregs, not poured from one jar to another. . . . So she tastes as she did, and her aroma is unchanged.

There are persons of advanced age who have allowed themselves to be tipped from one vessel to another, gradually leaving less of the dregs of grape skins in the bottom of the vessels. The purity comes from repeatedly tipping and pouring the wine into new, clean vessels. The eagle, whose appearance is renewed over the years, requires repeated molting. Each molt renders the mighty bird ugly, unkempt, and unattractive. And then the new feathers come. A price must be paid to retain the appearance of youth. Moab refused to be tipped. There are older people who also refuse to undergo the pressure of being separated from the dregs in their lives. They turn their backs on those who would tip their vessels. Their aroma remains—they are stale—they are rancid.

Old Wine and Renewed Wineskins: Exception to the Parable

In the parable of old wine and new wineskins (Luke 5:33–39), the discussion is about the Old Covenant and the New Covenant. It was common knowledge that new, unfermented wine should not be put into old skins that had lost their elasticity. How accurately this describes those of advanced age who, like the retiring old king of Moab, have lost their elasticity of thought and sentiment. New ideas, forms of worship, architecture, and music are the new wine. There are older people who just do not or cannot fit. They have confused form and function.

Jesus, for whatever reason, left it up to others to fill in the broader picture of the Lucan parable. Each year's grape production far exceeded the availability of new wineskins. Old wineskins had been emptied and were available if only the problem of stiffness could be addressed. The cool, pure mountain streams provided an answer: the skin flasks were cleaned and rinsed over and over in the clear streams, until they were refreshed and took on the form of new skins. Their elasticity was restored, along with the necessary strength to hold the new wine. We must be careful not to impose meaning, yet we know that the believer of advanced years who returns to the fountain of refreshing in the Holy Spirit will be renewed in spirit and will experience youth like that of the eagle. His or her mind, soul, and spirit are once again elastic and responsive to what God wants to do in his or her life. In the psalm about the exalted horn, the blessings of the Lord rendered older people like supple, pliable green boughs, full of sap—not dissimilar from the restored wineskins. The next generation is likened to new wine. It still must be mellowed. It does so in the presence of seasoned older adults who yield to the times of refreshing from the Lord.

It was said of the priest Eli that at ninety-eight years old, his eyes were set so that he could not see (1 Sam. 4:15). Eli's ability to discern spiritually the difference between right and wrong, however, had disappeared long before when he had refused to confront his wayward sons' improper ministry as priests in the temple (1 Sam. 2:12–17, 22–36). By contrast, Moses at 120 years old had eyes that were still sharp and vision that had not dimmed. Eli was fat, lazy, and unable to move from place to place. Moses' vigor had not diminished even on the day of his death. Moses is our model for the person of advanced years, not Eli who failed as priest and father.

We have considered the role of parents who surround their values with garments of character. Values are foundational, but character, like the sugar that makes the medicine go down more easily, is necessary as the vehicle through which values are passed on from generation to generation.

CHAPTER SIX

Early Transitions toward Latter Days

KING DAVID THE WARRIOR WAS GROWING OLD; ISRAEL FOUGHT AGAINST THE PHILISTINES, AND DAVID BECAME WEARY. NOWHERE ELSE IS HIS WEARINESS MENTIONED (2 SAM. 17:29). ON ANOTHER occasion, Israel readied for war, but the people said to him, "Do not go out to battle; it is better you stay in the city," and, again, "You shall not go out to battle, so that the lamp of Israel is not extinguished" (2 Sam. 18:3, 21:15, 17). Samuel served Israel as a judge for more than sixty years, and then the elders said, "no more," and demanded a king. Samuel was fired (1 Sam. 7–8). Elijah witnessed the deaths of four hundred heathen priests by the hand of God; he then ran, frightened by Jezebel, and when God found him hiding in a cave, he asked for death (1 Kings 19). John, the disciple who was "loved by Jesus," was nearly one hundred years old and exiled to the prison colony on the island of Patmos. Paul, his missionary journeys over, was imprisoned in Rome where he would later be beheaded (Phil. 1:7).

Giants in the kingdom of God: old, weakened, and no longer as active in their callings and purposes in God. Were their careers at an end? Not quite, but they were all in transition from where they had been when younger to new assignments from the throne of God. David continued as king and wrote a magnificent psalm of praise that was followed by what became his last song (2 Sam. 22, 23). Samuel pledged himself to pray for Israel and then formed the school of the prophets (2 Kings 2, 4, 6). Elijah was instructed to anoint two new kings and to prepare Elisha to succeed him as prophet (1 Kings 19). In what could have been isolated destitution ending in madness under the burning Mediterranean sun, John beheld a heavenly vision and recorded it in letters to the churches, which were included in the canon of Scripture. In his dark and damp cell, Paul pledged to never cease praying for the saints at large. Each of these giants transitioned in the hands of a loving God: they completed their assignments and then went to be with Him.

THE CONCEPT OF TRANSITION

Life is a series of transitions. The road we travel from birth to death is filled with signs, each marking the time when another transition will occur. The foregoing champions of the Bible are examples of transitions. The many references to the four seasons and other agricultural metaphors throughout the Bible are constant reminders of change—new life in the spring, the formation and ripening of fruit under the burning summer sun, celebration of the harvest in the fall, and lonely dormancy in winter.

Transitions are easier when there are well-established ceremonies, and rules are attached to them: confirmation, baptism, graduation, engagement, marriage, housewarming, and retirement. The rules are still being written about growing old and dying, and they change as society changes. But societies need principles that are substantial and lasting.

Many transitions are exciting and marked by a variety of personal, family, and community-wide celebrations: the addition of a child to the family; the circumcision of a male baby on the eighth day; bar mitzvah for sons and bat mitzvah for daughters when they graduate from childhood to adult privileges and responsibilities; marriage; the down payment on a first home; a first child or grandchild; getting a driver's license; going off to college; graduating; the first job; getting a promotion; buying a larger home or a luxury car.

Not all transitions are exciting. There are painful transitions such as widowhood, loss of a job, divorce, loss of security, miscarriage, a teenager's accidental death, a crippling sports accident, declining health, forced retirement, bankruptcy, increasing disability and illness, the death of a spouse, the sale of the family home, loneliness, and the death of beloved friends.

Growing and being old is relative across the ages and around the planet. In Western societies, the issue is more fluid. Because of medical and technological advances in nutrition and health-care, as well as new preventions for diseases, life expectancy is changing rapidly. Also, because people are freer to write their own rules, older people are less inclined to accept the stereotypes that continue to be held by the society around them. This can be aggravating to those who are closest: spouses, families, and churches, who often, for their own comfort, prefer what is convenient though inaccurate.

More people are living longer, and gerontologists anticipate that in a few years, living to be 100 years of age will not be unusual. By 2040, some will live to 120. Older people today seem younger and more active than in years past. Recently, an eighty-nine-year-old woman with arthritis made a two thousand mile trek across the country for her special social cause; a seventy-three-year-old man ran his first twenty-six mile marathon. The Senior Olympics attracts more participants each year. These clinical and demographic patterns frighten policy makers who don't know how to budget for 20 percent of the population who will live thirty or more years in retirement. While youth and beauty have historically received the lion's share of marketing attention, there is little doubt those seeking second youth are causing quite a stir. Early in the year 2000, both houses of the U.S. Congress unanimously passed a bill to remove the earning penalty for those who already were drawing social security entitlements. The reason? Unemployment was down and older people were needed—and wanted—to continue working in the marketplace.

The rules are still being written about growing old and dying, and they change as society changes. But societies need principles that are substantial and lasting.

The race toward and investment in vital, longer lives prolongs the transitions for which western society and non-biblical secular institutions have yet to write all the rules. Just beyond the second or third winds and the endorphin highs lurk new questions and apprehensions.

We need a fresh look at those in the Bible who have dealt with the inevitable. We need reassurance of the scriptural and spiritual foundations before the enticement and attractiveness of the spirit of the age overcomes and engulfs us in its grasp, and we find that in our blindness we have purchased a field where we mistakenly thought the treasure was hidden (Matt. 13:48).

A Biblical Standard

For the Christian, the issue is not what society does or does not provide, but rather what Scripture has always held is the standard for the person of advancing years. American Christians have long been guilty of assuming their brand of Christianity is the biblical standard. They criticize believers in less affluent nations for a moral failing if they do not have two cars in the garage and a chicken in the pot every day of the week. The issue is not one of affluence, but rather what Scripture maintains God's intention is for us all.

It is God's way—and a triumph—to grow old gracefully and graciously; not to do so is tragic. There are those who refuse to admit they may have passed the period of effectiveness and service, even though they have changed from one pursuit to another over the years in order to remain as effective and useful as long as they could. It is a wise person who can make changes in usefulness, relative to what he or she is capable of doing. There are some who harshly insist upon the place and position they have long since ceased to fill effectively. They become a grief to themselves and an aggravation to others. Transition, whether as a process or event, carries with it both anticipation and apprehension.

The Badge of Honor

Long before the transition of the old became an issue, God had already crafted a policy about older adults. Paul attested that Jesus Christ was the foundation of the new life, and each person in faith would build on that foundation (1 Cor. 3:10). The Lord had an unchanging plan for righteous ones who lived by faith (Hab. 2:4). "Listen to Me, O house of Jacob, and all the remnant of the house of Israel, you who have been borne of Me from birth, and have been carried from the womb, even to your old age, I shall be the same, and even to your graying years I shall bear *you*! I have done *it*, and I shall carry you; and I shall bear *you*, and I shall deliver you" (Isa. 46:3–4 italics added).

Other remarkable passages, such as the compilation here from the King James Version of the Bible, reassure us in present life and provide promises for our tomorrows.

> The hoary head is a crown of glory, if it be found in the way of righteousness. . . . The glory of young men is their strength, and the beauty of old men is the gray head. . . . The righteous man will flourish like the palm tree . . . . He will flourish in the courts of our God. . . . [He] will still yield fruit in old age . . . [and] . . . be full of sap and very green. . . . With the ancient is wisdom and in length of days understanding. . . . With long life will I satisfy him, and show him my salvation.[1]

The historical and cultural basis for old age as a badge of honor was everywhere throughout the ancient Near East where the old were acclaimed for their experience and wisdom (Job 12:12, 32:7). Among the Hebrews, this was not simply because of the outward sign of a gray beard or gray hair, but because having attained "fullness of days" or "entering into many days" was thought to be a sign of divine favor—a result of having feared the Lord and kept His commands (Lev. 19:32; Deut. 30:19–20). Fullness of days indicated one's lifelong dependence on God-appointed authority (Ex. 20:12). The linkage between old age and righteousness is called propositional truth: "*If* you are righteous *then* you will live long," as amply illustrated here:

> Thou shalt keep therefore his statutes, and his commandments, which I command thee this day, that it may go well with thee, and that thou mayest prolong thy days upon the earth . . . . Ye shall walk in all the ways which the Lord your God hath commanded you, that ye may live, and that it may be well with you, and that ye may prolong your days in the land which ye shall possess . . . . My son, forget not my law; but let thine heart keep my commandments; for length of days, and long life, and peace, shall they add to thee. . . . The fear of the Lord prolongeth days: but the years of the wicked shall be shortened. . . . Honor thy father and mother; which is the first commandment with promise; that it may be well with thee, and thou mayest live long on the earth.[2]

TELEOLOGY AND PURPOSE

The Bible enables us to go back to the beginning and look ahead to where we are today. Teleology is the study of beginnings. Our word *telescope* derives from the same root word, *telos*. We place the optics of a telescope up to our eyes and see the image of a distant object. The lenses control how the image appears to us. The image represents something distant, not in the here or now.

In life, we decide on a journey, and this becomes our purpose. Teleology and purpose are related. There is a beginning and an end. The end of our journey is more real than any image we can see through the telescope's lenses. Faith enables us to say this. The energy that pushes us along is called hope. At the other end, opposite hope, is faith. In between the two is purpose. Purpose is born of God.

This teleological exercise was expressed in Isaiah 46:3–4, which was quoted above. God gave us birth and carries us from the womb to time of old age. God established the goal for advancing years. He crafted the journey for us and promised us purpose for all our days. The value of the promise is predicated on who made it. Purpose continues; transitions occur during its course.

From the Life of David

David knew he was on a journey that involved God's purposes for him, he sensed the transitions, and as he neared the end of his days, he prayed: "O God, You have taught me from my youth, and up to this point I have declared Your wonderful works. Now that I am old and gray-headed, O God, don't forsake me until I have demonstrated to this generation the strength that comes from You and shown Your power to every one that is yet to come" (Ps. 71:17–18).

David's purpose in life was the kingdom of God. He expressed this often as in Psalm 118:17: "I shall not die, but live and tell of the works of the Lord." His approach varied from one stage of his life to another. As a young shepherd, he first expressed it through psalms, and these continued throughout his life. He killed Goliath, led an army, ruled a nation, prepared for construction of the temple, and chose a successor who would build the temple. The venue changed; the message was constant.

Since David's purpose was the kingdom, his purpose was also a prophetic one inasmuch as the kingdom continued to unfold relative to the sovereign purposes of God. David did not know about, or even anticipate, the canon of Scripture that would memorialize his life for our benefit. Still, he prayed to the Father with the long view in mind. God's eternal purposes were David's existential ones. He lived eternity in the present. This points to an important principle: It is not enough for man to be righteous so that he can live long, although longevity itself is worthy of thanksgiving to the Almighty. Rather, long life enables man to persist in carrying out the heavenly vision, the personal propagation of the purposes of God. Man's life is tied to God's teleology.

In life, we decide on a journey, and this becomes our purpose.

David's request for longer life to continue declaring God's strength to his generation was preceded by an impassioned plea: Do not cast me off in time of old age; do not forsake me when my strength fails (Ps. 71:9, 17–18). David was a prophet for us all. He cried out in behalf of every Christian and Jew who knows advancing age is catching up with him or her. He was sensitive to the waning days of others, such as when old Barzillai's health and strength had disappeared, and David offered to sustain him until he died. Appreciative of his master, the old man instead decided to return to his own home and die (2 Sam. 19:31–39).

David is not begging for his life in Psalm 71. Make no mistake about that! Rather, he had a task given him by God that he had to complete. Every fiber of his being was energized by God-given purpose. An impregnable wall of resolve, like that of old Otto whom I mentioned in chapter 2, drove David on. This was no self-aggrandizement. David's purpose in Israel was the personification of God Himself who lived in and through David. David is a model for every man who puts his faith in God: Do not allow my old age and lessening strength prevent me from declaring who You are and completing what You have given me to do! Was his prayer answered? Or was this merely the poetic, plaintive pleading of a fading voice likened to a declining shadow (Ps. 102:11–12)? The answer comes in Paul's testimony to the conclusion of David's life:

> And after [God] had removed [Saul], He raised up David to be
> their King . . . a man after [God's] heart, who will do all [His]
> will . . . [And] after [David] had served the purpose of God in
> his own generation, [he] fell asleep, and was laid among his
> fathers . . . (Acts 13:22–23, 36)

After he had served the purposes of God in his own generation! How unthinkable that God would have deserted David in his
old age. Whether David had ascended to the heavens, made his
bed in the nether world, taken flight with the rising of the dawn,
or dwelt in the remotest part of the sea, God was always there,
taking David's hand and leading him (Ps. 139:7–10). Could such
a God fail to sustain David in weakened old age when he was still
engaged in "serving the purposes of God in his own generation"?
As a shepherd, he killed the bear and lion. He dispatched Goliath
in the name of the Lord of Hosts (1 Sam. 17:45). During his life,
he wrote songs and poems that remain as a legacy of praise,
exhortation, and prophecy to all generations of mankind after
him. As a youth, he was chosen by God through Samuel to be king
over Israel and to rule righteously. Prior to death, he chose
Solomon to rule over Israel (1 Kings 1:15–31). But when he had
served God's purposes, he died. He knew death was at hand. In
his last days, his body turned cold, blankets would not suffice, and
a young virgin was recruited to lie at his side to provide warmth
(1 Kings 1:1–4).

The issue here is not David's longevity, the manner in which
he honored his parents in order to achieve longevity, or the
historical record which attests to his fame and productivity. No,
the issue is, and always has been, God's purposes. David prayed
that he would live long enough to serve God's purposes.

God's purposes and God's will are often confused, and the
distinction is very important. There are two words for "will."
There is *thelema* as used in Matthew 6:10: "Thy will be done,"
implying the desires, wishes, and will of God for the individual
which are found in the written Word, as in Psalm 119:11: "Thy
Word have I hidden in my heart that I might not sin against
You." Or "Thy Word is a lamp to my feet, and a light to my path"
(Psalm 119:105). Some suggest that 90 percent or more of God's
will for an individual's life can be derived from the written
thelema word.

The second word is *boulema*, meaning God's sovereign will: the unknown and unknowable purposes of God revealed at the appropriate time, which we have no control over. We can explain the difference by reference again to David. God's *thelema* for David was the *Shema* confession of faith of Deuteronomy 6, the Ten Commandments, and their derivatives in the Pentateuch. But God's *boulema* for David was a sovereign movement, first through the prophet Samuel and then from year to year, to bring him to the point of general, king, and prophet, so that when David had served God's various time-bound purposes or *boulema*, he died and was buried among his fathers.[3]

In Anticipation of More to Come
You may look on your own horizon, even as David did, and see a descending sun. You feel your life's work has been accomplished. Completed are the tasks connected with family and work, but you are not satisfied, for while you have lived your life faithfully in terms of God's *thelema*, there is a gnawing in the pit of your stomach that knows there remains the untouched, unrealized *boulema*—God's purposes that are yet to be translated into your purposes. Chapter 9 has been prepared for you, but let's first see how purpose plays out in the lives of Samuel and Hezekiah.

From the Life of Samuel

God's purposes for Samuel were for him to serve his people as judge and prophet, which he did for more than sixty years, willingly and patiently bearing the grief and burden of leadership (1 Sam. 7:15–17). As a child, he had been consecrated to serve God and country, and "all Israel . . . knew Samuel was established to be a prophet of the Lord" (1 Sam. 3:20). And then the inevitable—the forecast feared by us all: the elders, his peers, the ones he trusted and confided in, approached and said, "Behold thou art old, and thy sons walk not in thy ways; now make us a king to judge us like all the nations" (1 Sam. 8:5). They essentially said, "It's been sixty years, Samuel, you've had your chance, and still you have not prepared a successor for yourself. Besides, we want a king, not a judge." Was this the reward for long, unselfish service? Had he fulfilled God's *boulema* for his life?

Had his words as prophet ever fallen to the ground? Would displacement shortly be followed by death? Samuel prayed to the Lord, and the Lord answered His servant (1 Sam. 8:6–9). God was not finished with Samuel, which is to say, God's agenda was not over, and His *boulema* providentially involved this faithful servant. In response to his antagonists, Samuel said "Moreover, as for me, God forbid that I should sin against the [Lord's purposes for my life] in ceasing to pray for you: but I will teach you the good and the right way" (1 Sam. 12:20, 22, 23).

It is important to note that at this critical juncture, Samuel did not ask permission from the elders. After all, they were the ones who had dispensed with him and had snatched the mantle of their endorsement from his role as judge. Their loyalty could be counted on as long as he was in step with them, but they had changed their aspirations for Israel, and their plans did not include Samuel. His was an audience of One, now more than at any other time; he would bend the knee to the Father of all elders, but not to the elders themselves at this time, and he told them what he would do in and for Israel.

There comes a time in the life of the aged saint who has served God faithfully and been submissive to the authorities God has placed over him or her, when he or she must choose either to follow men who may be governed by cultural stereotypes or obey God. This is not arrogance or rebellion against legitimate authority. It is the decision of a man or woman who knows God and is determined to follow the purposes of God unhindered by control, manipulation, or intimidation.

Samuel's obedience to God's continuing purposes for his life led to recruitment of young men who were taught the Scriptures and mentored to become prophets among the people (1 Sam. 19:18–20). Thus began the school of the prophets, whose influence has continued to modern times and has had a profound effect for spirituality and godliness to millions in the church.[4]

The other purpose Samuel received from the Lord was that of unceasing prayer. When the days of active service were done, as defined by the elders, there remained the high priestly duty of intercession. This part of Samuel's life was so key that David memorialized: "Moses and Aaron were among His priests, and Samuel was among those who called on His name. They called upon the Lord, and He answered them" (Ps. 99:6). Who among the elders that forced his retirement would have thought that the heavenly epitaph of Samuel would place him as an inter-cessor alongside the lawgiver and the founding priest?

From the Life of Hezekiah

An interlude to a long run of evil kings in Israel and Judah came with the ordination of Hezekiah as king of Judah who ascended the throne at age twenty-five. Son of Ahaz and Abi (Abijah), the daughter of Zechariah, he reigned twenty years in Jerusalem. It was said that "he did right in the sight of the Lord, according to all that his father David had done," and that "He trusted in the Lord, the God of Israel, so that after him there was none like him among all the kings of Judah, nor among those who were before him" (2 Kings 18:3, 5).

Hezekiah was a breath of fresh air. He destroyed the places where heathen gods were worshipped, he clung to the Lord, and he prospered wherever he went. He did not align himself with heathen nations, and he defeated the Philistines. Through the prophet Isaiah came the prophecy concerning the defeat of Sennacherib, king of Assyria. Concerning these accomplish-ments, God gave a sign to Hezekiah which has served as an encouragement to many since: " . . . the surviving root of the house of Judah shall again take root downward and bear fruit upward. For out . . . [from] . . . Jerusalem [there] shall go forth a remnant, and out of Mount Zion [there will come] survivors. The zeal of the Lord shall perform this" (2 Kings 19:30–31).

Hezekiah also brought righteousness, holiness, and knowl-edge of God back to Judah, first by confessing his own sins and those of his fathers, and by requiring the priests to purify them-selves and cleanse the house of the Lord. He then called a congregational meeting of the princes of the city and ordered the Levites to sing praises to the Lord with the words of David and Asaph, so they sang praises with joy, bowed down, and worshipped. "Then Hezekiah and all the people rejoiced over what God had prepared for the people, because the thing came about suddenly" (2 Chron. 29). Revival, following this, spread to the entire nation (2 Chron. 30–32).

For most, this would have been legacy enough, but then Hezekiah fell mortally ill (2 Chron. 32:24; 2 Kings 20:1). Isaiah came to him and said, "Set your house in order, for you shall die and not live." 2 Chronicles 32:24 reports that he prayed to the Lord, and the Lord granted him extra life. In the parallel passage of 2 Kings 20:2–3, we learn he turned his face to the wall, beseeched God to remember his righteousness and good works, and wept bitterly. Notice the difference in the prayers of Hezekiah and of David. David wanted to complete the purpose God gave him to do. Hezekiah thought he was justified, based on past performance, to receive additional years.

In response, God told Isaiah, "Return and say to Hezekiah . . . 'I have heard your prayer, I have seen your tears; behold, I will heal you . . . And I will add fifteen years to your life . . .'" (2 Kings 20:3–6). Added to this, God provided a miraculous sign of confirmation to His promise: He made the shadow of the sun move backwards!

A strange turn of events provides further perspective on his later years. After he was healed, we read:

> Hezekiah gave no return [to the Lord] for the benefit he received, because his heart was proud; therefore wrath came on him and on Judah and Jerusalem. However, Hezekiah humbled the pride of his heart . . . so that the wrath of the Lord did not come on them in the days of Hezekiah. (2 Chron. 32:25–26)

Being a proud man, Hezekiah bragged to the king of Babylon about all his abundant riches that were warehoused throughout the domain. Isaiah denounced Hezekiah's overconfidence, pride, and disclosure to a heathen king and said ". . . the days are coming when all that is in your house . . . shall be carried to Babylon; nothing shall be left, says the Lord." Hezekiah naively and arrogantly interpreted Isaiah's words to mean "there shall be peace and truth in my days . . ." (2 Kings 20:12–19).

God knew that the fame, immense wealth, military positioning, and personal accomplishments of Hezekiah had made him overconfident and boastful, and they exposed an inherent weakness in his character. After he was healed, "God left him alone only to test him that He might know all that was in his heart" (2 Chron. 32:31). Hezekiah died, and the nation fell into disrepair under his evil son, Manasseh, who undid all that

Hezekiah had done. There are important lessons to be learned from the account of Hezekiah.

Hezekiah did the will of the Lord exceedingly well. He accomplished God's purposes for Judah and served as a witness to Israel. And God said, figuratively, "Well done, son; it now is time for you to return to me." Had Hezekiah accepted the loving, gentle beckoning of the Father to come home, the history of Hezekiah might have been written differently, bringing a perpetual remembrance to Israel. Unlike David and Samuel, Hezekiah's concentration on himself prevented him from seeing when his days were finished. He did not seek longevity to continue doing the *boulema* of the Father; rather, he sought it as a reward or payment for having "walked before Thee in truth and with a whole heart, and [having] done what is good in Thy sight" (2 Kings 20:3). In his later days, Hezekiah's piety was a righteousness of merit, not a desire to complete purposes born of commitment to a sovereign God.

The teaching of the Bible forces the people of God to ask, "Were we sensitive to what His calling and purpose for our lives was, and did we carry out that purpose in a manner that was pleasing to Him?"

Responding to God's Call

David, Samuel, and Hezekiah provide perspective on the character qualities of older men who have served God. God's sovereign purpose is distilled into a million pieces and distributed into the lives of those who follow Him. When the *boulema* for each of us is accomplished, the Lord in His mercy invites us to join Him. For Hezekiah, unlike David and Samuel, longevity was more important than satisfaction with a job well done. In the end, we are all expendable relative to having lived out His purpose in our lives. The teaching of the Bible forces the people of God to ask, "Were we sensitive to what His calling and purpose for our lives was, and did we carry out that purpose in a manner that was pleasing to Him?"

There is an inherent weakness in all men, and God tested Hezekiah to bring out that weakness so that today, we can be alert to the fact that in our self-sufficiency and, perhaps our longer-than-usual life span, we do not forget that a Sovereign God demonstrates sovereignty sovereignly!

Inevitable Judgment

By now it is clear that the theology of advancing years pertains to those who are righteous, but, as in the case of Hezekiah, aberrations provide perspective and a warning. During a time of national sin, Isaiah prophesied that the day would come when God would remove Israel's leaders, and the youth would not spare the life of the elder (Isa. 3:5). The account of Saul's death is a clear example of an ignominious ending of an anointed man who disobeyed God (1 Sam. 13). And because of Moses' intemperate and impulsive striking of the rock twice, the great prophet and his brother, the priest, were forbidden entrance into the Promised Land (Deut. 34:4; Num. 20:23–24). Even in the face of overwhelming accomplishments by anointed and commissioned men, God's holiness prevails to establish a higher level of expected righteousness for some, whereas men of lesser stature, such as Caleb, were allowed to enter the Promised Land and take possession of their inheritance.

BEYOND THE PURPOSES OF EARLIER YEARS ——————

The person of advanced age whose life has been in fellowship with God and who has walked in righteousness and holiness must recognize that God's purposes do not stop at the point of diminishing productivity, the time of retirement, or even when anticipating death. The wisdom and experience of many years brings a sobering maturity to the elderly person's prayers. He or she has walked with the Father in times of service in the presence of others; in old age, he or she communes silently at the foot of the throne in prayer. Each person who lives this way walks in the footsteps of the patriarchs, who in their later years were no longer preoccupied with the problems of the present.

The prescription of Luke 14:25–35 was to become unencumbered. When children are educated, grown, and no longer dependent on their parents; when the wardrobe no longer requires annual updating; when the home is paid off; when the family car is no longer strained by hard trips; these are occasions when advancing age is witness to lessening encumbrances, and one can turn his or her mind to intercession. The work of God continues when the elder statesmen call upon the Lord in behalf of the next generation. Abraham prayed for Isaac, Ishmael, and Lot; Job for his sons and their households (Gen. 48–49); Moses for Israel to find a righteous shepherd (Num. 27:15–17); Samuel for Israel and Saul; Elisha for Samaria (2 Kings 13:14–20); and Paul, as quoted here, prayed in a dark and damp prison cell for those he had introduced the kingdom:

> I bow my knees before the Father, from whom every family in heaven and on earth derives its name, that He would grant you, according to the riches of His glory, to be strengthened with power through His Spirit in the inner man, so that Christ may dwell in your hearts through faith. . . . (Eph. 3:14–17)

Purpose Overcoming Challenges

The successful transitions of David, Samuel, Paul, and others in their declining days are skills to be learned—if not by the example of others, then through trial and error. Even Elijah, who told God he wanted to die, nevertheless was given a new (although brief) purpose prior to ascending to the heavens in the chariots of God (2 Kings 19:4).

Disciplines of the spirit and mind are not easily taught. Older persons given to intercession for children, sinners, church, and nation are often challenged to develop these disciplines more often than are those who are not similarly committed. To enter the hallowed ground of intercession often means taking on the equally difficult task of learning to live with adversity. In the midst of ministry, why do we still experience the pruning knife, refiner's fire, winnower's flail, and scalpel's circumcision of the heart? Such questions are too often born of a Westerner's conception of comfort-laden Christianity.

Adversity in the midst of ministry renders the prayers brought before the throne of God with a laser precision, purity, and purpose. The prayers actually become the word of God redirected back to God Himself, in fulfillment of the formula that "they who pray according to the will of the Father know the Father hears and answers" (1 John 5:14–15). The challenges to spirit and mind eventually make the intercessor more immune to the encumbrances most people encounter in their prayer life. The challenges excite an exchange of concentration on the natural world for the effectiveness of the inner world and the solitude of doing business with God.

In the midst of God's promises to bear us up, He reserves for elderly intercessors the privilege of interludes laced with disease, desolation, desperation, and darkness. These do not result from sin, moral failing, lack of faith, or some mistake buried in a distant past. Rather, God seeks those who, in times of trial, will humble themselves, pray, and stand in one of a thousand gaps. Our theology of advancing years cannot ignore this.

Disease

Created from the dust, we are subject to the ways of the dust, a point made in chapter 2. Knowing that we are creatures helps to protect against presumption and pride of past performance. In Ecclesiastes 12:1–7, the preacher decries the vicissitudes of old age and returning to the dust. In societies given to health, wellness, and excellence of medical care, it is easy for illness or disability to be attributed to a moral failing, and we ask "Why this illness? What did I do? Am I at fault and therefore held accountable for my pain?" Today's accusers are no different than were Job's friends or the disciples when they asked the questions in John 9:2, "Who sinned, this man or his parents?" In religion based on righteousness by merit, illness and disease are explained by a twisted system of justice and retribution for wrongdoings. Cruel, insensitive people rush to unjust and un-Christian judgment. Under what conditions does illness lay a foundation for personal growth?

In religion based on righteousness by merit, illness and disease are explained by a twisted system of justice and retribution for wrongdoings.

Disease and Sin

Not all sickness is due to sin, but Scripture supports the relationship. Deliberate or careless treatment of our bodies comes under the dictum of "whatever a man sows, he also shall reap." This was true when Miriam murmured against Moses and turned leprous (Num. 12:10); when King Asa spurned the prophet's rebuke later in life and trusted more in riches and physicians than the Lord (2 Chron. 16:12); when King Jehoram did evil in God's eyes and incurred plague for his people, his children, and himself (2 Chron. 2:14–15); and when Gehazi coveted Naaman's reward contrary to the counsel of Elisha and became a leper (2 Kings 5:27). Sin also may have been the cause of illness of the palsied man as suggested by Jesus' comment, "Son, thy sins be forgiven thee" (Mark 2:5).

Disease and God's Glory

It may be that illness comes as a vehicle by which the works of God can be made manifest—to make His glory known (John 11:4). He chastens us by any means so we may share His holiness (Heb. 12:6), however, Hebrews 12:11 states, "no chastening for the present seems to be joyful, but grievous: that it may yield the peaceable fruit of righteousness." David said in Psalm 119:67, "Before I was afflicted I went astray, but now I have kept Your word," and, on another occasion, "We went through fire and through water, but You brought us to a wealthy place" (Ps. 66:12).

Long before there were prayer summits, citywide prayer rallies, and prayers around the school yard flagpole in the late–twentieth century, there was the World Prayer Movement led by men like Thomas Carruth, Glenn Clark, and E. Stanley Jones, on whose shoulders modern warriors stand. My wife Carolyn's mother, Nettie Lou Bradley Lawrence, was part of that movement and represented the United Methodist women at its conventions and prayer retreats. In her latter days, Mother was dying from the horrible interstitial lung disease that progressively deprived her of breath. Death came by suffocation when withered lung tissue finally failed to retain air. Carolyn assisted in cleaning out her mother's room at the nursing center and found a prayer journal, dated up to the day of her death. There in almost indecipherable scribbles were the names of children, grandchildren, and friends who were prayed for moments before she drew her last breath. During the last months and weeks, her range of attention to things of the Spirit became more focused and precise. Death at age eighty-seven was merely a door through which she stepped to continue doing what she had been practicing for a lifetime.

Disease and Satan's Work

The ancient book of Job is the first to report on the drama involving Satan's efforts to search out and destroy. Job was blameless and upright in God's sight, and the tempter asked permission to afflict him in order to challenge and hopefully diminish his commitment to God. Permission was granted, but Satan was kept short of destroying him. The modern American Christian's sense of justice cannot easily accept that righteous men will be turned over to the evil one or that God would participate in such a macabre scheme. But this limited perspective is blinded to the concept of the sovereignty of God; we are brash in imagining that man's holiness, even in its most elevated form, could even begin to approach the holiness of God. In fact, the Scriptures frequently say illness can come from the Evil One. For example, in Luke 8:35, Jesus cast out the demons of a wretched man of Gadara, restoring the man's right mind.

Illness, in the hands of a loving Father, is a means to bring us to greater humility and to challenge longtime defenses, pride, resistance to Him, and preoccupation with the things of this world. When we agree our times are in His hands and that pain and weakness can be for His glory—whether by life or by death— then God can move in the sickness for purposes beyond those of the present (Ps. 31:15; Phil. 1:20). If, on the other hand, the illness is of the enemy, we can recognize how he works, whether in the dark of night or through the terrors that visit when we least expect them. David foresaw this when in Psalm 118:18, he said: "The Lord had disciplined me severely, but He has not given me over to death."

The experiences of older Christians are no different than those who do not have a relationship with God. And while this is true, the resources are demonstrably different, whether in sickness or in health.

Desolation

Desolation follows the loss of hope. Hope is the energy that drives us toward goals in which we have faith. Challenges or threats to hope, when finding no reprieve, mercilessly lead to desolation.

Desolation is the lonely widow, the abandoned retirement home resident, or the man who gazes blankly out a window at children playing and wonders when his own grandchildren will call. Desolation is the retiree shooting below par golf and asking, "Is this all there is to life?"

Desolation can be surrounded by luxury and lack of purpose. Desolation looks at a canvas and can't choose from among brushes, oils, or even subjects to paint. Desolation is an author looking at all his books, thinking, "There is nothing else to write." Desolation sees the exciting experiences and journeys of the past and realizes the photograph album no longer holds any interest.

Desolation, your name is advancing age! The challenge or loss of hope can be caused by illness, disability, or a major life-changing event that is suddenly an unrelenting diversion from the desired path. When there is no respite from the absence of hope, desolation has arrived. The similes of Psalms 102:4–6 and 11 sum up these thoughts:

> My heart has been smitten like grass and has withered away
> . . . My bones cling to my flesh. I resemble a pelican of the
> wilderness; I have become like an owl of the waste places. . . .
> I have become like a lonely bird on a housetop. . . . My days
> are like a lengthened shadow, and I wither away like grass.

Desolation is the day one discovers that he or she has invested all of his or her worldly riches in a deal gone sour, and there is no retreating to another loan. It happens at all stages of life; it is ubiquitous among those of advancing age. Desolation is having everything, sensing its emptiness, and missing life's purpose. I have met hundreds of older adults who, dressed in their finery and sitting behind the wheel of a comfortable car, say: "I have no purpose and do not know where to go to find it." And these are Christians! Oh, how we need this theology of advancing years.

For the octogenarian who knows and has walked with his God, desolation is a new venue in which to trust and prove Him worthy to follow during lonely winter days.

The psalmist describes the deliverance of mankind from desolation in Psalm 107:

> They wandered in the wilderness in a desert region; they did not find a way . . . They were hungry and thirsty; their soul fainted within them. . . . He delivered them out of their distresses. He led them also by a straight way. . . . There were those who dwelt in darkness and in the shadow of death, prisoners in misery and chains. . . . He saved them out of their distresses. He brought them out of darkness and the shadow of death, and broke their bands apart. . . . He changes a wilderness into a pool of water. . . . and there He makes the hungry to dwell. . . . When they are diminished and bowed down through oppression, misery, and sorrow. . . . He sets the needy securely on high away from affliction, and makes his families like a flock.

Is there no end to transition? Who among us can claim we have arrived as a finished work? Throughout life, there seem to be challenges—if met head on and with the grace of God—that will introduce us to yet another period of transition. It is in the nature of God to treat us as He would have treated Moab had the region been willing. However, it refused the tipping of his vessel. Had it willed, would not the dregs have been left behind, and each successive pouring of the wine brought greater clarity and mellowness?

Desperation

"Lord, save me!" This was Peter's scream of desperation in Matthew 14:30. "My despair is too great. I am in the pond of despond," cries the pilgrim, "I have no way out, none to help." Desperation. Life expectancy has increased, but longer life carries the lingering pain and physical disintegration brought by chronic disease—diabetes, osteoporosis, dementia, osteoarthritis, pancreatitis, cerebrovascular attack, myocardial infarction, and high blood pressure. Many older people will experience one or more of these afflictions. Christians are not exempt. How does our theology deal with such desperation?

> For we do not want you to be unaware, brethren, of our afflic-
> tion which came to us . . . that we were burdened excessively,
> beyond our strength, so that we despaired even of life. . . .
> (2 Cor. 1:8)

> I was afflicted and about to die from my youth on; I suffer Thy
> terrors; I am overcome . . . Thou has removed lover and friend
> afar from me; My acquaintances are in darkness. (Ps. 88:15, 18)

There are experiences whose dimensions our imaginations cannot fathom, and our ability to overcome is sentenced to helplessness. Such was the condition of Peter on the water, Paul in Asia, and the psalmist at the hands of God. Peter was saved, Paul lived for another day, and the psalmist continued to compose poems and songs.

How many times have we heard, "The just live by faith, and without faith it is impossible to please God"? Without faith we cannot pursue the purposes of God in our lives. But times come in all lives, and especially those of advancing years, when faith seems not to suffice and one is in a powerless place. In addition, our friends accost us for failing faith, desperation becomes interpersonal, and connectedness to the body of believers is threatened. Trust is the sentiment of last resort. In desperation, I throw myself on the mercy of One who shall help and trust that He will preserve my life.

Desperation for the believer can be a good condition, though utterly painful, for it brings us face to face with where the Lord wants the righteous to be—fully dependent and abjectly reliant on Him as a source and a resource.

In my journey to reach a goal, I may encounter a barrier and experience anxiety, which, if unrelieved, turns into fear. It is fear that I may lose my way or never reach my destination; it causes me to strike out in anger and hate to destroy the thing or person who obscures my path. There have been times when I have panicked—this is fear and anger out of control. I slump down, depression takes hold, and I pray or quote passages of Scripture. But I feel nothing. "Are you there, Lord?" Despairing of even life itself, I cry out, "Save me." Job cried out that even if God slay him, he would not curse God—but moments came when he wished for death.

In despair, the social and emotional veneers are peeled away. No more than the shell of a man or a woman is left. However, there is no distance between where despair is and where Jesus stands. The victory song of older parents' character comes when they can do no more than make their hands available to the One whose grasp is sufficient and superior to save.

The victory song of older parents' character comes when they can do no more than make their hands available to the One whose grasp is sufficient and superior to save.

George Matheson speaks of victory in his chronicles of the discipline of despair by asking a question of saints of old: "What was the occasion for your prosperity of career, the critical event bringing your purpose to maturity and worthiness?" For Abraham, it was the sacrifice on Moriah; Joseph would point to Potiphor's dungeon; Moses would date his destiny from the danger in the Nile; Ruth would remind of her submission to Naomi and her field of toil; David would consider the night watches; Job would tell you of hearing God out of the whirlwind; Peter's was his stinting obedience on the sea; John would brush the dust of Patmos from his brow and make an offering of it; blindness on the way to Damascus would be the *tour de force* for Paul. And Jesus? He would recount the cold ground of Gethsemane which He anointed with sweat of blood. These people knew something about desperation.[5] During times when a loved one is on a deathbed or is otherwise in the midst of desperation, we often forget that the Lord Himself is party to the deathwatch: for, as the psalmist wrote in Psalm 116:15, "Precious in the sight of the Lord is the death of one of His loved ones."

Darkness

The older person who says he or she has never been in darkness is one who likely has never experienced the light. Darkness is the absence of light, for how else would we recognize and call it by name? Darkness is promise denied. Darkness is God's presence having been withdrawn. Old age can be a time of living in vision-obscuring darkness. Has God died? Did I hear Him incorrectly? Have His ears turned to brass? Did He discover that I had a hidden sin I failed to confess, and is He now extracting some macabre justice from me?

The promise to Abraham, and the seemingly endless wait by Sarah, Moses' forty years herding sheep, Joseph in the pit and then in the dungeon: these are examples of a pattern—promise, vision denied, testing by the darkness, and vision realized.

Darkness and the dark night of the soul are common among God's children of advancing years. For example, Job had a busy, productive, socially active, and rewarding life in younger years with a quiver full of many arrows—sons, daughters, and grandchildren. Then came the suffering. Job had walked in the light, upright before men and approved by God, a man of deep piety and great prosperity.

Transition: The Concept Expanded

Transition from productive and healthy old age to less productive and diseased old age removes the predictive security of prior regimen and schedule. Memories of the recent past are obscured with the newness of the unknown. We are not where we were; we have not quite acclimated to where we are going. It is a social and psychological limbo. We are unsure of ourselves, and our neighbors and loved ones find us unpredictable and sometimes frightening. Where is God? In darkness, all are strangers. Isaiah 50:10–11 sheds light on how the older adult must apprehend the challenge to pursue the course:

Who is among you that fears the Lord, that obeys the voice of His servant, that walks in darkness and has no light? Let him trust in the name of the Lord and rely on his God. Behold, all you [who wrongly] kindle a fire, who encircle yourselves with firebrands [of your own choosing], walk [then] in the light of your fire and among the brands you have set ablaze. This [is what] you will have from My hand; and you will lie down in torment [because of your own devices]. (Annotations added.)

The disciplines of darkness, disease, desolation, and desperation require quoting the adage: "Never doubt in the dark what God told you in the light." For those whose minds are stayed on Him, He will keep in perfect peace. "Unto the upright there arises light in the darkness; He is gracious and full of compassion and righteous" (Ps. 112:4).

These disciplines are signatories to the latter day transitions where victory is only for the person of advancing age who says no to strange noises that otherwise would clog his hearing. We seek to hear His voice clearly and to be precise in our appeals to Him. The challenges resulting in the disciplines of darkness, desolation, desperation, and disease are inevitable foretastes for the child of God, and, as such, trophies for His glory. This theology of advancing years rejects sociological simplicities, secular stereotypes, and strange doctrines that offers a partial and imperfect Gospel.

Chapter 1 concluded with a statement about the cosmology of the church—the bride reigning with Christ, and every moment of every day in this present life serving as preparation for that ultimate purpose. Transitions in declining days, while disheartening to many, are designed to elevate to a new and higher level the criticality of purpose of the older adult who rests in the assurance that what God has provided is sufficient for the trials at hand.

CHAPTER SEVEN

Later Transitions and the End Game

CHAPTER 1 IDENTIFIED THE CHURCH AS THE CULMINATION OF GOD'S WORK ON EARTH (EPH. 3:9–11). ITS TASK IS TO PREPARE, THROUGH PRAYER AND PRAISE, TO REIGN WITH CHRIST. ALL THAT OCCURS during the church's sojourn is defined as training the bride for her exalted position of co-ruling with Christ. "All that precedes the marriage supper of the Lamb from all eternity is preliminary to God's eternal enterprise."[1] The "all" includes our advancing years. No theology of advancing years can leave out the cosmology of the church and the role of older adults within it.

Chapter 6 described the changes of growing older: physical, sociological (separation from loved ones and loss of status), and psychological (anxiety and depression). God designed suffering to produce, particularly in the older righteous person's life, character and disposition—the compassionate spirit required for ruling in a government where *agape* is supreme.[2]

The biblical references and non-biblical sources on suffering are not part of this discussion. We accept that the biblical record is clear—suffering is a part of the Christian life, it has a special part to play among older adults, and it is an integral part of God's inclusion of His children into His greater plan. The role of suffering among older adults involves what we call the end game.

All older people eventually experience disability in varying degrees, diseases, and the lessening of strength, vigor, and function. The essential difference between believers and non-believers in times of suffering is that the former and their believing relatives and friends have different resources, purposes, and a promise for the future. These do make a difference! The older believer for whom these truths are unknown, undeveloped, or inconsistent is miserable, and is easily overcome with resentment, bitterness, and lack of forgiveness. While we feel sorry for such people, ignorance of Scripture does not absolve one from the consequences of living in ignorance.

It is instructive to pursue the killer-trilogy: resentment, bitterness, and lack of forgiveness, and I will do so in part 2. Medical researchers and clinicians have tied these character defects to many chronic illnesses, examples of which include arthritis, gastroenteritis, chronic bowel syndrome, migraine headaches, cardiac hypertension, angina pectoris, and others. In old age, the linkage between spiritual disability and physical disability grows stronger.

THE END GAME

The later-life transitions of chapter 6 continue as one moves toward the end game and the moment of death. Our concern is with how the biblical record handles the subject. The end game is a concept familiar to any one experienced in sales, sports, chess, or warfare. Entire books are written by and for chess masters on how to bring the game to checkmate. The final move has been planned sometimes dozens of moves earlier, and the player's strategy leads deliberately to the final move. The moment of truth occurs when the anticipated final move reveals whether the strategy was right or wrong. Even in the sedate and refined confines of chess tournaments, there is anxiety and sweat. Generals in charge of great armies begin a battle with an exit strategy. Forsaking the presence of an exit strategy, wars can go on and on. As some are want to say, "If you don't have an exit strategy, almost any one will do." Every athlete is familiar with the end game and what is necessary to force the *coup d'etat*— the final blow. Many reasons account for delaying the end game: the superior athlete's apprehension that he might not win, lack of confidence in his own prowess and resources, or overlooking or underestimating the opponent's final and often "all-or-nothing" daring. The brilliant marketing of a product and gaining entry to a valued prospect's place of business accounts for nothing if the sales person is unable to close the sale. In all of these, the issue is closure! In all of life the end game, or closure, is crucial and critical. We are all required to negotiate a personal exit strategy. Many prepare by writing wills, signing powers of attorney, establishing a family living trust, purchasing more life insurance, etc.

Our deaths are not just as bodies, but as people in our entirety, in the totality of our being.

Geropsychiatrist Adrian Verwoerdt years ago coined the phrase "life review." It describes how many old people prepare for their final days by writing an autobiography, but leaving out the bad and selecting the good, to cast in portraiture "my story, of which I am well pleased." There is much more to the human end game than the life review, and I address it in this chapter.

Death's Sentence in the Old Testament

Death in both the physical and spiritual sense was first mentioned by God Himself in Genesis 2:17. Physical and spiritual death came about because of the fall of man, and Paul clearly summarizes this in Romans 5:12–21. Unlike the death of animals, the death of human beings is not the end of life. Death is a threefold event. The first physical death recorded is the murder of Abel by his brother Cain (Gen. 4:8). At the moment of man's sin, spiritual death occurred, although it was many years later that Adam and Eve died physically. The first and second deaths, physical and spiritual, are recognized in the Old Testament. The third death is an eternal one and is best articulated in New Testament doctrine.

We should understand that death involves the whole person. Our deaths are not just as bodies, but as people in our entirety, in the totality of our being. The Bible doesn't make a sharp line of demarcation between physical and spiritual death. The former, in its essence, is a fitting symbol and expression of the more serious spiritual death that sin inevitably brings.[3]

For whatever reason, the Old Testament record is limited and sometimes encouraging in its progressive revelation of the idea of death. We are left with a mixed bag that ranges from dread to anticipation. Short of details, which varied over time, the Israelites clearly knew God was the ultimate Ruler of life and death (Deut. 32:39). This point was first made in the Creation (Gen. 2:17) and reaffirmed when God constrained Satan, first from harming Job physically and, second from taking his life (Job 1:12; 2:6). Despite God staying Satan's hand, Job, whether fatalistically or philosophically, commented on the fate of all men:

> One dies in his full strength, being wholly at ease and satisfied; his sides are filled out with fat, and the marrow of his bones is moist, while another dies with a bitter soul, never even tasting anything good. Together they lie down in the dust, and worms cover them. (Job 21:23)

The ancient Hebrews regarded death as entrance into Sheol (the grave), where they were cut off from everything dear in life, including God and loved ones. Sheol, or the realm of the dead, had gates and chambers, and the path of the wicked lead to this abode (Ps. 9:13, Prov. 7:27).

It wasn't until God's revelation to the psalmist, however, that Old Testament Jews benefited from knowing a Redeemer God who is both in heaven and in Sheol (Ps. 139:7–8), and who can bring a person out of Sheol (1 Sam 2:6). In one of his experiences, David composed a psalm describing how close he came to death: "For the waves of death encompassed me; the torrents of destruction overwhelmed me; the cords of Sheol surrounded me; the snares of death confronted me" (2 Sam. 22:5–6). During his shepherding days as a youth, David wrote of the valley of the shadow of death, of wanting to know the measure of his days as an indication of his constitutional frailty, and of a final indictment that man's flesh was as the grass of the field that first flourishes and then is gone (Ps. 23:4, 39:4, 103:15–16). Fatalism is seen in these passages, but it intensifies with Solomon.

Solomon's Ecclesiastes was preoccupied with many vanities, and death was not the least of them. The wise man died just like the fool (Eccl. 2:14–18); there was a season to live and a season to die (Eccl. 3:2); men differed little from the beasts in death, since neither knew the destination of the spirit (Eccl. 3:19–21); one comes forth naked from the womb and takes nothing with him into death (Eccl. 5:15); and man has no power to retain his spirit or withhold death (Eccl. 8:8).

Isaiah's prophecies were the first of the Old Testament to anticipate New Testament doctrine. He predicted that the Suffering Servant was cut off from the land of the living for transgressions done by others, and His grave was assigned with wicked men, yet He was with a rich man in His death (Isa. 53:8–9). Nevertheless, "He will swallow up death for all time, and the Lord God will wipe tears away from all faces, and He will remove the reproach of His people from all earth . . ." (Isa. 25:8). Paul later argued in 1 Corinthians 15:54 on the basis of Jesus' resurrection that this event had already taken place, but John looked forward to the hope of the resurrection when God would wipe away our tears (Rev. 21:4).[4]

Life's Promise in the New Testament

Within New Testament doctrine, the third, eternal aspect of death is articulated with greater clarity. Revelation 21:8 refers to eternal death as the second death, equated with the "lake that burns with fire and brimstone." The New Testament reminds us of our Old Testament legacy; through Adam, we are born with death in our genes, and therefore we are terminally ill and life is limited by time. We must wrestle with this issue early in the twenty-first century with its forecast of longevity reaching, some predict, to 120 years. *Will longevity, as an object of devotion in the westernized church, eventually become the subject matter of sermons? Will it be held out as a desirable way for the Christian to postpone negotiating the spiritual issues of terminal illness?*

In league with man's physical limitations is the reality of being born morally imperfect and bankrupt (Phil. 3:3). For Paul and others, moral imperfection renders us incapable of solving our problems; we do not have the ability to rationally put any confidence in the flesh or to trust ourselves (Rom. 3:23). All life is a risk. The soul that sins shall die, and in this sense, Paul speaks of death as an enemy in 1 Corinthians 15:26: "The last enemy that will be destroyed is death." In His resurrection, Jesus conquered death—physical, spiritual, and eternal. However, man's fear of death is bondage (Heb. 2:15). We forget that "our Savior Jesus Christ . . . has abolished death and brought life and immortality to light through the Gospel" (2 Tim. 1:10). There are Christians who fear death though they have been freed from it. Not infrequently, fear takes cover under the mask of a pantheon of lesser gods—extreme sports, super health, and regained youth, which are marketed as aggressively to older adults as they are to the younger under the illusion that they delay the inevitable. People attempt to believe that what happens to all men will not happen to them. In the natural world and secular way of thinking, all life is a crap shoot.

The arresting feature of New Testament teaching on death is that its emphasis is on life. The Bible faces death just as it faces all reality, but its main focus is on life, and only incidentally on death. Christ conquered death and the one who holds death, namely the Devil (Heb. 2:14). The Devil's power has always been subject to God's overrule (Job 2:6; Luke 12:5). For those separated from Christ who lack faith and obedience, death is the supreme enemy and the symbol of our alienation from God—the ultimate horror. If the soul that is alive is conscious presence with the Father, than the soul that is dead is conscious absence from Him.

Contrasted to the inevitability of eternal judgment of those outside of Christ, there is little doubt about the promise of life for those in Christ. Jesus refers to believers as children of the Resurrection, having a God who is of the living (Luke 20:34–38); He has gone to prepare a place for them (John 14:1–4). Paul wrote that those planted in the likeness of Christ's death shall also be like Him in the likeness of Christ's resurrection, and because of the Resurrection, death had lost its sting (Rom. 6:4–11; 1 Cor. 15:55–57). John the revelator quoted Jesus as saying He was alive forevermore. He has the keys of death, God shall wipe away all tears, and there shall be no more death, sorrow, crying, or pain (Rev. 1:17–18, 21:4).

Our purpose recognizes that even though those who are in Christ have the promise of eternal life, they still carry in their genes a predisposition that is selfish, earthly, contrary, temporal, and oriented toward self-gratification, self-aggrandizement, and consumption. These abide in all of us, including those who are of advancing age. The physical body always presents us with its limitations: sin, death, temptation, and disease. We need to determine how the aged Christian is supposed to negotiate faith and prepare for death.

Paul had to grapple with such a negotiation. His anticipation of death took a sobering turn from which our theology benefits.

Paul on Death

What was the effect of Paul's suffering on his ideas about death? The inevitability of death universally concentrates a person's thoughts and emotions on that event. In the absence of impending death, we are cavalier, complacent, and careless about the affairs of life and its indulgences, pleasures, and excesses.

Upon learning of the sudden and unexpected death of a friend or family member, we are sobered and make resolutions on how we will act differently, especially in terms of how we will relate to others whom we may have previously neglected. Or we may take a more serious attitude toward various duties we have put off. Someone else's death, however, is not impending death for us; the concentration of thoughts and emotions is usually short-lived. All people seem to be in denial about death. This is best illustrated by how little time it takes for us to forget even the most significant of people. Fame, for all it's worth, still requires marketing to keep it alive. In the annals of world history, relatively few enjoy the notoriety of a national holiday. Christianity's Christmas is about birth and its Easter is about resurrection. Every Christian has experienced a new birth and is privileged to look forward to eternal life. Spiritually, we must die to self to experience the new birth, and we must physically die in order to inherit the promise of eternal life. Our culture comes in between the two to prolong the inevitability of the latter. This is denial.

Spiritually, we must die to self to experience the new birth, and we must physically die in order to inherit the promise of eternal life.

If it can be shown from Scripture that Paul changed his thoughts about death because of the sentence of death upon him, we will have a biblical case for why even the sentence of death itself concentrates our attention suddenly on eternal things and better prepares us for eternity.

Living until the Parousia

In Paul's earlier writings, there was an expectation that he would survive until the second advent or coming of Christ, otherwise known as the *parousia*. The imminent second coming was one of the most widely held beliefs in the early church, and a potent hope throughout the apostolic age. The early use of the invocation *maranatha* bears witness to the disciples' lively expectation of Jesus' *parousia*, his advent in glory intended to consummate the kingdom begun by His death and resurrection. Acts 3:19–21 is one of the most primitive eschatological passages and carried with it the expectation that early repentance by the people in Jerusalem (on behalf of all Israel) would speed the *parousia*.[5] This was a remarkable incentive for aggressive evangelism, resulting in the spread of Christianity to the known civilized world during its first one hundred years. We know now, despite the evangelistic fervor, that it was not based on historical fact: Christ has not yet returned, but Christians since—particularly in the last years of the twentieth and first years of the twenty-first century—have again mobilized a massive worldwide evangelistic effort—all in anticipation of Christ's prophesied second coming.

Paul's early reference in 1 Thessalonians 4:15 to the second advent associates himself with those who will still be alive: "We who are left alive until the Lord comes shall not forestall those who have died"; where those who have died are mentioned in the third person but the survivors are mentioned in the inclusive first person plural. "In 1 Corinthians 6:14, the first person plural is used of those who will experience resurrection . . . but no distinction is drawn between those who have died and those who will still be alive and 'we shall not all die, but we shall all be changed,' for at the *parousia*, 'the dead will rise immortal and we [who are still alive] shall be changed [in the sense of getting a new body, while living, at the moment of His coming].'"[6]

Paul truly believed he would be alive at the second coming of Christ, and there have been thousands of Christians throughout the ages who have agreed with him, each in his or her own time. Some anticipate the joy of rising up into the air to meet Him, others anticipate using the physical ascension to meet Him in the air as a way of cheating death itself. (I often wonder if our religious beliefs are a veiled way to hide fears that may be a more real part of our psyche than spiritual truths are.)

Death Prior to the Parousia

Probably no more than a year separated the writing of the two letters to Corinth, and 2 Corinthians brings a significant change in the perspective of Paul. The difference in the two accounts raises interesting questions about biblical interpretation and the necessity for scholars to distinguish between an author's personal views and the revealed theological importance of Scripture. He could say some months before that "I die daily" in the sense that he always considered himself to be a living sacrifice for Christ in all that he did (1 Cor. 15:31, Rom. 12:1). Some consider 2 Corinthians as Paul's testimony and defense of himself as an apostle, but rather than boast of his accomplishments, he instead catalogues his sufferings (2 Cor. 4:7–12, 6:4–9).[7]

However, 2 Corinthians 7:5 reports something quite different: "For even when we came into Macedonia our flesh had no rest, but we were afflicted on every side: conflicts without, fears within." Dancing with death was no stranger to Paul, but on the occasion of the Macedonian visit, he felt like a man who had received the death sentence (and some scholars feel this referred to an actual threat from one of the local leaders). On earlier occasions, escape had accompanied the threat, but now escape seemed beyond all expectation. Escape did come, however, and Paul welcomed it like resurrection from death. He had been forced into a new dimension and concentration of focus. Whatever other changes took place in his outlook resulting from this experience, the prospects of dying before the *parousia* were now more probable than otherwise. He looked into the mirror of his circumstances and saw staring back at himself the picture of death. Hence, there is a personal confession of faith when he writes in 2 Corinthians 4:14, "Knowing that He who raised the Lord Jesus will raise us also with Jesus and will present us with you [who are still alive]."

Paul makes his most personal contribution to the subject of immortality in his second letter to Corinth (2 Cor. 5:1–10). It may have been his own expectation of death that precisely shifted his focus on living and serving to concentrating his mind on the question of death in the months preceding the writing of 2 Corinthians. This is his most personal letter, as if agreeing with the earlier mention that the sentence of death causes one to focus and predisposes him to gentleness and character. Paul knew the reality of *agape* in his life. But, it would appear in the second letter to Corinth and the subsequent one to Philippi, that during his imprisonment in Rome a loving softness emerges expressed as radiance amid the storm and stress of life.

One implication of this apparent shift in the apostle's views on his personal demise is that it was allowed by the primary Author of Scripture. And, as another possibility, it may actually have been more than allowed, but rather planned to occur in the life of Paul as a caution to the rest of us that we should not presume too much on our own ideas of the *parousia* or our own longevity. If Paul could not anticipate such a change in his personal theology, should we? Further, if only the Father knows when He shall give the order for the Son to return, is it unreasonable to assume that our own death is likewise of His sovereign purposes? The unknown encourages us to plan for the end game, and the scriptural formulae for this are more detailed than accounts of how we should prepare to meet on some mountaintop with others of like mind awaiting the second coming. Too many latter day prophets have been mistaken on this event, and we need to take care to not be enticed and captivated by prognostications merely to appease our own gratifications.

If these observations are correct, we conclude that suffering at a new and intensified level prepared Paul for his execution and departure to be with the Lord.

Suffering as Strategy for the End Game

The place of suffering in the Christian life requires little documentation and little justification of its role in producing godly character. At least this is true for the more serious of believers. Well known passages include 1 Peter 1:6–7; James 1:2–4, 12; and Romans 5:3–5. These are common experiences of the believer committed to following Christ as Lord, and the results of suffering are desirable goals toward which sincere pilgrims of all ages travel in their daily walks.

In addition to suffering which culminates in godly character, there is a suffering that points to the final transition—the penultimate end-game closure—of the aged person into the presence of the King. Paul, writing to Timothy in 2 Timothy 2:12, repeated a common theme: "If we suffer [in an acceptable godly way], we shall also reign." The old apostle John records Jesus' words in Revelation 3:21: "He who overcomes, I will grant to him to sit down with Me on My throne, as I also overcame and sat down with My Father on His throne."

Paul's suffering in Macedonia, in a manner of speaking, decentralized some of his preoccupation with survival during the course of ministry and forced him as never before to consider physical death as imminent. Any modern minister who focuses on the ministry to the exclusion of the full counsel of the Word is courting problems. In regards to the future and more particularly to future death, the minister of the gospel is no different than the minister in the marketplace, to whom James wrote (James 4:13–16), saying:

> Come now, you who say, "Today or tomorrow, we shall go to such a city, and spend a year there and engage in business and make a profit." Yet you do not know what your life will be like tomorrow. You are just a vapor that appears for a little while and then vanishes away. Instead, you *ought* to say, "If the Lord wills, we shall live and also do this or that." But as it is, you boast in your arrogance; all such boasting is evil. (Italics in original)

The most immediate consequence of Paul looking death in the face, other than stirring a revision of his ideas on the Resurrection and the resurrection body, was that it softened his letters: he began addressing converts as precious friends for whom he had a deep warm affection. Paul knew love for the saints, but in his latter days, it took on a new softness and tenderness. In *Don't Waste Your Sorrows*, Billheimer summarizes a principle applicable to Paul:

> All born-again people are in training for rulership. Since the supreme law of that future social order, called the kingdom of God, is *agape* love, therefore their apprenticeship and training is for the learning of deep dimensions of this love. But deep dimensions of this love are learned only in the school of suffering . . . [where maturity] . . . comes only through years of suffering. "If we suffer, we shall also reign"—because where there is little suffering, there is little love; no suffering, no love; no love, no rulership.[8]

I recommend caution in taking this quote from Billheimer as a stand-alone perspective, and it would be an injustice to him not to recommend a full reading of his thesis contained in both *Destined for the Throne* and *Don't Waste Your Sorrows*, which still serve as resource books.

A lifetime in the world system with its experiences, accomplishments, and affections are now brought into juxtaposition with the late life focus that Billheimer encourages. In my view, it is a difficult juxtaposition, but it is necessary. Because of death's inevitability, the older Christian has to juggle the affairs of this world with the affairs of being present with the Lord. This too is elemental in a theology of advancing years. There is a final season of calling to account the blessings of the Lord over a lifetime and the purposes to which He has called us. Among the most difficult of tasks is how to hold onto a God-given earthly existence over which we have a measure of stewardship and which we admit is in God's hands, and at the same time hold onto that stage of our eternity when we are in His presence to perform the kind of ruling with Christ for which Billheimer so convincingly argues.

There is a seed of discontent with this present life once we become Christians because our spirits have been given a gyroscope, which steers toward a final destiny in Christ . . .

When I write as a gerontologist and a behavioral scientist, I recognize the social psychological problem this challenge poses. For the mature committed believer there is a kind of constitutional schizoid orientation—he or she has behavior and affections on the present world, while trying to include in everyday life the teachings of the gospel which tell of a life to come—"look up from which your salvation comes," and "anxiously anticipate the coming of the Lord." Many a Christian is exposed to the two orientations from the earliest days of faith. It is only when the time comes for developing an end-game strategy that we, like Paul, begin to sort out the sociological, emotional, and spiritual options. Some writers have speculated that the uneasy feeling many Christians have is really "homesickness." There is a seed of discontent with this present life once we become Christians because our spirits have been given a gyroscope, which steers toward a final destiny in Christ rather than making us fully comfortable with the present world system. The words of the old gospel song, "This world is not my home; I'm just passing through," express this spiritual homesickness.

Transitions

A premise of all behavioral science, amply supported by the Scriptures, is that transition is a stress-provoking experience which causes anxiety and makes a person unpredictable, even to those closest to him or her. In times of transition, we become different people.

To be unpredictable is to provoke anxiety. In Matthew 6, Jesus told the disciples six times not to be anxious, but they were, because what He was proposing—a new government—had unpredictable outcomes in the minds of the disciples. Paul in Philippians 4 said not to be anxious, but his beloved church still was. Transition is difficult because we prefer the familiar and avoid the unfamiliar. Those closest to us prefer us when we maintain a familiar stance and therefore remain predictable. They don't want us to change (assuming, of course, that our behavior is essentially acceptable behavior). This is often true of adult children who resist later-life changes in their parents who are adjusting values and behavior to suit themselves. Many church members have stormed the gates of heaven with their prayers, if not demanding then certainly imploring God to grant continued life to an aged saint. They refuse to release a loved one; they refuse to let go.

Transition involves being pushed out of an old situation and pulled into a new one, and the two occur simultaneously. Seldom is the Christian deprived wholly of the old comfort zone without already moving toward a new position in God. The overlap often involves contradictory values and ethics. He or she is less than a citizen of the past while still unacceptable as a patriot of the future. Transition is never easy, and we cannot lose track of this fact when applying it to older people whose relationships and patterns of behavior have, in many instances, been set for many years. We benefit when we have insight on how God prepares us for that final transition from this life to the next. John Calvin's insights help.

Calvin on the End Game

Little doubt exists as to where John Calvin stands on the topic of Christians transitioning from things of the world, and through God-ordained suffering and deprivation, centralizing on heaven. Calvin's interest does not include, as does Billheimer's, the marriage supper of the Lamb and subsequent co-ruling by the bride with Christ. Rather, he is concerned with "meditating on the future life" and "how to use the present life and its comforts" without losing a perspective of [the] Christian's place in God's economy.[9] We may take comfort in Billheimer's systematic theology, but it is Calvin's practical theology that charts a course for the here and now.

Calvin's interest is for all Christians, not just the elderly; age is not a concern in his theology as it is in this book. He begins: "Whatever be the kind of tribulation with which we are afflicted, we should always consider [what its] end [may] be, that we may be trained to despise the present, and thereby stimulated to aspire to the future life."[10] Calvin rejects any idea that says material possessions, worldly blessings, and pleasures are bad. Rather, they are to be defined as gifts of God's unmerited favor, seen as evidence of His love, and used for His purposes.

God knows how strongly we are inclined by nature to a slavish love of this world, so in order to prevent us from clinging too strongly to it, He, in His love and mercy, employs reasonable devices to call us back to center, remove our lethargy, and impress on us the transitory and deceptive ways of the world. Calvin, writing in 1559, could have been describing present day America when he wrote: "Hence, our stupidity; our minds [are] so dazzled with the glare of wealth, power, and honors, that they can see no farther. The heart also, engrossed with avarice, ambition, and lust, is weighed down and cannot rise above them."[11] He was describing the religion of *eros*!

More recently, Donald McCullough offered a modern slant to this part of Calvin in *The Trivialization of God*, where he identifies illicit affections within the modern church for gods of success, political party, social cause, comfort, doctrine, and experience.[12] The theme is a common one. Herbert Schlossberg joins in criticism of the institutional church in *Idols for Destruction—The Conflict of Christian Faith and American Culture*. There he identifies conformity to and identifying with the economics and politics of the current culture (thus preventing a focus on the kingdom of God), a loss of theological underpinnings, humanism, and a bewildering kaleidoscope of conflicting and shifting beliefs all too ready to reflect the *ethos* of the day.[13]

Calvin says our minds are incapable of seriously desiring and aspiring after the future of heaven until they learn to despise the present life.[14] Aversion to the present life, however, should not result in ingratitude to God for His blessings. We are to be thankful, while recognizing that blessings are deceptive: as symbols of God's grace, they too easily can usurp the authority of the grace they symbolize. Calvin wrote, "Let believers, then, in forming an estimate of this mortal life, and perceiving that in itself it is nothing but misery, make it their aim to exert themselves with greater alacrity, and less hindrance, in aspiring to the future and eternal life."[15] It is in the contrast of the present and future life, that Calvin comes closest to our theology of advancing years:

> If heaven is our country, what can the earth be but a place of exile? If departure from the world is entrance into life, what is the world but a sepulcher, and what is residence in it but immersion in death? If to be freed from the body is to gain full possession of freedom, what is the body but a prison? If it is the very summit of happiness to enjoy the presence of God, is it not miserable to want it?[16]

As if in anticipation of our discussion on transition and its anxiety, Calvin says we all want to remain in the comfort of where we are, avoiding change, since " . . . everything longs for permanent existence. I . . . therefore contend that we ought to look to future immortality, where we may obtain that fixed condition which nowhere appears on the earth."[17] Paul agrees in 2 Corinthians 5:2 and enjoins believers to hasten cheerfully to death, not because they "would be unclothed, but clothed upon."

The Supreme Basis for the End Game

Most men die without ever having sensed, grasped, and lived out their God-given calling and purpose in life. To know and live out one's calling and purpose is the most important evidence of affection on things above rather than on things below. We live for Him and we die for Him. Purpose makes all things fade into irrelevance (Phil. 4:12). With it, we can be full and grateful, and we can be in want without complaint. With every distinct purpose, Calvin says, God provides whatever is needed to perform it.[18] I would add that jealousy and envy are foreign to the man who walks in his purposes. When David had served the purposes of God, he died. He had asked for no more than to live out what it was God wanted him to do (Acts 13:36). A purpose can so captivate our affections that we are not drawn to want more than is necessary to carry it out. Calvin concludes:

> The call of the Lord is the foundation and beginning of right action. He who does not act with reference to it will never, in the discharge of duty, keep the right path. He will sometimes be able, perhaps, to give the semblance of something laudable, but whatever it may be in the sight of man, it will be rejected before the throne of God . . . Hence, he only who directs his life to this end will have it properly framed; because, free from the impulse of rashness, he will not attempt more than his calling justifies, knowing that it is unlawful to overleap the prescribed bounds . . . Under the superintendence of God . . . the magistrate will more willingly perform his office, and the father of a family confine himself to his proper sphere . . . This, too, will afford admirable consolation, that in following your proper calling, no work will be so mean and sordid as not to have a splendor and value in the eye of God.[19]

From the beginning, this book's emphasis has been on the purposes of God for Israel, for the church, and for individuals irrespective of era. The person, young or old, who has grasped his or her genuine and divinely crafted purpose will see reality validly. God's grace will provide in the world whatever resources are needed to perform effectively for the glory of God. What is in excess of what is needed will be enjoyed but never so much so as to usurp the higher purposes of God.

The Defining Call

Christians have a defining moment in their spiritual walks when they know what it is for which God has apprehended them, and that moment defines for them the purpose of their remaining days. For some, there is a single purpose. For others, relative to God's sovereign plan in reference to the kingdom, there may be a succession of two or more courses they will pursue. Paul's defining moment occurred on the road to Damascus. He described what occurred in his life in the years immediately following. They were years of decentralization from worldly affairs, referred to by Billheimer, and a time of focus on the future life, referred to by Calvin. Paul catalogues his past accomplishments: circumcised on the eighth day, an Israelite of the tribe of Benjamin, a Hebrew of the Hebrews, perfect in obedience to the Law, and a highly regarded Pharisee. A Roman citizen trained in Greek culture, it is speculated that by age twenty-one he had the equivalent of two doctoral degrees. Paul's credentials were impeccable. His devaluation of these, written in latter days when decentralization from life was a more critical issue, is classic:

Christians have a defining moment in their spiritual walks when they know what it is for which God has apprehended them, . . .

> But whatever things were gain to me, those things I have counted as loss for the sake of Christ. More than that, I count all things to be loss in view of the surpassing value of knowing Christ Jesus my Lord for whom I have suffered the loss of all things, and count them but rubbish in order that I may gain Christ (Phil. 3:7–8).

In Philippians 3:12, Paul refers to the purposes for which Christ had laid hold of him. His calling and purpose were clear. He was to be an apostle to the Gentiles. He put off his worldly credentials as a badge of identity (without forsaking what he had learned in reference to the world) and he put on the badge of his purpose in God.

As he pursued his calling and purpose in God, Paul confessed that he had not yet become perfect. He was still a work in progress (v. 12). This was not how God saw him, however. God saw him as a finished, perfected work—not in Paul's time, but in God's (v. 15). In the course of his journey in Christ, Paul later incurred the critical Macedonian threat on his life, and this further centered his affection on God and impending death, so that he could say in his last communication to Timothy:

I am already being poured out as a drink offering, and the time
of my departure has come. I have fought the good fight, I have
finished the course, I have kept the faith; in the future there is
laid up for me the crown of righteousness, which the Lord, the
righteous Judge, will award to me on that day; and not only to
me, but also to all who have loved His appearing. (2 Tim 4:6–8)

Little doubt exists that Paul could have been compared to
King Hezekiah who failed to be thankful for all things, including
those which otherwise were anxiety provoking (Phil. 4:6). Paul,
like David, continued in sufficient strength to declare God's
purposes through him to the world of his day, and when he had
completed God's purposes, he was beheaded. The end game had
been played and won. We remember Paul; the name of his execu-
tioner is long forgotten.

The latter days need not be the same for every older person,
but it shall be the end game given by the Father. In final days of
waning strength, each must determine through divine illumination whether he or she continues with what has been on his or her
platter for prior months or years, or whether a shift is necessary
to a new, albeit short-lived, purpose for which God's grace is sufficient unto completion.

CHAPTER EIGHT

The Body of Christ Revisited

THE EMPHASES OF CHAPTERS 6 AND 7 ARE INCOMPLETE WITHOUT A SCRIPTURAL REVIEW OF WHERE THE CHURCH FITS INTO THE LATTER DAYS OF BELIEVERS. SHORT OF THIS PERSPECTIVE, SOME MAY COME away from prior chapters excessively sobered—others angry. After all, much of what has been presented is not the usual kind of comforting words we hear or read about declining days. In order to properly understand the role of the church, we need to first make observations about the family.

FAMILY AND CHURCH IN PERSPECTIVE

Some skeptics speculate that historians have idealized the existence of a so-called noble extended family, seeing it as something more desired than real. This does not stop us from wanting the ideal. We like our myths for the comfort they provide because we see them as being in stark contrast to the modern American family many of us experience or hear of others experiencing. Myths serve more than the occasion for reminiscence, however; they also are models toward which we move as the occasions arise. In the present case, the myth may not return us to the idealized extended family, but it does make us more sensitive to the possibilities found in the social trust fund.

The Social Trust Fund and Community

Regardless of era, the social trust fund has been the perennial safety net for the weakest of families and an integral component of the strongest of them. Where the family fails, the community, with its own self-interests, enters to compensate for family weaknesses. This safety net does not exist in any visible, highly organized, or institutional sense. It comes in different forms—relatives, friends, associations, churches, and public agencies. The amazing reality is that the resources are there for the taking, and we can structure our own social trust fund by selectively choosing from a variety of options. The farsighted head of a family has this kind of strategy in mind. Let's explore why this is true.

Most wise and experienced heads of families know that they do not possess total control over their family members or the events that impact them. Societal competition for individual member loyalty has existed in all societies, and the more complex the society, the greater the competition. Modern mass society is defined as one where the flow of information occurs without restriction. Not only is it accessible when people seek it out, but it also comes into every person's living room, den, or bedroom through a variety of telecommunications—radio, Internet, and television being the prime examples.

The events of living also challenge every head of family; some are easier to deal with than others. The competition for family member loyalty and the events of life are spurs to seek assistance from the outside. Since searching for extra-family resources is biblical, there is no shame or admission of weakness for the Christian when the wise head of family seeks help.

When adult children watch a parent in their declining days, they, too, want the support of friends who will stand alongside and provide comfort. They need their own social trust fund that supports, surrounds, and encourages. Adult children of a parent with dementia, Parkinson's, Alzheimer's disease, or rapidly debilitating cancer want support. Even when an aged parent still communicates and otherwise participates in family life, the adult child appreciates someone who is able to provide perspective of what can be expected in the next six months, or five to ten years.

The community provides the basis for direction as we move from one season of life to another, and it comprises for us our social trust fund—not to replace the family, but to augment it.

The Church as a Social Trust Fund

For the Christian, the institutional church has been a part of the social trust fund in varying degrees. Our purpose here is to explore the implications of the church for the elderly, particularly in their waning years, and thereby prepare for part 2.

Our reference to the church is in its institutional sense, not to all the people—past, present, and future—expressing faith in Jesus Christ. This is the universal church, and, in its collective sense, is referred to as the body of Christ and the bride of Christ. The institutional church is sociological in nature and is comprised of all denominations, doctrinal streams, cults, sects, and ecclesia that represent man's effort to understand biblical truth and organize around that understanding to provide a practical theology for everyday church life.

The institutional church is expected to be an important participant in the Christian's social trust fund, if not the main one. Ideally, it is supposed to be more than just any other organization among a potpourri of options. For many, however, the institutional church is just one *The institutional* of a broad spectrum of voluntary associations, and *church is expected* in this sense it is part of a gigantic smorgasbord *to be an important* from which modern man picks and chooses to have *participant in the* his needs met. Humans gravitate from one group to *Christian's social* another; sometimes it's the church, the lodge, or *trust fund . . .* the monastery that is sought out for its isolation and solitude. Or it may be a cult of peyote or LSD devotees, a homebased small group meeting for Bible study, or a weekly game of bridge, golf, or poker. These all come under the umbrella of what we call community—people gathering for a common purpose (although not all are considered appropriate for Christians).

In modern society, again because of religious diversity, the institutional church has also been treated as its own kind of smorgasbord, and this helps us to understand what some call "member transfer." We go from one congregation to another, tasting the worship service and musical program here, the teaching and preaching there, a seminar or conference somewhere else, and the architecture still elsewhere. Smorgasbord tables, however, have a hard time meeting one's needs for community. For that, we have to be planted and then grow and mingle with others who eventually know, appreciate, and tolerate us. Community, and thus the social trust fund, only exists when there is a greater degree of relationship and continuity to that relationship. In the diversity of modern mass society, the easiest thing to do is get lost and not even be missed. But it takes effort to get connected so that you are missed when absent. I assume it was "easier" to get sick and die in pre-modern societies, since community was more intense, and family and friends gathered around the sick and dying person to express love, comfort, and assurance that they would be missed and would eventually meet again.

God created the church and has used it for two thousand years to provide community for those who believe in Christ. The Bible is rich in describing both the broad parameters and the finer points regarding the church's role. The primitive church had its origins in the form of house churches comprised of families or households. These would meet on the sixth or seventh day of the week for corporate celebration and worship. Sociologically, the first institutional churches were shaped by the collective qualities of those who comprised them. Paul recognized this model and gave instructions to the Corinthians on how they were to worship, manifest the gifts of the Holy Spirit, and conduct the sacraments. Each person was known for his and her spiritual gifts, and they were depended upon to provide for the general welfare out of those spiritual resources.

More formal structures of church organization arose around 300 A.D. when the Roman Emperor Constantine institutionalized the church under what became the Roman Catholic model. Doctrinal and theological changes took place at the time of the Protestant Reformation, but the institutionalized structural and organizational form of the church did not change dramatically. More or less, the Roman model of the church remains throughout most of Christendom today. Church organization was not a doctrinal issue, but rather a sociological one, in which the church adopted the archetypical model of the Roman Senate.

Students of human organization tell us that once an organization is established, it takes on a life of its own, despite its origin in the ideas and styles of its founders. In this sense, the institutional church as organization can assume a certain sacredness, and any effort or proposal to change it is met with the typical "we can't do that; we have done it this way for forty or fifty years." The reason "we can't do that" is that within the traditional structure, members have become predictable to each other in terms of the organization's culture and not in terms of what unique skills each individual brought to the organization when they first joined and helped organize it. Hence, we all give up a piece of ourselves when we join any organization, including the church. Some parts of us are left at the door when we enter. Some parts are changed after we get inside and begin to adapt to the local culture. This is true of our affiliation with the majority of organizations to which we belong. It is this kind of social-psychological fact that helps explain what was earlier referred to as "member transfer," or the periodic effort to find the best fit for who we think we are or want to become.

In its most general sense, the institutional church is an opportunity for and a source of community where we can contribute to church life as well as derive the benefits that church has to offer. Within this environment, both contributions and benefits are problematic. Older adults and their adult children may or may not be able to derive certain ministry benefits; the church may or may not be a place where the older person can minister in terms of God's calling and purposes in his or her life.

The Church as a Reflection of Society

Sociological observations repeatedly confirm that religious institutions in America usually do not teach values distinctive to their own traditions. Instead, religious terminology approves of the values of the society at large. Peter L. Berger noted that religious institutions so much defer to society's norms as their own that any kind of distinctiveness seems odd.[1] More recently, pollster George Barna in *The Second Coming of the Church* summarized surveys showing that Christians do not score better than non-Christians in many biblically prohibited behaviors, and, further, non-Christians do not score radically worse than professing Christians.[2] In 1999, Dr. Henry Blackaby, speaking at a conference at the Billy Graham Training Center in Cove, North Carolina, echoed Barna and others by saying the incidence of abortion, divorce, and gambling was as prevalent among church people as those outside the church. The church, said Blackaby, had lost its light and the consequent darkness of the world should come as no surprise.

Notable theological works of the twentieth century, as summarized by Herbert Schlossberg, support the preeminence of society's norms in the teachings of the church.[3] He notes that Paul Tillich and Rudolf Bultmann, as examples, hoped to make theology engage the process of correlation, or conformity to secular systems such as Jungian psychology, linguistic philosophy, popular sociology, and Marxist economics. Enlightenment scholar Crane Brinton concluded that mainline Protestant denominations had already completed correlation and had become indistinguishable from the Enlightenment orientation that dominated American society. Therefore, the master of the American church is likely to be whatever cultural or intellectual fad is in vogue. Christology displays this, writes Schlossberg, when the "real Jesus" becomes the champion and prototype of the American middle class—perhaps a guerrilla fighter, a social democrat, or a model of psychological fitness. This produces intellectual and spiritual sterility where the church functions to justify the political and sociological establishment, and rather than being a restorative body for biblical authenticity, the church merely transmits society's values to the next generation.

Has correlation taken place in the church in regards to the elderly? In congregations generally, there is little doubt that correlation has occurred regarding stewardship over money. The amount of private and corporate debt is equally as great inside the church as outside. When we extend this to families, few adult children have the resources to care for their parents when there is an unexpected major financial need, and it is an amazing—almost unprecedented—congregation that can meet the major needs of older adults when children fail to do so, as required by Scripture. In this instance of benevolence, the church has indeed achieved correlation.

The defining moment for the social gospel in the early–twentieth century was when the institutional church succeeded in lobbying for laws to establish entitlement programs for disadvantaged groups. Each time federal law provided for taxation to support a social need, the institutional church was able to relinquish another biblical mandate. The literature is rich regarding the defects of socialist entitlement efforts and their efforts to help those in need compared to the advantages of private benevolence.

I will not develop this here, except to say that government-managed housing, health, and welfare programs have essentially freed the church from historic responsibilities.

In addition to Schlossberg, referenced above, Marvin Olasky in *The Tragedy of American Compassion*, Rousas Rushdoony in *The Politics of Guilt and Pity*, Helmut Schoeck in *Envy: A Theory of Social Behavior*, and Colonel Doner in *The Samaritan Strategy*, all attest to how organizations, inclusive of the institutional church, assume the vocabulary of the secular world as a means of accommodating their version of the gospel to it, thereby making the church a comfortable place to be. Semanticist Edmund Burke long ago referred to this as "the rhetoric of motives." Chapter 10 recommends surveying church leaders and program managers to determine the degree to which they hold to the same stereotypes or misconceptions of the elderly as held by secular society.

THE INTEGRITY OF THE CHURCH AS AN ORGANISM

Two doctrines apply to the place of older adults in the church. The first is the church as the representative of the spiritual body of Christ, and the second is the church's ministry of restoration. Both are applicable to the biblical view of benevolence whose frequent beneficiaries are older adults.

The Ethics of New Testament Gerontology

The list of New Testament passages regarding parents and the elderly is brief. It includes Paul's repeat of the Fifth Commandment for children to honor them so that their days may be long (Eph. 6:1), and a related injunction to not rebuke older men (1 Tim. 5:1–21). Jesus scolded the Pharisees for feigning loyalty to the tithe rather than caring for their parents (Mark 7:11), and for foreclosing on the houses of widows (Matt. 23:14). Honor is required for widows, and children and grandchildren are to practice piety for their older members and provide for them and others of their own house as a return for their earlier sacrifices (1 Tim. 5:3–4, 8). And, finally, the practice of visiting widows is singled out as a measure of true religion (James 1:27).

With the exception of reference to the Fifth Commandment, these other New Testament prescriptions on behalf of the elderly are primarily ethical in nature. They become theological when they are tied to a much larger context. David Wells has stated that systematic theology takes into account the full counsel of God, predicated on the unity of Scripture and on other theological assumptions which are outlined by Bernard Ramm in his book, *Protestant Biblical Interpretation* (Baker Books, 1981). The ethical dimension derives from systematic theology. Systematic theology cuts across all of Scripture—Old and New Testaments alike. Hence, whatever the Old Testament had to say about the place of older adults in God's scheme of things still applies to the New Testament church, as well as the contemporary church. Further, we seek what is new in the New Testament and what impact this has on our subject.

The Body as an Organism

Three concepts describe the biblical view of the body of Christ and how it is supposed to be lived out on a day-by-day basis. Weaving in and out of the Scriptures are the ideas of relatedness, interdependence, and complementarity in reference to the body. The body is a fellowship of persons placed and jointly fitted together for purposes of mutual support and edification, building one another up, growing to maturity, and loving one another (1 Cor. 12; Col. 2:19; Eph. 4:16).

- To be *related* means that a person is placed into a larger group with which he or she shares some identifying quality. The group doesn't consist of dissimilar people, all randomly dumped together without consequence.
- To be *interdependent* means that no one member of the body is sufficient unto himself or herself, and that each member depends on others in order to function. In interdependence, a person is a function of factors uniquely intrinsic to him or her as well as to those extrinsically tied to others.
- To be *complementary* means that each member of the body has a unique quality that adds to or augments the qualities of some other member.

The biblical body is an organism, each part strategically, purposefully, and integrally placed in conjunction with every other part, whether that part is five years of age or ninety-five. Irrespective of age, all believers come to God through faith, are baptized into Christ, and have Christ within them. Paul makes an amazing pronouncement that all but destroys demographic classifications: "There is neither Jew nor Greek, there is neither slave nor free man, there is neither male nor female; for you are all one in Christ Jesus" (Gal. 3:26–28). Why didn't Paul mention "neither young nor old?" The reason was that age, unlike other demographics (race, economics, education) and culture (language, religion, values, styles of life), didn't have to be mentioned. It just did not play a role in determining who was born into the family of God, nor do these distinctions have any future significance in who is retained and fitted into relationship with others in the mystical organic body. The bride of Christ, in the end, turns out to be heterogeneous without that making any difference.

The all-inclusive quality of the body of Christ is further seen in the well-known passages where the Holy Spirit parcels out gifts to all believers . . .

The absence of any reference to older adults in Paul's listing purposefully retained for the New Testament family culture what was radically and thoroughly understood as integral to Old Testament family structure. Jesus retained the honor due older parents, and, for that matter, all older people. A strange paradox was taking place in the newly minted body of Christ. Age didn't make any difference to salvation. As to family structure and the culture, the honorific role of the elderly continued to make a difference. Older adults continued to be considered seasoned and wise. They had equal status to all other believers as it pertained to salvation; they had honor as older believers. Nevertheless, trouble loomed on the horizon of the New Testament family.

Paul's frequent reference in his letters to the carnality of Christians and particularly to jealousy, envy, and factions suggests that the full significance of the church as an organic phenomenon was difficult to grasp and equally difficult to live out.[4] It is no different today.

The all-inclusive quality of the body of Christ is further seen in the well-known passages where the Holy Spirit parcels out gifts to all believers, and God places each person in the body as He desires

(1 Cor. 12; Rom. 12). Each sacrifices himself to serve others, being "devoted to one another in brotherly love; [giving] preference to one another in honor . . . fervent in spirit, serving the Lord . . . contributing to the needs of the saints . . ." (Rom. 12:10–11, 13). None of these provide for differential treatment or performance based on demographic qualities. In a word, age is an irrelevant factor in receiving and utilizing gifts.

The organic model of the body of Christ, when operating this way, differs greatly from what social theorists have referred to as an atomistic social model. These two models have received attention for several hundred years, and the distinction first became evident at the time of the Renaissance when humanism was given its birth. Atomism is individualistic and reminiscent of what in an earlier chapter was referred to as Hellenistic *eros*. The human being becomes the measure of all things, is reliant only upon what he or she thinks is right, questions others, creates values, and rules as desired, all to his or her own benefit. The atomist is a law unto and for himself or herself. In the extreme, atomism is anarchic, and a society committed to this model is self-destructing. Will Durant described the events leading up to the increase in individualism:

> The instincts formed through a hundred thousand years of hunting and savagery had reemerged through the cracked shell of a morality that had lost the support of religious belief, of respected authority, and established law. The great Church that had once ruled kings could no longer govern or cleanse itself . . . and where there had been citizens there were now only individuals.[5]

On the other hand, the organic social order is integrated, interdependent, stable, and enduring—all qualities we attributed to families and the social trust fund in Old Testament times. The more tightly people are bound to one another, the more members perform as a group for the welfare of individuals.

The biblical formula for the body exempts no one from individual responsibility for personal sins, and each is accountable for obedience and stewardship over gifts and purposes to which one is called. The gifts are, nevertheless, given for the benefit of others, so while every person is responsible for their own behavior, that behavior is integrally tied to the manner in which others are dependent on it for their own welfare and function. This has great implications for the involvement of older adults in the body life of the church.

- The institutional church, as an organic entity, is expected to fully integrate the older person in a functional way into the life of the church. This will appropriately be done in terms of (1) the older person's spiritual and ministry gifts, (2) the perceived calling and purposes of God, and (3) natural talents and experience. This is body ministry with focus on the individual.
- The church must also exercise every effort to provide for the welfare of each individual part to keep it tied into the whole, providing support and care where it is necessary. This is body ministry with focus on the integrity of the body itself.

For the most part, the church's body ministry is confined to the second option—to define the older adult in terms of requiring but not contributing services. Hence, older adults are primarily perceived as objects of benevolence, and this stereotype is derived primarily from fifty of years of governmental entitlement programs that at the beginning of the twenty-first century are increasingly recognized as only half a biscuit.

THE MINISTRY OF RESTORATION

The final word of God in the Old Testament is the prophecy in Malachi about restoration. God will send the prophet Elijah prior to the great and dreadful day of the Lord (Mal. 4:5–6). Jesus reiterates this prophecy in Matthew 17:11–12, saying: "Elijah is coming and will restore all things; but I say to you that Elijah already came," implying three different appearances. First, Elijah came through Elisha, who continued in the spirit of Elijah. Second, Elijah came through John the Baptist (Luke 1:17). Third, Elijah will return through the body of Christ as intercessors fulfill the Elijah task. The old are uniquely set aside to intercede in their latter years because this is the time when they are able to decentralize from the affairs of the world and recenter on the things of the Spirit (James 5:17–18, Eph. 4:11–12, 1 Pet. 5:1–4).

The Elijah task is to restore all things as the Father intended from the beginning. In the mid–1970s, my wife and I travelled a total of 140 miles each Friday evening to meet with others in the home of Harold Hill (author of *How to Live Like a King's Kid* and *From Goo to You by Way of the Zoo*), a tough consulting engineer who was an early convert to the charismatic renewal. We were going through the Twenty-third Psalm one evening and Harold asked the question, "To what was David asking God to restore his soul?" After lots of discussion, the agreement was "To whatever it was that God had in mind at the beginning."

Two important areas of restoration are the family and the church. Correctly understanding the implications of this, the institutional church has no choice but to foster restoration if it expects to properly retain its place in the sun, and the restoration is primarily the responsibility of older members skilled in the business of prayer.

Restoration of the Family

Restoration of the family occurs at four levels: between generations, within family leadership, through the cleansing of the conscience from guilt, and by coming against false family gods.

Restoring Relationship between Generations

Malachi's prophecy in Malachi 4:5–6 told of Elijah restoring the fathers' hearts to the children and the children's hearts to the fathers. On Mount Carmel, Elijah reminded Israel to return to the faith of the fathers—Abraham, Isaac, and Jacob—in order to reestablish the flow of blessings from generation to generation, as expressed in the covenant promise of Deuteronomy 5:16: "Honor your father and mother, so that you may live and that it may go well with you in the land." In the Old Testament, land was a metaphor for the inheritance that passed from one generation to another. In the New Testament, our inheritance in Christ is comprised of the calling and purposes of God that are expressed in the blessings of parents and grandparents to their offspring. The prophet Malachi established that the continued stability and continuity of the family was to rest with praying parents and grandparents. Societal survival was placed in front of them as a mandate.

The older generation is to live in such a way as to pass on to younger generations whatever was received from the Father. And the younger generation is to honor the older with an attitude of willingness to receive their blessing. The Elijah task of the church counsels both generations of their respective responsibilities. Short of turning the hearts of the generations, the land will be smitten with a curse; but compliance with the injunction brings protection of the inheritance. In the Old Testament, protection was to be found in the rooms of households under the protection of the blood (Ex. 12:1–4, 7, 15). In the New Testament, families were to clear out the yeast of malice and wickedness, so that sincerity and truth could reign in the home, because a home divided against one another will not stand (2 Cor. 5:7–8, Matt. 12:25).

> *The older generation is to live in such a way as to pass on to younger generations whatever was received from the Father.*

I was involved in a situation that illustrates how the ministry of restoration worked in the relationship between a young man and his father, and particularly how restoration results in physical health and healing. Dave was in his mid-twenties, and he came to the front of the church for ministry one Sunday morning, asking for prayer and anointing with oil so his cold symptoms would be healed. It wasn't an unusual request—it was typical of the kind of ministry we offered. As I approached him I sensed a deep down, very authoritative voice saying, "Don't touch that man!" I stopped, inasmuch as I try to be obedient when I sense that God is talking. Then I had another impression: "Ask him about his relationship with his father," and I subliminally said, "Yes, Sir." I asked Dave what was going on with his father. He looked startled and let loose with an expletive or two, followed with a snarl. "Look, Dave, I think you had better go home, make things right with your Dad, and then come back for prayer and the oil," I said. He got up right then and left the church. The next afternoon he called and said, "I did what you said, I got things straight with my father, and I immediately got well." Had Dave not done what I told him to do, he would have missed the blessing of restoration and likely would not have been healed. Had I ministered to him prematurely, our church would have missed this remarkable opportunity to restore one generation to another. For that moment, at least, we retained our place in the work of the Son.

Restoring Family Leadership

Elijah put man's relationship with God right. At Mount Carmel, Elijah may have challenged four hundred heathen priests under the control of Jezebel, but at the heart of Israel's sin was King Ahab who acquiesced and fled the responsibilities he had as the head of his unprotected family and royal office (1 Kings 16:31, 21:25). At the heart of family dissolution, more than any other cause, is the lack of viable fatherhood. Elijah challenged that weakness, and the church's call to restore the family requires prophets who will do likewise. The destruction of the four hundred priests was symbolic of the destruction of sulking, paralyzed, inactive heads of families as personified by Ahab.

The act of restoring leadership to the family recognizes that it is the husband and father (at least in intact families) who is the rightful leader in God's sight. To assume otherwise pits the church against what we call divine order. Even when the husband or father is not a believer, Scripture still maintains that he is the authoritative conduit through whom ministry can still flow to wife and children. I have ministered many times to wives and children at the altar, in counseling sessions, and in home group meetings, and whenever I ask permission of the husband or father to minister, the results are remarkably greater than if the divine order is circumvented by ignoring the father's rightful place as head of the family.

If they happen to be attending a church service when wife and children need ministry, I have invited permission of even unbelieving husbands and fathers to minister to needy family members. There have been times I have gone so far as to instruct the unbelieving father or husband himself on how to minister—a simple prayer, a laying on of hands. So surprised and impressed to be recognized for their authority in the family, many of these men have made commitments to Christ without even hearing the gospel message as it would usually be presented.

While not universal, a similar pattern must be followed regarding the elderly, many of whom are set aside as no-longer viable members of the family. Considered irrelevant, they are held out more as fixtures than functioning personages. The repository of experience and wisdom of the years has not disappeared, and restoration is to be encouraged as long as older adults can draw breath. Again, we often call upon the family patriarch to minister restoration rather than using the altar worker for that purpose.

Restoring Right Conscience and Removing Guilt from Sin

Elijah was the instrument by which guilt, derived from sins of the past, was erased. He visited the widow of Zarephath, and her son became ill and stopped breathing. She said to Elijah, "What do you have against me, man of God. Did you come to remind me of my sin and kill my son?" (1 Kings 17:17–18). Elijah ministered to the boy who returned to life, and Elijah returned him to his mother. She was full of joy, free of the guilt of sin, and returned to joyful relationship with her son. A child of death was restored to life, and modern day Elijahs can also return generations back to each other and to life in God. The generation gaps can be bridged, and God's wrath can be turned aside.

The sin that separates generations resides with the children, the parents, and just as often with the grandparents. Guilt at any level, accompanied with resentment by those who have been the victims of sin, separates the generations. In the hands of a godly grandparent, the later-life blessing can be a time of restoration that assures the younger person that he or she is forgiven and accepted, much in the same way the father received the prodigal back into the fellowship of the family. It is a beautiful thing when an aged father, son, or grandson are brought together to reconcile to each other and restore the fellowship that existed in earlier years.

Restoring Holiness and Righteousness

Finally, modern day Elijahs can battle, as their namesake did against the Asherah cult, against the powers and principalities whose earthbound counterparts destroy the family—pornography, pre- and extramarital sex, and homosexuality. But the Asherah cult symbolized more. It stood for any pantheon of contemporary lesser gods and deities whose worship was joined with the worship of the Lord. In modern America, this includes the deities of success, comfort, or the adulation of youth, personal cause, private doctrine, and personal experience; these are today's Asherah and represent the sin of mixing the authentic with the counterfeit.

The church can never take the place of the family and should only serve a surrogate role when the possibility for a viable family no longer exists. Its function is to do all it can to restore the family to wholeness. It should be an extension of the family rather than the family being an extension of the church.

Restoration of the Church

Prior to the active ministry of Elijah, prophets in Israel had been put to death with the sword. Elijah poured his heart out to the Lord in 1 Kings 19:14, "The Israelites have rejected your covenant, broken down your altars, and put your prophets to death with the sword. I am the only one left." In the place of the Lord's prophets were the prophets of Baal and Asherah, the official leadership recognized by the state. Obadiah had hidden one hundred prophets in two caves and provided them food and water. Under Elijah's ministry, they were freed from fear, and under the later prophetic leadership of Elisha, a school of prophets was started, and they ministered openly in Israel as leaders to the nation (2 Kings 8:4–5). A prophetic leadership raises up leaders, restores fellowship among believers, and restores the church through the training of disciples and placement of believers in their rightful calling and purposes in God.

The search for godly boldness in proclaiming a message of restoration is found more among older mature Christians than in any other group.

The prophetic ministry within the church requires of men and women a boldness that grows as the entanglements of this world diminish in the life of the individual. It is a badge of honor worn by those of advancing age who no longer strive for position, are unafraid, and are immune to the envy, control, threats, or blackmail of others.

The search for godly boldness in proclaiming a message of restoration is found more among older mature Christians than in any other group. They have walked the trenches of life and emerged victorious with scars and limp in tow. They have, by virtue of prolonged holiness and righteousness, struck bedrock, and from the church's standpoint, contain in their being the mother lode.

Restoration of the Church's Disenfranchised

The disenfranchised most frequently referenced include the widow and the orphan. These, however, are more illustrative rather than exclusive of the recipients of benevolence.

In Galatians 6:1–5, Paul recognizes the possibility that there will be some who sin, and others are counseled to restore them to fellowship with a spirit of gentleness. Each member of the body is given a ministry of reconciliation, with the end goal that the body will not suffer dismemberment, since the suffering of one part brings suffering to the whole (2 Cor. 5:18–20). Ministry to the disenfranchised has as its focus the care of the ill member, in which there is the legitimate motive of maintaining the integrity of the corporate body. It is as if the senior pastor were saying, "Our desire is to minister to you and serve your personal needs. However, there is another side to this: we consider your place here vital, and we don't want the church to suffer from your absence from us."

All too often, however, isolated, independent, self-sufficient, and self-reliant people suffer and die alone. I have heard leaders say of such people, "They went their own way; they wouldn't listen to counsel." But the message of Matthew 18 is a forceful, almost threatening, directive (see verse 35) to rein such people in and return them lovingly, although sometimes forcefully, to fellowship.

It is painful to see situations where it is more politically and socially expedient for church leaders to allow a person out of joint to silently disappear rather than pursuing such a person and restoring them to fellowship. There is no biblical principle that tolerates this kind of benign neglect. Part of the problem here is that members often think that the responsibility for restoration lies completely with the salaried ministers, when in fact it resides with all members of the body of Christ. There is no group of people more uniquely designed and prepared to assume a restorative function than older members who have likely experienced restoration at some time in their lives. The remarkable truth about this kind of body ministry is that no pastor has to be asked permission by a parishioner to restore a wayward or hurt brother or sister to full functioning participation in the church. Restoration belongs to us all.

The body functions as each person who is jointly fitted with another is called upon to minister to that person's needs and help carry his or her burdens. Put even more simply, isolated older people provide a prime opportunity for others to learn to minister to those in isolation.

Paul developed the idea of complementary roles in his discussion of the distribution of the gifts of the Holy Spirit (1 Cor. 12:20–26).

There appears in his instructions justification for deficiency-by-design among some members of the body. There are strong members and weak members. The former have much to offer others, including those who have less. In fact, the apostle is saying (much to the consternation of moderns), that the weak and deficient members of the church are specifically intended to provide occasion for those abundant in gifts to serve them so that a leveling factor occurs in the church.

We seldom consider that God purposefully designs defects into the church, not as a consequence of any one's sin or neglect, but so that the integrity of the body is strengthened as we find occasion to minister to one another.

This provides new insight on the need for those who are sick, widowed, orphaned, in jail, caught in a trespass, old, weakened, disabled, or confined to home, hospital, or nursing home. To be disenfranchised from the company of the strong is not to be disdained; they are also integral to God's plan to bring the bride to maturity so she can rule with Christ.

From this perspective, the body of Christ gives occasion for all its members to minister in sickness and health, in poverty and wealth, so that the abundance of some becomes the abundance of all.

To be a member of the body is to function forever relative to other members. The old who otherwise may be disabled, disdained, and potentially disenfranchised are as necessary to the body as are the old who are still healthy and pursuing goal-oriented purposes. The bride of Christ daily makes itself ready for the Groom, as each member ministers to others, whether they are well or sickly and disabled.

PART 2

THE CHURCH MINISTERS TO OLDER ADULTS
A PRACTICAL THEOLOGY

Foundation for Practical Applications

PRACTICAL THEOLOGY CAN BE COMPARED TO AN ENGINEER WHO HAS JUST FINISHED LOOKING AT DIAGRAMS AND MATHEMATICAL FORMULAS THAT EXPLAIN A COMPLICATED MECHANICAL DEVICE. HE STEPS BACK and asks, "Does this thing work? Does it fly?" Systematic theology, when applied to practical theology, goes beyond faith and asks if practical theology stands the proof of testing and time.

Practical theology is not a free-for-all of taking a verse of Scripture here and there, devising some action plan reflective of what is already happening in the world, reattaching some Bible verses to the plan, and calling it "God's way." Practical theology is ideally expected to derive from soundly established systematic theology. This is the stuff of Scripture.

Church doctrine and a practical theology of aging are not intended to incorporate the prevailing cultural *ethos* into their preaching and teaching. They are not intended for sending Christians into the world to mimic what they find others doing. Rather, the church is to indoctrinate believers to radical truth, and to be a change agent by example. This was the intention of the New Testament. This is the essence of being light, salt, and yeast to an unbelieving and searching world. The same is true of ministry to older adults. Something redemptive and restorative must be done to proclaim, "Look, this is the way of love, this is the way of Father God for all those with hoary head."

Our job is not to reflect on what the world is doing. The best way to make the distinction is through some basics.

"You cannot serve God and mammon." Jesus thus threw down the gauntlet of no compromise. Six times in Matthew 6, the disciples were admonished not to be anxious. Their anxiety had arisen from having one foot on the path heading for the kingdom where Jesus was leading them and the other foot on the path to the world's system, or mammon. They learned that distraction and divided loyalty give rise to anxiety. The story of ten Israelites who sought the Promised Land is one example of the seriousness of distraction. The spies were distracted by giants, took their eyes off the promises of God, became anxious and fearful, and returned to Moses with a negative report. Displeased, God sentenced two and a half million men, women, and children to forty years of aimless wandering around a desert. It is wise to remember these sobering stories when we are tempted to mix the world's ways with God's.

There is a tendency for many Christians in America to equate the ideologies of conservative political parties with the gospel.

Ministry can reflect either serving and worshipping God by following biblical principles, or serving and worshipping mammon by following a self-serving world system standard. The thesis of part 2 is that there are reasonable ways to minister to the elderly without becoming entrapped by wrong sets of values and solutions.

There is a tendency for many Christians in America to equate the ideologies of conservative political parties with the gospel. Perceptive people, however, have come to realize that capitalism can be as heartless and selfish as liberal philosophies that redistribute wealth through taxation. Economic ideologies of any persuasion that promise material prosperity and the elimination of poverty, pain, and discomfort can become idolatrous.

Social and health resources in America are available for many older adults, but not for all. Many of those denied these resources are Christians, and we must be careful not to attribute relative deprivation to some indictment by a God who withholds grace, mercy, and favor from people at random. In common jargon, many Christians are just not in the loop of social provision, and this does not suggest that they are living in sin. This poses a question: is there a biblical standard for older adult ministry that is useful for all Christian families and churches irrespective of economic and social status? Taken to its logical limit, this question also asks if that same biblical standard can be applied to all Christians who live in other nations where the per capita income is remarkably less than in the United States. Can churches and families in those countries also live according to the biblical standard, or is it reachable only by Americans and others in modern industrialized Western nations? We may have missed something in our hermeneutics if we assume that the biblical standard is in some way dollar and status related.

It is not in the nature of any ideology, liberal or conservative, to satisfy anyone—especially Christians. The Christian position is that people are satisfied when reconciled with God. Christian leaders are advised to take account of this when choosing from among options on how to minister to older adults. The idolatry of mammon disagrees with Jesus' warning that a man's life does not consist in abundant possessions (Luke 12:15), but that sufficient quantities of food and clothing can provide contentment (1 Tim. 6:8, Heb. 13:5). Through public policy and government-sponsored programs, the U.S. government has in fifty years all but destroyed the immense wealth it accumulated in the first 250 years. It has created value out of nothing through entitlement programs, and it has given people a false sense of expectations associated with a debt-laden standard. It then seeks to redeem the consequences of debt and false value through the policy and practice of redistribution. Herbert Schlossberg summarizes these issues:

> Idols of mammon invite us . . . to place our hopes on wealth, [it will] tell us that taking is better than giving, tempt us to covet what our neighbor has, convince us that we have been wronged because we do not possess as much as we desire, and, finally pervert the sense of justice that alone can preserve peace. If we continue to worship them, the unrest and discontent that mark our society now are only a sample of the destruction that is to come. Insatiable greed placing infinite claims on finite resources can have no other end.[1]

The Process of Arriving at a Practical Theology

A practical theology of ministry to older adults derives from the systematic theology of how those of advancing age fit into the unity of Scripture. Part 1 organized the biblical data on those of advancing age in a logical rather than historical manner. Three purposes have been accomplished:

- First, we have seen how God's activity and purposes with mankind tell a story as individuals advance in age.
- Second, we have seen how the past activities of older people have established their identity in God's scheme of things.
- Third, we have now come to a point where we can look at the past, and in obedience to it and with faith in God, write a practical theology of advancing years: to address how we ought to minister to the elderly, and how they can uniquely minister in, to, and outside the institutional church.

As we move into the chapters on practical, or applied, theology, we are reminded of the responsibility C. S. Lewis has laid at our feet. "You must translate every bit of your theology into the vernacular. This is very troublesome . . . but it is essential. It is also of the greatest service to your own thought. . . . Power to translate is the test of having really understood your own meaning."[2]

There may be some who challenge my proposals, particularly those who feel I fail to meet the standard set by C. S. Lewis. Others will be challenged to take these proposals and run enthusiastically with them, expanding them as they go. In the end, both groups edify.

A Demographic Overview and Stereotypes

The purpose of this overview is to emphasize the magnitude of ministry potential within the institutional church itself. There is probably no age category in the Western world that has received as much attention as those of advancing years. "Old" was initially considered age sixty-five, and this was tied to the arbitrarily determined U.S. Social Security Administration policy of beginning retirement payouts at that age. The Germans under

Count Bismarck a generation earlier had chosen sixty-five as the retirement age, recognizing that the average mortality at the time was sixty-seven. In America's hurry to provide a safety net for its own seniors, the same age was uncritically used. Today the figure is obsolete, and the life expectancy of men and women is much higher and increases each year.

In 1997, the U.S. Bureau of the Census reported that almost forty million people were aged fifty-three to seventy-one, and another twenty million were aged seventy-two and older. Each passing year finds fewer working-age persons available to pay Social Security taxes to shoulder the burden of each retiree. When the system began, forty workers helped support each retiree since there were so few of them. Today it is less than six, and everyone born today and living to mid-century will watch a mere two workers making social security payments for each retiree's monthly entitlement.

From an economic standpoint alone, this trend is a clarion call to working children and the institutional church relative to caring for elderly members—to children who are challenged to forsake a secular model of eldercare and to the church who is called upon to reexamine and reestablish the biblical standard of body life.

The elderly, using age sixty-five as the starting point, are the most diverse age category of people alive. Many are living to the mid- and late-eighties, and it is common to talk to people who are living witnesses to the events of almost one hundred years ago. In all age categories, there are those who are healthy and productive and those who are frail and fully dependent on others. Where age may have been a reasonably good predictor of one's functional capacity two or more generations ago, age is now less of a factor in its ability to accurately predict the capacity of older adults.

The diversity of potential among older adults, along with their contributions to families, organizations, and society, cannot help but challenge the many stereotypes about the elderly that have persisted for decades. In my book *Foundations of Practical Gerontology*, my colleagues exposed the prevailing myths of the 1960s and earlier at the first statewide conference on aging in South Carolina.[3] Thirty-one years later, the MacArthur Foundation sponsored a decade-long project whose results likewise challenge the myths of aging. Authored by John Rowe and Robert Kahn, *Successful Aging* presents findings on stereotyping remarkably similar to earlier findings, which speaks to the persistence of stereotypes![4] Comparing the studies done thirty years apart illuminates the following similarities:

- Old does not necessarily mean sick.
- Old is not a barrier to acquiring new skills, making new mental connections, and absorbing new data.
- Old is not a hindrance to major increases in functional capacity, and an increase in healthy status results if unhealthy habits are stopped and proper diet and exercise become a way of life.
- Old is not influenced more than 30 percent by genetic structure, and among those eighty and above, genes play a decreasing role in determining longevity.
- Old does not put a padlock on sexual desire or activity, which although tending to diminish with age, are more related to cultural norms, health, illness, and the availability of partners.
- Old does not mean diminished in productive behavior; evidence shows that millions of older people are capable and desirous of engaging in either paid or voluntary activities.

Two major barriers to overcoming stereotypes are cultural-psychological and organizational. First, it is much easier to continue with one's stereotypes, for explanation of behavior is easier if one has a ready-made answer based on long held perceptions. The attractiveness of stereotypes is that they make decision making less troublesome. Second, unless the institutional church has a trained specialist in aging, church programs are left to untrained volunteers whose perceptions usually mimic the prevailing stereotypes. A recent summit of well-known church-based senior program specialists convened to develop a national strategy to capitalize on the remarkable potential of older adults. The nation's outstanding programs were represented, and there was unanimous agreement that the days of pink lemonade and cookies had to come to an end if the church was going to fulfill its mandate to minister in a biblically authentic way to older members, as well as then employing them in ministry.

Preview of Part 2

Chapter 9 introduces a radical dimension to the way the church should minister to older adults. *Radical* derives from the Latin *radix*, which speaks of fundamental or foundational things, first principles, and essential basics. The radical person, therefore, returns to first causes. The creation event began with a purpose-driven God instilling purpose in man. Our guiding premise is that the institutional church must restore biblical truth in such a way that it salvages any person in whom purpose was never established in the first place or ignites places where purpose has lain dormant among Christians. I believe this is the greatest ministry the church can provide persons of any age. It is remarkably critical when applied to older adults, for the simple reason that it restores to eternal purposes those who have been created in the image of God and who have not yet tasted of those purposes.

Chapter 10 builds on chapter 9. It is my conviction and that of prophetic leaders of the twenty-first century that true ministry to the elderly is more than a pacification of unsettled spirits; more than compensation for lack of beauty, strength, productivity, and youth; and more than demeaning infantilization and compartmentalization of people who don't happen to fit the stereotypic mold of having to run the races of yesteryear. These are the ministries of entertainment, consumption, and self-aggrandizement.

Ministry beyond entertainment seeks to free people from disability and declining capacity and to remove any barriers in order to continue God's age-graded purposes within them.

Hence, we see true ministry as a means to an end, not the end in itself. Ministry beyond entertainment seeks to free people from disability and declining capacity and to remove any barriers in order to continue God's age-graded purposes within them. It addresses mundane issues: health, housing, finances, and others, but with the long view of perpetuating optimal functioning until the time when they go to be with the Father.

Chapter 11 has two emphases. It first encourages a public accolade during congregational meetings that older adults were important in the past and remain so in the family, church, and community today. The second edge is a reminder to the present generation that it stands on the shoulders of prior giants, that history is prologue, that inheritance reckons back to our ancestors, and that the proper posture of the young, productive, healthy, and strong today should be that of humility and recognized limitations so they may benefit from those who have sat on the pews for a longer period of time.

CHAPTER NINE

A Purpose-Driven God

I HAVE WORKED IN GERONTOLOGY AND GERIATRICS SINCE 1960. MOST OF MY WORK HAS BEEN IN THE SECULAR MARKETPLACE AT EVERY CONCEIVABLE LEVEL OF POLICY AND PROGRAM DEVELOPMENT. I SAY this to emphasize a point: During this time, whenever I saw a persisting pattern among the elderly, I felt safe in concluding that it was predicated on some essential principle that generally applies to older people. I may be accused of stereotyping, but future studies are invited to disprove my observations.

There is such a principle. To miss or ignore it is one of the grossest errors the Christian community can commit in behalf of its members. As it applies to the elderly, neglect of this principle can turn into a cruel and macabre joke. This chapter exposes the joke and provides a remedy that I consider to be one of the institutional church's most fundamental responsibilities.

It has been my privilege to talk to many Christian and secular audiences, and whenever I discuss the issue of life purpose, there is a similar response, nicely expressed by Edmund Sinnott. Dr. Sinnott, dean of the Yale University Graduate School, observed and gave expression to this pattern from his vantage point as a world-renowned research biologist half a century ago. He wrote that all the natural world moves purposefully toward some goal; purpose never is in question; it is everywhere and in all places; but purpose is a philosophical rather than naturalistic phenomenon. Sinnott concluded that purpose is to be found only with a "purpose giver."[1] Oliver

Wendell Holmes, that great jurist and associate justice of the U.S. Supreme Court, said, "Most people go to their graves with their best music still in them." The issues for Holmes, like that of Sinnott, were the universality of innate purpose and the challenge of how to bring that purpose into the everyday life of each individual.

There is a story in the New Testament about Jesus being summoned to heal His good friend, Lazarus; alas, Jesus took too long to arrive at the village where Lazarus lived, and Lazarus succumbed to death. When Jesus finally arrived, the family was grieving, and Lazarus had been several days in the tomb. The story continues with Jesus praying to God and then commanding Lazarus to arise and come forth from the grave, which he did. Great story. Today it would likely result in shouts of joy from among the congregation and perhaps be worth an article in the miracle section of the obituary columns. But Jesus didn't stop there: He commanded those standing around to unwrap Lazarus—to set him free from what man had done to him when they prepared him for burial, and to give him some food—the symbol of fellowship. What does this mean? Simply, life itself is not the end goal. But purposeful life among family, church, and community serves God's purposes.

At the conclusion of my lectures on calling and purpose, those who most frequently exhibit excitement are older adults. A light bulb has come on, a key has turned, and there is illumination regarding new possibilities which perhaps had their origin somewhere in the distant past. They would crowd the lectern. They wanted to talk about some idea or venture they had years ago, only to have been squelched by the affairs of life or some institutional barrier.

The excitement was greater among Christians. They had known there was something more than paying a tithe, attending meetings whenever the church doors opened, and dutifully sitting and taking notes of sermons year after year. For them, there was something more than being on a welcoming committee, ushering, or helping with the Communion service. Rather, they recognized a spark, a burning deep within, that had been awakened by a sermon or teaching, and they realized they still had somewhere to go, something important to do, often in contrast to the "pink lemonade and cookies" mentioned earlier.

Loren Cunningham, founder of Youth With a Mission (YWAM), related how thousands of short-term missionaries raised their own support, boarded ships and planes, and went to every conceivable tongue and tribe on earth. As Cunningham continued, I watched older adults, first sitting on the edge of their seats, then responding to invitations to participate in YWAM's Cross Roads ministry for older persons where, after a season of training, they would head to the four corners of the globe for mission assignments. Examples include a retired teacher, now in her late sixties who established a ministry for handicapped children in Mongolia. Another woman many years earlier had planned to go for several months to Amsterdam, Holland, to help at the YWAM base, but had remained there for more than twenty years overseeing a ministry to Spanish-speaking Amsterdam residents. Today she is in her late seventies. Yet another woman is an unsung heroine behind the scenes, well past seventy, and preparing for retirement from her position as a YWAM accountant in Canada.

It was also the awakening of calling and purpose that resulted in a remarkable turnaround of a woman in her mid-seventies. I met her at a religious conference. She asked for prayer and ministry for unbearable depression that began after a nephew had ruined the family business following her husband's death. I quoted many of the Scriptures about the eagle and honored horn mentioned earlier, prayed for her, and impressed upon her one of the strangest, most foreign concepts she ever had heard: God had a calling on her life and a purpose for her to fulfill. She graciously accepted my ministry as I laid hands on her and blessed her. Then we went our separate ways. The next year I saw her again at the same conference with a bounce in her step, a wide smile on her face, an obvious determination, and a sense of purpose and confidence. I asked the conference director to tell me about her. He confided, "She's a modern-day miracle. With no business experience, she went home, received the counsel of management consultants who mentored her, got rid of her nephew, took over the helm of the business, and in less than a year brought the bottom line into the black." Purpose!

A GOD WITH PURPOSE ————————————————————

God's creation of the natural order and man had the eternal purpose of making His glory known throughout the earth and of having a bride who would rule with Him. The Bible is rich, from start to end, with the purposes of God and the strategy He has used to endow man with specific elements of the grand purpose that would be lived out in the lifetime of each individual.

God does not stint. Some express faith in Him at an early age, others come late in life. He withholds purpose from none. We do not stop with basic salvation and discipling. By the time a person, irrespective of age, has learned the basic doctrines of the church, come to understand what it means to follow the Lord by obedience to scriptural precepts, and embarked on a journey of developing the character qualities of the Holy Spirit, that person will begin to have awakened in his or her spirit a divine spark that says, "I have something special for you; I am prepared to give you a piece of myself." Paul made this simple in Ephesians 1:18–19: the Father calls us, we share an inheritance in Christ, and we are empowered by the Holy Spirit to carry it out. This becomes our driving force. The French refer to it as our *raison d'etre*—our reason for being, a personification of the living God in and through our lives, with boldness and a singularity of focus.

The Father calls us, we share an inheritance in Christ, and we are empowered by the Holy Spirit to carry it out.

We cannot manufacture this purpose; we can't force God to give it to us; the prophets cannot make it happen; prayer and fasting only make us aware of its presence once put there by God. But in the fullness of time, when the Lord can trust us with it, He will entrust it to us. But alas, many go to their graves with their best song never having been sung. How different our eulogies for the deceased would be if in confidence we could say, "He knew and lived out his purposes for God, and when he completed those purposes, as David did, he died."

There is no finality to life, no closure, if one dies without having known, followed, and lived out his or her unique purposes for God. The body is dead; the purpose remains unfulfilled. Teleology fails. A life ended without having discovered and lived out divine purpose is like the gunman's hang fire; he pulls the trigger, but the cartridge doesn't discharge. A journey was started, but a destination was never reached. We feel the pain of parents, and sometimes our own, when a child or young person's life is snuffed out, and we say, "Too soon—he or she never had a chance to live," meaning that purpose was aborted. The memorial service or eulogy never suffices, regardless of how elegant and erudite, if God's purpose in the life of the deceased was a hang fire.

Now, think of those of advanced age, and inquire how many older Christians sit in the pews with tears streaming silently down their cheeks when they hear the testimony of one of their peers who has discovered and lived out purpose. They later seek audiences with the ministerial staff, but don't quite know how to express and put their finger on "this pain that aches in my belly; this gnawing from which I cannot escape, and which I know wants and deserves to get out." God's purposes for all of mankind were intrinsic to the creation of man. It began with Adam and Eve. The charge for them was to subdue the creation and then exercise stewardship over their piece of it. Aged Anna ministered in the temple until her ending years after her husband's death. Simeon's purpose late in life was to behold the new Messiah. The Apostle John had numerous age-graded purposes: to be a disciple of Jesus, care for the Lord's mother, write letters to the churches, and still be sensitive enough to behold and record the apocalyptic vision. For a fleeting moment in the biblical record, Ananias was commissioned to lay hands on blind Paul, pray for return of his sight, and then slip into oblivion within the annals of the early church. How surprised would Ananias have been had he only known that his divine purpose in the kingdom was to minister to the one who would become the greatest apostle? Suppose he had reneged on the spontaneous urging of the Holy Spirit. But he did not, and there lies the tale of purpose.

Purpose does not lend itself to planning and scheming. It often emerges from the crucible of difficulties. In *The Hidden Price of Greatness*, Ray Beeson and Ranelda Mack Hunsicker catalogue the purposes that were deeply hidden in and emerging from suffering in the lives of Monica and Augustine of Hippo, Susanna and Samuel Wesley, Francis Schaeffer, Charles Spurgeon, Blaise Pascal, Fanny Crosby, and many others.[2] In a prior generation,

V. Raymond Edmund wrote the classic *The Disciplines of Life* that described over thirty disciplines (doubt, disappointment, delay, and defamation) and identified saint after saint whose purpose was discovered in the midst of difficulty.[3]

There are countless Christians, such as children of the Great Depression and the two World Wars, whose responsibilities for family and homestead faithfully kept their hands to the plow, lathe, or sewing machine, or who dutifully sat alongside the bedside of a loved one who seemed to linger too many years. Now, free at last from yesterday's labors, they once again turn their thoughts to "Is it possible, just remotely, that God will reawaken what I knew as a young person?" And so they pray for revival of their own purpose. Many, like Lazarus, await removal of the shrouds and an invitation to break bread and be a vital part of family, church, and community.

Discovering Purpose

I can think of no greater responsibility of the institutional church than to bring its members to purposeful maturity. I do not presume to know what God sees as the most important role of the institutional church. We do know He expects His glory to be known throughout the earth, and that He wants to prepare the church to reign with Him. But the breadth of His ingenuity knows no limits. He invests unimaginable infinite variety in His children. One of the most intimate partnerships the church can have with the Father is to discover and bring to maturity the purpose of every believer in order to prevent any member of the family of God from wasting their lives—particularly those of advancing years. Herein lies the ultimate ministry to older adults!

The fruit of an evangelistic message places thousands of spiritual acorns into churches all over the world. The church's task is to bring them to the point of being fruitful oak trees. This is not an easy task. Five percent of a woman's effort is to endure nine months of gestation and then give birth to an infant. Ninety-five percent of parents' efforts are to produce an effective human being. The goal of the epistles is not simply salvation, but rather Christian growth and maturity out of which comes the purpose that each believer is to live out in doing the work of the church. We would be derelict to restrict our definition of purpose to the usual list of ministerial vocations. Rather, it is the responsibility of church leaders to assist each member to discover where in the kingdom he or she fits—whether it be in the institutional church, a parachurch organization, or the secular marketplace as a business person, executive, laborer, soldier, or professional. Whatever is biblical in ethics and goals is a legitimate target of the church's commitment to its members.

Theological Basis

The basis for God's purpose in the lives of any Christian is His love for us. The theologian Anders Nygren, in *Agape and Eros,* identifies the four components of *agape.*[4]

First, *agape* comes from God to man; it is His initiative and is exercised in terms of His sovereign will.

Second, *agape* is spontaneous and unmotivated. There is no personal attribute of man so great as to warrant *agape* (it cannot be earned), nor is there any sin so great as to prevent God from acting. This is critically important for those of advancing age, for it says the effects of delays in one's younger years or prior sins can be erased; second chances are in the Father's way of doing things.

Third, *agape* confers value on man without reference to qualifications or characteristics. Youth, strength, beauty, and productivity are not criteria for receiving *agape*; old age is not a barrier. The content of that value is measured in terms of one's calling and purpose.

Fourth, value, as calling and purpose, becomes the basis for man's fellowship with God. These are testimonies to the Father's continuing desire to restore to each child the fullness of life that He has predestined from the time the foundations of the earth were set in place.

Sources of Insight

There are at least ten ways an older person can discover or resurrect sense of purpose. All are biblical in nature. These can be discussed in a class devoted to discovering purpose, summarized in a private or small group counseling sessions, or be part of a questionnaire the older person completes prior to a counseling session.

- **Prayer and fasting**—These heighten our sensitivity to God's will. They are the biblical way to humble ourselves; God gives grace to the humble. The person may have to be taught how to fast and pray as a task in his or her own personal commitment to the discovery process.
- **Placement within the body of Christ**—Fellowship with others exposes our natural and spiritual gifts, whereupon we are known for those talents and skills. What have others said about our contributions? Do they lend themselves to our identity?
- **Personal prophecy**—As in the case of Timothy, prophetic ministry can reveal our place in the kingdom. Personal prophecy should be done under the supervision of church leadership, even when a visiting prophet may be ministering. Church leadership should follow up the prophetic ministry to assist the older adult on how to respond to it in a biblical manner.
- **The church's ministers**—Pastors, apostles, prophets, evangelists, teachers, elders, mentors, small group leaders, or those in charge of accountability groups—all have the responsibility of maturing each believer to do the work of the church. Leaders may need to be interviewed to get their observations of each member's past performances in group, work, or social situations.
- **Godly family members**—An aunt, uncle, or grandparent may have made observations years ago during one's childhood or teen years about certain traits which were encouraged during earlier years. Or they may have said, "Someday, you will . . ." and given a glimpse of the future.
- **Inclinations**—What evidences exist regarding gifts, bents, or talents? What gives the person pleasure? Where does he or she seem to gravitate in a work, leisure, or social situation?
- **Life's circumstances**—Have there been dramatic events in which the person has performed admirably, even out of the usual, to solve problems or meet needs? Has there been an injury or some other difficulty that was overcome, so as to be an inspiration to others?
- **The *rhema* word**—Someone might read a passage of Scripture and a verse "jumps off the pages" and unduly

impresses him or her, in a way that says, "This is you; do it!" It can also come from a book, play, or movie, but the impact is the same: the older person identifies with it in such a startling way that he or she feels moved to action.

• **Sovereign epochs**—There have been periods of history (economic depressions, wars, natural disasters, widespread revivals, terrorist threats or attacks, population migration) in which direction as a leader emerged or talents were developed and put to the test, now awaiting reemergence in later life.

• **The autobiography**—The tenth source of discovering purpose is through confessional writing, which has been around since the Renaissance. New research now supports that the insights that can come from an autobiography can literally be the gateway to reducing depression, physical symptoms, and anxiety. All of those problems, while common among older adults, are also emotional barriers to thinking clearly about one's aspirations and goals. The most prolific autobiographer was the psalmist David, and what he wrote about his fears, anger, guilt, sorrow, depression, source of joy, and object of praise has been comforting, challenging, liberating, guiding, and insightful to generations of readers. The autobiography, coupled with any of the other sources of insight, will go far in accomplishing the most important ministry the church can offer to those of advancing age.

The autobiography begins as far back as one cares to retreat and builds on dreams, talents, and gratifying experiences, as well as events that were hindrances. The intention is to resolve the past, put it in perspective, and thereby start on a path now paved with the purposes of God designed for the traveler—a modern day pilgrim. Irrespective of one's perceived calling and purposes in God, this exercise will be one of the most gratifying the older adult can have. Those who complete it will also be issuing a challenge to others.

There could be no part 3 of this book without a part 2. There is no purposeful pursuit of latter-day destiny without first removing the barriers to purpose. Three times in Luke 14:25–35

Jesus says that those wishing to follow Him *cannot* if they are improperly related to others, are obsessed by seeking status and reputation, or have placed too a high a priority on material things. He could have listed a dozen other hindrances as well, but He declined their desire to follow Him not as a matter of permission but rather as a matter of their inability to follow. This was not a natural inability of skills and talents, but instead an inability caused by being chained down and thus being unable to arise out of the captivity to hindrances that robbed them of opportunities. Early in the same gospel account (4:18), Jesus declared His mission: to proclaim release to the captives, recovery of sight to the blind, and freedom to those who are downtrodden. Was He talking about older adults? Were they also included among those who were to be enabled to find their divine purposes, even if in latter days? Chapter 10 elaborates on the barriers to purpose.

CHAPTER TEN

Ministry beyond Entertainment

THE DEPARTURE FROM JUDEO-CHRISTIAN VALUES IN POST-CHRISTIAN
AMERICA HAS SEVERELY THREATENED, IF NOT ALTOGETHER DAMAGED,
THE PRIMARY FAMILY AND HAS NEUTRALIZED THE EXTENDED FAMILY.
Our secular and humanistic society emphasizes individualism
and personal fulfillment—the essence of Hellenistic *eros*
referred to earlier. This sort of belief system is acquisitive, self-
aggrandizing, and aimed at creature comforts. The social,
emotional, and economic fallout resulting from these values is
extreme and requires little elaboration here.

Many churches offer ministry that likewise caters to creature
needs. This is the clinical approach to ministry which often
neglects promotion of spiritual and behavioral growth and maturity. Public policies and programs are a poor model for the
church. They cannot possibly remedy the outstanding problems
of families in the secular arena, simply because their agents are
products of the same value structure that has caused the problems. When the institutional church adopts the same strategies,
the kingdom is not served.

This chapter defines a practical theology on how the church
can minister to those of advancing age and their families. The
recommendations are practical, but they are not ends in themselves. Rather, they enable older adults to live out their
God-given purposes.

BIBLICAL GUIDELINES

A practical theology of ministry to those of advancing age requires biblical principles to guide the *choice* of ministry as well as the *manner* in which that ministry is designed and carried out. I draw these from part 1.

Integrity of the Family

At the heart of the church is the family. The church's mandate is to see that whatever support is needed beyond what the family can provide for itself will be provided. This is the essence of biblical church-based benevolence.

The integrity of the family extends to intergenerational issues, inasmuch as each generation has something to pass on to succeeding generations, and younger generations are supposed to honor parents and grandparents in order to receive whatever the older generations have to give them.

Therefore, the church does not leave the welfare of older adults to their children alone, but provides support and counsel to adult children, where and when needed, for the care of their parents as well as providing care directly to older adults. The church of the New Testament is tantamount to being equivalent to the social trust fund of the Old Testament.

Integrity of the Body

The finer points of body life are overlooked in the rush to organize and conduct the more familiar congregational meetings and church educational programs. The principle better pursued is that each member of the church is jointly fitted to others with the purpose of promoting interdependence—each part supporting, edifying, and building up the others in love. This is a sociological phenomenon in evidence of spiritual verities.

The corporate body is to assure that no part of itself is put out of joint, for when one part suffers, the whole body suffers. The genius of the Holy Spirit in choosing metaphors and similes to describe the body of believers cannot be over emphasized, and the analogy is even more relevant today when we know more about the integral wholeness and interrelatedness of the physical body. The person who is ill, institutionalized, or otherwise indisposed or absent from his or her usual place, remains an integral part of the body of Christ in the Father's eyes and is to be cared for as such. Wondering where an absent member is, inquiring of their welfare, and hastening to provide assistance is as important as greeting and embracing a member in person. The writer of Hebrews comments on this when describing those who undergo the disciplines of God.[1] Because trials, tests, and suffering challenge our mettle, whether because of illness, a financial setback, or interpersonal failure, the writer says in Hebrews 12:12–13, ". . . strengthen the hands that are weak and the knees that are feeble . . . so that the limb which is lame may not be put out of joint, but rather be healed."

Integrity of Calling and Purpose

The kingdom of God is a complex, interwoven matrix of persons, each of whom has a calling and purpose to foster the purposes of the kingdom. Purpose does not cease upon retirement, nor when one becomes ill, disabled, or dependent on others. Social psychologists use the term "role complementarity" to connote interdependence in such a way that each person's purpose is dependent on and contributes to the purposes of those with whom he or she is in relationship. Role complementarity is everywhere: shepherd/flock, husband/wife, parent/child, pastor/parishioner, counselor/counselee, doctor/patient, teacher/student, he who is dependent/he who supports, he who is dying/he who comforts and releases the loved one to the Father. All have their purpose.

Our calling and purpose in life is for kingdom purposes.

The issue here is the kingdom. Our calling and purpose in life is for kingdom purposes. Hence, maintaining the calling and purpose of each person, even when old and dependent on others, is a kingdom requirement.

While purpose in the older person's life continues until he or she breathes his or her last, purpose nevertheless changes during what Tim Stafford refers to as the "Seven Days."[2] Writing with a compassionate and gentle style, Stafford gets into the minds and hearts of older persons, friends, and family, and sketches aspirations, dwindling anticipation, and the emergence of new purpose with each step toward the time of death. It is a ripening process of humankind resulting in family unity and mutual commitment to the living truth of the kingdom.

These guidelines, with their focus on family, church, and kingdom, provide the framework within which we minister to the elderly. One other guideline applies to all three: the programs have to be within the reach of the majority of churches.

Feasible and Reasonable Ministry Options

The standard I propose is reachable by the majority of churches whose memberships are 250 adults or more. For smaller churches, two or more churches can pool resources through a cooperative relationship called a consortium (see chapter 12).

My recommendations for ministry do not include social or recreational programs, the usual spate of which includes potluck dinners, outings, vacation conferences, and the like. There seems to be no end to the creativity with which these are thought up. There seems to be a shift in the tide, however. Numerous national leaders of aging programs in major churches, denominations, and parachurch organizations are beginning to deride the philosophy behind "the pink lemonade and cookie" bunch, or the "feed 'em, burp 'em, and send them home" crowd. Fellowship and friendships are important, but my emphasis is elsewhere. I'll focus instead on a range of ministry options that have been tested, and because of my personal and corporate experience, I know they can be implemented in congregations of moderate size.

LAYING A FOUNDATION FOR MINISTRY

Getting beyond the stereotypes about advancing age requires information that liberates the professional staff of the church and prepares the members and the elderly to support and participate in older adult ministry. Leaders do not need to reinvent the wheel. The amount of information and available resources is so extensive that one can find whatever is necessary to launch a successful program. The information explosion of the 1990s has robbed any person or organization of using ignorance as an excuse for not investigating age-graded services.

Information and Referral Services

Most of those who work with the elderly agree that information and referral services are foundational to all other ministry. I&R, as it is known, has become the mainstay in community after community and is indispensable for quickly identifying those in the congregation who can provide services for older people. Anyone who has ever started to enroll in Medicare, Social Security, or Medicaid knows the details can be overwhelming, if not downright frightening.

Each generation has its own spate of bureaucracies and regulations ranging from social welfare, legal aid, community housing, health, education, and others. When the Scripture says "be anxious for nothing," the church is called upon to allay the older person's anxiety about negotiating the affairs of everyday life. Those in the church must help carry the burdens of the old, so they won't be put out of joint.

The I&R center also identifies services that can be mobilized efficiently by utilizing a member's skills, which have been honed over a lifetime of work. Some of these skills will duplicate what is already available in the community. The urgency and frequency of need will determine who can be called on to provide for it. Over time, I recommend that the church strive for self-sufficiency.

Volunteers can manage I&R services once the required information has been compiled. Several older members can staff the I&R center in the church or from their own homes, rotating responsibility from day to day, using a phone forwarding service to refer calls from one volunteer to another. There are few pastors who would not welcome a ready resource to respond to the dozens of emergency requests for assistance that come in every week or month.

Internal Assessment of the Church

Churches need specific information on its own members, and I recommend this be compiled on all persons age fifty and above. This lays a foundation for identifying needs and problems, assigning priorities among them, assessing how church leadership perceives older people and the aging process, assessing how older people perceive themselves, and determining the resources already available within the congregation to provide the ministry. The internal assessment should include examining the degree to which church leaders may hold stereotypes about the elderly. These come in two forms: stereotypes about facts and about attitudes or perceptions.

Inventories on facts address matters such as the physical, mental, legal, financial, and social conditions of the elderly.[3] True and false statements are accompanied by a commentary explaining why any statement is true or false. The purpose is to measure the respondent's opinions against facts, expose stereotypes, and thereby measure how tuned in church leaders are to the actual lifestyles of its older members.

The inventory on attitudes addresses such things as plans for retirement, being young at heart, persistence and endurance, and perceptions about being old.[4]

Resource assessment

The assessment of needs determines the potential demands that may be placed on the church and the kinds of resources in the church that can be mobilized to meet the needs. The value of knowing resources beforehand is that leaders will not have to scurry around trying to find a plumber, homemaker, carpenter, or caregiver every time the occasion arises. Having a profile of needs within the congregation becomes the basis for establishing a resource clearinghouse that can be accessed and mobilized at any time.

Leadership

Smaller churches of less than five hundred members usually use volunteer leaders, and these are frequently older persons with backgrounds of having worked with older adults: a retired nurse, social worker, physical therapist, hospital discharge planner, senior center director, geriatric case manager, or someone who has had management experience in a nursing home or home health agency. Medium-sized churches of five hundred to one thousand members will usually have a part-time church professional who is assigned responsibilities for the older adult ministry in addition to having the usual five or more other responsibilities. Churches over one thousand members are capable of supporting a full-time minister of senior services.

External Resource Assessment

There is no way to exhaust the fund of information available to locate the resources of public agencies and private organizations. Most of this information is free to the user. The National Institute of Aging (NIA) is a premier source of information, and its annual *Resource Directory for Older People* compiles information on hundreds of organizations. Other publications can be ordered from NIA by Internet, fax, phone, or mail and include reports on the most recent findings about older people's health and emotional well-being. The *Age Page* series addresses major health concerns such as osteoporosis, arthritis, cardiac hypertension, and many others. Each state has a commission on aging, usually located in the state's capitol, and the commission sponsors or cooperates with a statewide network of area agencies on aging from which publications and information can be obtained on services in local communities. It is possible for any church, regardless of size, to establish an extensive library of technical and practical information at little or no cost.

Community resources should be listed in the church's information and referral services and augment what the church itself organizes in behalf of elderly members and their families.

From 1989 to 1996, I designed a number of community-based programs throughout the southeastern United States and the Midwest making use of the resources of the National Institute of Aging, the U.S. Administration on Aging, the Health Care Finance Administration, and state and local affiliates. All told, the locally developed programs served more than forty-five thousand older Americans age sixty-five and over.

MINISTRY NEEDS ———————————————————————————

Numerous organizations provide for the needs of older people. If the church fails to offer some of its own, however, it deprives members of the opportunity to serve one another.

The Motivational Mandate of Church Ministry

Ministry is not an end in itself. Ministry has a redemptive and restorative purpose, to be sure, but it leads to goals beyond those who are ministered to. First, ministry must be dedicated to increasing the strength of the primary and extended family. Family integrity laid the basis for bringing the kingdom into all sectors of our endeavors, it formed the basis for transmitting spiritual and material inheritance to succeeding generations, and it promised health and welfare to its members through acts of honoring one another and bestowing a blessing.

Second, ministry to those of advancing age provides for the integrity of the church itself. No member can be set aside because of declining years or because they frequently miss meetings. Mere absence does not mean "out of joint." Until the older person dies, he or she continues to serve a purpose, if for no other reason than to provide the occasion for others to minister to him or her in gentleness, understanding, and love.

Third, ministry to those of advancing age means supporting their respective callings and purposes in the kingdom. Every believer has an integral place in God's scheme of things, until, like Jacob, he blesses his children and goes home to heaven.

Financial Issues

Many churches offer seminars on financial management. Older people, many of whom are on fixed incomes, have a more difficult time managing their budgets since a fixed income budget cannot anticipate increases in the price of goods and services. The rapid price increase in medicines is only one of a host of such unexpected inconveniences. When we remember that the best of us become anxious, fearful, and even depressed at times because of financial problems, it is easy to appreciate that the usual biblical prescriptions to avoid anxiety can be remedied only by helping another carry his burden, rather than giving a lesson on character development.

Common Issues

The more common financial issues include negotiating Medicare and Medicaid reimbursement for health care bills; being sure Social Security and Supplementary Survivors Insurance forms are correctly filled out; deciding whether retirement checks will come directly to the recipient or be deposited directly into the bank; assisting in developing a household budget; and helping in estate planning and management.

Often the older person wants to continue in some salaried or self-employed work opportunity. Assistance in this pursuit includes helping them develop a job search or providing a cash flow analysis for services or products they sell and how they will be remunerated.

Long-term Care Insurance

Only a minority of people will require institutional nursing home care. Most of us, however, will require some kind of oversight by community-based long-term care (LTC) services. These include day care, adult day health care, home health care, assisted living, and home-based hospice care for the terminally ill. These services are listed here in ascending order of complexity, and are inversely tied to a decline in the patient's level of functional ability. Functional ability is measured by the person's ability to carry out activities of daily living—eating, toileting, bathing, moving from place to place, and dressing one's self. As functional ability decreases, the level of care is expected to increase.

Some policies provide for geriatric architecture, in order to remove barriers to movement and make the home safer. This includes widening doors to accommodate a wheelchair, building a walk ramp with handrails in place of steps, or installing grab bars in the bathroom in the tub, shower stall, or adjacent to the toilet.

The younger a person is when they purchase long-term care insurance, the less the lifelong total of premiums will be. A good policy should provide for up to seven years of intermediate (not skilled) nursing home care. Intermediate nursing care costs are among the more expensive long-term care services, ranging from thirty-five to fifty thousand dollars a year. Seven years in an intermediate long-term care facility is usually longer than is needed by the majority of people. The policy also preserves the assets of an older couple as well as the assets of adult children, who, without their parents' coverage, may have to use their own money to support an ill parent. Asset protection comes under the biblical principle of stewardship and assures passing an inheritance onto the next generation, which is also a biblical principle. When the value of long-term care insurance is recognized for all it provides, adult children may wisely pool their resources to purchase a policy for aged parents. And the church does its members a service when it promotes the purchase of LTC policies.

Household and Daily Living

The list of basic and otherwise simple considerations of everyday household issues, while taken for granted by most people, can become stumbling blocks for the elderly.

Geriatric Architecture

After my father-in-law's third stroke, my wife's brothers and sisters prevailed on us to move in with her parents for a brief time to assist in preparing their home to accommodate an invalid. We did the usual: replaced torn carpeting that would cause Dad to trip; replaced floor-level cabinets with shelves attached to the walls, so he could get around with a walker or wheelchair; replaced steps with ramps; and rearranged furniture to allow easy movement from place to place. The home was inspected for potential safety problems. A handyman or carpenter can make these adjustments at little cost or trouble.

Day Services

Day services include transportation to church, a doctor's appointment, a shopping center, the bank, or the pharmacy. A friend may be recruited to come to the home to prepare meals, or, if there are several or more older people who are homebound, meals can be prepared in the church kitchen and delivered to members. Meals-on-wheels have become a staple service in most all programs for the elderly, and meals delivered by a friend fulfill the scriptural prescription of fellowship and breaking of bread. Sometimes all the older person needs is someone to sit, visit, and help them to the bathroom or the sun porch. Perhaps they need help with meals if the older person is recovering from surgery or has a hard time feeding themselves because of a stroke. Other services include doing the laundry, cleaning house, and feeding the pets whose presence has now been determined to be a valuable asset for lonely homebound members.

In most congregations, there will be licensed plumbers, electricians, carpenters, and skilled craftsmen who can repair furniture. Even as Bezalel was called upon by the Lord to build the tabernacle in the wilderness and to fabricate the clothing for the priests, modern-day artisans have been endowed with gifts and talents that are needed by older members so that they can continue as integral members of the body. Utilizing skills in "such a time as this" (to quote from Esther), gives meaning, calling, and purpose to the lives of modern-day artisans and tradesmen.

Accessory Housing

The time may come when the older member is no longer able or willing to care for his or her home and needs living arrangement alternatives. Consensus has been building among gerontologists that the older a person is, the less wise it is to move to a new city, unless they are approaching dependency. It is difficult to find one's way around new surroundings, make friends, and become part of a new congregation.

The alternative to moving into a retirement home or apartment may be accessory housing. This can be as simple as renovating living space in an adult child's home, adding a "mother-in-law" apartment by converting a double garage, or building an "echo structure." These are off-site cottages, which may be stand-alone structures joined to the main house by a covered walkway. In many of these, the proceeds of the sale of the grandparent's home can be used to prepare a place for them to live with or near their children and grandchildren. This comes close to the biblical standard of perpetuating the extended family, it provides repeated occasion for bestowing a blessing to offspring, and it allows older people to receive honor from family members. An added benefit to renovation, adding an apartment, or building echo housing is that the value of the adult child's property is increased through inheriting, reinvesting, and perpetuating the parent's assets—another example of biblical stewardship.

Health Care

Many of today's older people grew up thinking of health and healthcare issues as residing in the hands of the family physician. This may have been true a generation ago, but Drs. Kildare and Welby (whose names are not even recognized by many of today's young and mid-aged adults) are characters of the past. Seldom is health care today conducted by a single physician, or, for that matter, physicians generally. The complexity of the health industry challenges even the most knowledgeable people. Providers are a highly diverse lot. Insurance regulations are difficult, if not impossible, to understand (experience has taught that some are even deceptive). Insurance companies often hinder referrals from one non-member medical specialist to another. This is particularly true of health maintenance organizations (HMOs). The diversity of other professionals such as physical therapists, podiatrists, chiropractors, and optometrists renders access to the "system" a veritable sociological and emotional nightmare. For a population of older people who grew up trusting a single family physician and his nurse to provide for most health care needs, this is enough to require massive infusions of remedial counseling and pastoral care by the church's professional staff, or those volunteers in the church who are health care specialists.

The diversity of other professionals such as physical therapists, podiatrists, chiropractors, and optometrists renders access to the "system" a veritable sociological and emotional nightmare.

Fortunately, the complexity of the healthcare industry has come with an information explosion enabling anyone to acquire abundant information prior to visiting the doctor. With information comes more control of one's fate in the health care marketplace. (See the final section of this chapter on the church's role as advocate and ombudsman.)

Information Revolution

There is no shortage of information available for older adults, their adult children, and others who provide a supportive role. The number of newsletters targeting an older population continues to increase. Excellent ones are published by the Mayo Clinic, Johns Hopkins University, the University of California at

Berkeley School of Public Health, Mount Sinai Medical Center in New York, Harvard Medical School's Men's Health Watch, the Cleveland Clinic, and others. These are world-class publications and provide reliable information for modest costs. Any or all of these could be added to the church's library and accessed through its information and referral services.

However, as many as seventeen thousand web sites dealing with various aspects of health care are now accessible through cyberspace. Anyone with a computer can access numerous cyberdocs, cyberpharmacies, and on-line technical libraries. Any church can enlist a computer-literate person, preferably a health care professional, to download hundreds of pages of good information for the church's elderly population and include this information in the church's geriatric information center.

No church has an excuse not to develop a healthcare library for the modest cost of Internet access and printing multiple copies of downloaded documents.

Healthcare Coordination

The church of average size will have members who know their way around the health care marketplace. It may be a physician, registered nurse, or mid-level practitioner (these are highly trained professionals such as nurse practitioners, physician assistants, or nurse midwives whose competencies fit somewhere in between those of a physician and a nurse). Then there are physical therapists, pharmacists, optometrists, chiropractors, medical social workers, case managers, and hospital, home health, or nursing home administrators.

The church has a number of options in assisting its older members in navigating through the health care maze whenever their own private physician has not been meeting their needs. Information and referral services may identify a person or a small task force of people in the church who can provide counsel to the older person or adult children. If the I&R service is managed by a single person who also acts as the advocate or ombudsman, it can be extremely helpful in this regard. The church can also retain (for a moderate fee) a local professional other than a physician who works as a part-time independent contractor to assist in health care coordination.

The care coordinator, sometimes referred to as a case manager or geriatric case manager, is a specialist in health related I&R, and can expedite what professionals call continuity of care, to provide counsel on how the older person can best navigate among several specialists or services. Most providers of long-term care insurance provide a case manager as a no-cost service in connection with using the long-term care insurance benefits.

Caregivers and Respite Care

One of the fastest growing industries in America today is that of the caregiver. Unfortunately, caregivers are not usually a reimbursed service under insurance policies, and studies have shown that the cash equivalent of volunteer caregiving by families and friends is in excess of $3 billion a year. The charitable contribution of volunteer caregivers is admirable and is evidence of the value of the extended family and ministry by the body of Christ. Caregiving takes a toll, however, on those who provide it. The most common caregiver is the adult daughter from fifty to sixty years of age, who cares for an invalid mother. Without relief from others, she ages more quickly and begins to have many of the same mental and physical disabilities as the one she cares for.

This is a major challenge for the church committed to family and church integrity. A single, disabled, and dependent elderly member can easily pull others into the vortex of illness and disability unless provision is made for respite care for the primary caregiver.

The challenge goes beyond merely mobilizing the resources within the congregation; it means setting priorities and making decisions on the allocation of resources. Body ministry such as this may compete with the traditional programs of the church. This emphasizes the gravity of having someone with the gifts of management and administration to oversee the older adult ministry. Since most seminary-trained graduates— by their own admission—do not have the gifts of administration or management, others from the congregation who do have these gifts must be recruited to oversee this ministry area of the church.[5]

Day Care and Adult Day Health Care

In the absence of members who are willing and prepared to provide respite for the primary caregiver, some churches establish day care centers for older adults whose needs require simple oversight for feeding, toileting, managing medications, and occasional recreation. Many churches have combined the adult day center with the one for children, and this encourages intergenerational relationships of benefit to both children and older adults.

A variation on the adult day center is the adult day health program which, if licensed, will have its costs reimbursed by most long-term health care policies. The additional services of physical therapists and occupational therapists are provided on an as-needed fee-for-service basis. Day care and adult day health care provide opportunities for ministry by salaried staff and volunteers, some of whom will be older adults themselves.

Disease Prevention

The twin strategies leading to healthy longevity are disease prevention and health promotion, which I will elaborate in the next section. Disease prevention involves updated vaccinations, particularly winter flu and pneumonia shots. It also includes a variety of common hygiene and sanitation measures, which older adults approaching dependency take for granted or overlook because their attention is turned to concerns of a more immediate nature. One example is leftover food. Church volunteers who help in homemaker and caregiving chores need to see to the sanitation of food-preparation surfaces. And, of course, sanitation applies to matters of bathing, toileting, and laundry.

Prevention also applies to home safety: non-slip flooring, grab bars in the bath or shower and next to toilets, replacement of torn carpets or vinyl flooring, and clean and sanitized ducting in the heating and air conditioning systems. As one gets older, the immune system is depressed, and in high-risk areas for pollen and mold spores, the older person is more susceptible to respiratory diseases. Remedial measures on controlling the humidity and installing low-cost, high efficiency furnace or air conditioning filters can reduce discomfort and disability. The Scripture is rich in promises of God's readiness to heal and

Shema
love God with all my heart, strength, soul, mind

provide for good health. But stewardship over the immediate environment and ourselves means that we cannot rely on the prayers of friends as a sole means of supplying the needs of others.

Health Promotion

Health promotion is the most biblical of all principles when it comes to the care of our bodies, minds, and spiritual health. No Israelite was able to commit to the *Shema*—to love God with all his or her heart, soul, strength, and might—without defining himself or herself in an all-encompassing way. What he or she ate, listened to, said, meditated on, and otherwise did with his or her body, were all expressions of obedience to God's mandate to demonstrate stewardship over that part of the creation that was under his or her immediate control. In believing he or she was created in the image of God, promotion of one's own health assured that he or she would continue to live as the image of God.

Both disease prevention and health promotion are matters of health education. In ignorance we suffer and perish, but knowledge brings life and prosperity. There is no excuse to neglect health promotion. The available information is in excess, and the healthier a congregation is, the more it is able to carry out the responsibilities of the kingdom. The three sides of health promotion for our physical bodies are diet and nutrition, aerobic exercise and strength building, and refraining from substance abuse. Application will vary from person to person, but the principle remains. Several examples suffice to illustrate the point.

Gluttony is frequently railed as unscriptural. It results in unhealthy obesity. The National Institute of Aging now reports that every animal species eating a diet reduced by 30 percent has had remarkable increases in longevity. In humans, it is known that being overweight is associated with cardiovascular hypertension, diabetes, and high cholesterol levels, which can increase risk of heart attacks.

Physical inactivity, instead of being a measure of earned rest, limits the older person in numerous ways. Contrasted to this, the studies on nursing home patients who participate in daily exercise show an increase in their muscular strength by 15 percent in six months. The average age of those in the studies was eighty-five. With muscular strength comes increased balance, less tripping, stronger grasp of handrails, increased cardiovascular capacity, better sleep patterns, and diminished loss of bone mass which otherwise leads to osteoporosis. Every YMCA provides special exercise classes for older adults; a church van can get them there and deliver them back to the church for a healthful fellowship meal.

In 1998, the National Institute on Aging published one of the most comprehensive handbooks to date on exercise for older adults. It includes diagrams of recommended exercises, basics of motivation and safety, self-tests to measure progress, the overall benefits from exercise, and the best kind of nutrition to couple with exercise. Single copies are available without charge, and the entire handbook is accessible from NIA's web site at www.nih.gov/nia. Again, information is readily available to enable Christians to live out biblical principles supported by the best of modern clinical research and practice.

Substance abuse may not seem to be a high priority topic for the church crowd, and it usually isn't—except when it comes to self-medication, overmedication, improper mixing of medications, and unsupervised scheduling of medications. Having a prescription drug written by a physician does not make the medication any more holy than illicit addictive drugs, tobacco, or alcoholic beverages. It all boils down to misuse of the temple of the Holy Spirit. It is now well known that abuse of medicine among the elderly has reached epidemic proportions and is causing new illnesses as well as compounding existing ones.

Spiritual and Ethical Issues

Suffering has meaning in life; in God's mercy, love, and grace, it continues to have meaning in declining days. The dying person may have no conscious awareness of himself or his suffering. But in the interdependent body of Christ, the suffering person complements the ministry of the one who ministers by providing the occasion for their ministry. I once shared this with a group of leaders of older adult programs, and sighs of relief echoed throughout the room when they realized that healing and yet another extension of life was not the goal, but rather that dying and death in themselves were meaningful, particularly for those who minister. One of the younger leaders, who had always defined his success in ministry by improved health or added longevity of the older member, expressed with tears that a heavy load of guilt had been lifted from his shoulders when he saw God's handiwork in the final days of the dying person. We often tell both our Christian and non-Christian friends that Christians experience the same suffering and challenges as non-Christians, since all live in an imperfect, unredeemed world. Kingdom principles are unlikely to be promoted in a non-kingdom world. But the faith and resources unique to Christians are sufficient to avoid and overcome unethical solutions to common problems. Two areas addressed in spiritual ministry are counseling and the ministry of Word and sacrament.

In the interdependent body of Christ, the suffering person complements the ministry of the one who ministers by providing the occasion for their ministry.

Counseling by Healthcare Professionals

Pastoral counseling, whether by pastoral staff or mature volunteer church members, is important for the elderly person as well as his or her family, friends, and acquaintances. Some volunteers will have dealt with illness, disability, and dying in their secular professional pursuits and possess God-given gifts, which are amplified by professional training and practice. In my experience, registered nurses who are mature, biblically literate believers have greater sensitivity to the needs of the dying and their families than many physicians whose skills focus on preserving life rather than on ministering during death.

Many Protestant churches (the more ecclesiastical ones often being the exceptions) lack a well-defined doctrinal position regarding declining days, disability, dying, sudden death, and how the role of healthcare operates at each level. More knowledge in this area would help many families as they walk the path with their loved ones towards the final moments of life. One comprehensive statement is found in *Ethical and Religious Directives for Catholic Health Care Services*.[6] In the general introduction are statements based on the parable of the Good Samaritan, encouraging local communities of men and women to exemplify neighborliness to those in need. Laypeople are invited, by virtue of their membership in the church, to participate actively in the church's life and mission.

Ethical issues have assumed major importance in recent years because of the ability of medical science to prolong biological life beyond the usual signs of viable existence. In response, sophisticated secular statements have developed concerning physician-assisted suicide and euthanasia, and many in the Christian community find themselves swayed by these arguments. Often public policies against prolonging meaningless suffering of loved ones are uncritically accepted by adult children or by the elderly themselves, given as they once were to unquestionably accept a physician's advice. Each advance in medical science brings new challenges to the pastoral staff that seeks to guide congregational members in arriving at answers that satisfy but also comply with the teachings of Scripture. To shirk from providing counsel, or providing it only superficially, fails to minister to the old person in his or her declining days and does a disservice to family members seeking answers to life's final questions. This is one of the most critical ministry issues for an aging population.

The literate adult of today cannot help but increase his and her familiarity with new information on health, wellness, disease, and death. The mass media have performed an exemplary job in increasing awareness. The announcement of every medical advance presents new information for those who listen and mentally record the possibilities for themselves or some friend or relative they know has a particular disability.

The Ministry of Word and Sacrament

The ministry of the Word and sacrament is the primary ministry of the church for all people, and it is especially important for the elderly. The Word reaffirms the later years of a person's life as seen from the vantage point of the Father. It is His promise for forgiveness of sins long unconfessed, for bringing peace and reconciliation in the face of bitterness and resentment, and for reassuring the person confined to home or institution that he or she has not been abandoned. Chapter 8 addressed the ministry of restoration. This is one of the most needed ministries, and it fulfills Malachi's prophecy that the hearts of parents and children will be turned to each other. I am reminded of the dying lady who, because of her own history of emotional distress and interpersonal conflicts, found it impossible to forgive, lay aside resentments and bitterness, and become free enough to give a final blessing to her children. It is a wise pastor who brings parents and children together, and in the spirit of the Beatitudes, makes peace between them an act of reconciliation. Without this, the integrity of the family is insulted, the connectedness of the body of Christ is given short shrift, and members of the community lurk in the shadows of the memorial service or funeral wake gossiping that an old friend died, having failed to restore relationships with children and friends.

There is no more sacred sign of the intergenerational covenant family than to share in the Lord's farewell meal.

The truth of Hebrews 12 and the discipline of the Lord is no less applicable for those of advancing age and their relations with children than it is for any person younger in years who is still learning the early lessons on the disciplines of God. Failing to live by God's discipline, the writer says, leaves one less capable of repentance and gives rise to a root of bitterness. We have been sensitized to the positive side of declining days and illness by focusing our hearts and minds on things of the spirit, inclusive of restoration and reconciliation. The sick and those on their deathbeds are remarkable opportunities for those who counsel to bring spiritual and emotional health and healing in the midst of physical decay.

The one ministering requires only the confidence that it is the Holy Spirit who gives life to the spoken Word and who personally witnesses to the heart of the older person. The pastoral call or visitation of shut-ins is a way for the older person to sense his or her continuing place in the body. There may be numerous people who perform this service for those who cannot attend the regular worship services, but if the older member has been associated with the local congregation for some time, a personal visit from the senior pastor is more meaningful, since the pastor personifies the church more than any other single person.

Larger churches do well to ordain or commission in congregational meetings those who will minister to members confined to home or institution. The more public the ordination, the more the roles of ministers are legitimized, thereby opening the door for parishioner acceptance. During these ordination services, older members will be assured that when they are ill and among final days, these ordained people will be at their sides. They will go home from church that day comforted.

Throughout pre-modern societies, rites of passage mark the significant transitions from one stage of life to another. In modern life, graduation from high school and college, confirmation, baptism, and marriage all are meaningful rites of passage for those who are living. Memorial services and funerals, on the other hand, exclude the most important participant—the one who has died. These ceremonies are a source of comfort to those who remain, but the more the church institutionalizes a member's importance, the more that member retains his or her place in the fellowship of believers while still alive.

Paramount among the ways Word and sacrament are carried out is for family members to gather with the ill parent and grandparent, sing a familiar song, read favorite passages from the Word, and share in the breaking of the bread and drinking of the wine. There is no more sacred sign of the intergenerational covenant family than to share in the Lord's farewell meal. As a closing testament to the blessings assured by the Father, the ill elder will be asked to give a blessing to each person present; he or she will be reaffirming his or her calling and purpose in latter moments. To die in the midst of administering purpose is the most fitting conclusion of having walked with God.

Ombudsman and Advocate

It is amazing that essential principles found in Scripture continue to find expression in a modern society that long ago forsook active acceptance and pursuit of biblical principles. Despite the secularization of the ombudsman and advocate, at heart these roles enjoy strong scriptural roots and are therefore exceptional additions to any church program for the elderly.

The Ombudsman

Armed with the resources of the information and referral ministry, the ombudsman has as his or her main quality the ability to cut through the red tape of agency, bureaucracy and resistant professionals (Does this sound like the elder, mentor, or kinsman-redeemer of old?). He or she does this by virtue of familiarity with community resources or his or her ability to mobilize others to open doors and influence people. Likened to the case manager for health care, the ombudsman could be welcomed as much by the court as by the person being helped, because he or she knows the language, regulations, and channels through which options are weighed and decisions made. In a very real sense, the ombudsman is not only aware of local resources, but he or she is also knowledgeable of how one organization depends on or contributes to another; that is, the ombudsman knows the system and how to work it.

The church's ombudsman ought to be one who knows governmental, legal, financial, and church-related resources and becomes the human conduit, whose efforts readily assist the elderly person and his or her family in important matters. In the best of all worlds, this person will be on the professional staff of the church and will always be in the process of mentoring other members to perform similar ombudsman services in their time.

The Advocate

God's passion for justice, particularly for the orphan and widow, stands alongside His passion for redemption and grace. Carrying the life of Christ to the body of Christ means pleading the case of brothers and sisters before the world seeking justice and mercy, just as the Lord pled our case before the throne of God. This is the role of the advocate, and a fitting conclusion to our consideration of the church's ministry to older persons. There seems to be no one more defenseless in America today than the unborn child and the lone older person. In the case of the latter, protectors and companions of a lifetime have either died or deserted, adult children have moved away, and friends of long standing find it difficult to keep in touch. An advocate is needed, and the body of Christ is the most logical place for such a person to be found. A summary of Arthur H. Becker's description of the elements of the advocacy role of the church is enlightening:

- Every congregation should seek to be known in neighborhood and community as a place where those concerned for justice gather to worship the Lord of justice.
- Every congregation ought to become a haven and resource for anyone and particularly the elderly who are so often victims of injustice.
- Advocacy in the congregation requires leadership, which can come from the pastor and lay leaders as well.[7]

Three primary functions adhere to the advocacy role: the correction of injustice, the positive pursuit of justice, and the prevention of injustice. Illustrations of occasions when the advocate exercises his or her skills include (1) threat of assault or stalking; (2) notifying the police to exercise surveillance; (3) pressing for indictment and persecution of offenders involved in fraudulent business schemes; (4) organizing elders to be court watchers when crimes against the elderly are tried; or (5) serving as a friend in court of both the older adult and the family.

The senior advocate, like the senior ombudsman, would explain the advocacy role to the congregation and recruit volunteers from the congregation to be mentored as advocates. Could there be any greater testimony for the ministry of Christ than the church that is protecting the elderly in the courts of the community?

CHAPTER ELEVEN

On Shoulders of Giants

THERE WAS A TIME WHEN I WOULD WAKE UP IN THE MIDDLE OF THE
NIGHT AND JUST LIE STILL SO I WOULDN'T DISTURB MY WIFE. WE
HAD BEEN CONCERNED ABOUT A FAMILY MEMBER, AND MY INSOMNIA
was linked to my inability to be of any help. I was also frustrated
because I couldn't get back to sleep. Then I got a small gift. I
remembered Paul's counsel in Philippians 4:6–9 to be thankful and
not anxious. This began a simple ceremony that has worked ever
since. I would choose a category of people from my past—close
relatives, university professors, men who mentored me during my
days on the family ranch, others who had influenced my spiritual
life, friends, work associates, or antagonists, and I would make long
mental lists and thank God for them. These weren't little perfunctory notes of gratefulness. I got detailed and told God how they had
made a difference; they had all made contributions to my life.
After about thirty to forty minutes of thanking, I would fall asleep
and awake two to three hours later perfectly rested and refreshed.

In the early days of thanksgiving-in-the-dark, I became more
tuned in to how much I had grown up standing on the shoulders
of big, medium, and tiny giants. God had been good.

One Sunday, my thoughts wandered from the sermon to the
padded oak pew I was sitting on, similar to the thoughts attributed to Dr. James Wiggins who was cited in the preface and
acknowledgments. I, like Jim, hadn't made that pew, I didn't help
build the church, I wasn't involved in the calling and purposes of
several generations of Christian leaders who established that

church; but there I sat, surrounded by the spirits of now-departed saints who had paved the way for me. There were similar experiences when I attended university. Sitting at the feet of intellectual giants, I often speculated about the kind of people their parents and grandparents must have been—the kind who produced these geniuses from whose wells I eagerly drew. One professor's parents were interned in the Japanese relocation camps during the Second World War; another's died during the Holocaust in a Polish concentration camp; another professor came from an Austrian family of Nazi sympathizers and had been one of Hitler's Youth. Another professor was from an Old South family, a remnant of Civil War aristocracy; still another was from the Midwest, born and bred in traditional virtues like hard work on the farm, respect for neighbors, friends, and individual differences, and commitment to intellectual honesty and excellence of effort. One professor's ancestor was a member of French aristocracy who had fled to Canada to avoid execution for seducing a member of the royal family.

Millions want to know about their roots. For hundreds of years, Jewish priests and kings called Israel into congregation and read the story of Abraham, Isaac, and Jacob, the flight from Egypt, entry into the Promised Land, and recited the Law and the Deuteronomic Code. History was reaffirmed, and each generation was exposed to the old stories, which allowed them to envision their source.

One of the greatest ministries the church provides to those of advancing years is to provide them the opportunity to teach us, making us aware of our heritage.

Only the arrogant, self-willed, and self-aggrandizing consider yesterday to be irrelevant and tomorrow to belong to him or her alone. Be that as it may, we all stand on the shoulders of those who preceded us; we all carry the genes of a thousand years; we are all shaped by parents we did not choose. Paul wrote in Ephesians 3:14–15 that every family derives its name from the Father above, and the gospel story of Jesus began with His genealogy in Matthew 1 and Luke 3.

As Christians, we stand on the shoulders of giants—men and women of legend. Some are in our churches today, and they can tell us of yet others whom we may have forgotten or never met. We cannot forget our past.

One of the greatest ministries the church provides to those of advancing years is to provide them the opportunity to teach us, making us aware of our heritage. This ministry stands at the intersection of where the church ministers directly to older adults and where they minister to others in and out of the church. Two types of ministry to older adults illustrate the value of the influence of past generations on our lives.

Families: The Body in Action

When the institutional church and church leaders look at members as disjointed individuals rather than as members of families, the most important God-ordained element of church life has been dismissed as irrelevant. When the institutional church places itself over the family, it is no different from secular governments whose totalitarian tendencies claim parental responsibility for individuals rather than placing the responsibility and accountability for what happens in the family on the shoulders of fathers and mothers.

The plan and purpose of the Old Testament family, as discussed in chapter 3, was to be the vehicle whereby culture was transmitted and to be a source for recruiting leaders. In the New Testament, the household became the focus for salvation and faith, but the biological family remained the bedrock sociological group which the social order relied on for stability and continuity.

Some ordained elders in church-based counseling take it for granted that a wife is not to be counseled without the prior endorsement by her husband, and preferably with him present. This is a common practice among many counselors who wisely wish to avoid appearances of impropriety. More importantly, the counseling session is an opportunity for the husband to learn to counsel his own wife, just as the Bible instructs. I taught altar counselors for many years. When a child or wife came to the altar, we inquired if the father or husband was in the congregation. If so, we asked him to come up during the time of ministry. On occasions, it was not unusual for an unbelieving husband to respond spontaneously to our invitation to commit his life to Christ. Then he would be taught how to lay hands on his wife and pray for her to be healed—and she immediately was! God has a special affection for family integrity.

I believe there is a kind of spiritual magic (no irreverence intended) whenever we do something that contributes to the strength of families. This is no less true regarding the extended or surrogate family.

The Extended and Surrogate Family

The requirement to care for women who are widows also extends to care for any other person who, because of disability, may become isolated from the body of Christ. Widows and widowers should not be isolated, alone, neglected, or closed out from active involvement from the body. They may find fellowship with the usual over-fifty group, make occasional trips, and attend potluck dinners. But every older person wants and needs family. The church therefore performs a service by connecting every older person with a church-sponsored surrogate family where grandchildren can have an extra set of grandparents, and grandparents will continue to live our their purposes in God.

Genealogies

The older person has a personal and spiritual genealogy. He or she may never have been asked what his or her "historical Rolodex" looks like, but sensitive pastors and the congregation need to know who these older people are and what they bring with them to the local body of Christ. I have known of honest-to-goodness twenty-four carat spiritual giants who have walked among the congregation and talked with the pastor without ever being asked details about their lives in Christ. Pitiful! Many are the men and women who have walked the paths of adversity and remained faithful to the precepts of the Word. Still, they have never been asked to share where they have come from or why they have affiliated with their present church. Nor has anyone inquired what God is saying to their hearts about how to share from their life experiences and pour into the lives of those who need a new challenge in their walk in the Lord.

A common thread that moves from start to finish in the Scriptures is to honor all those who have gone on before. This kind of ministry accomplishes several things. First, it publicly recognizes older Christians and gives them honor in the presence of the entire congregation. It says, "You are important to us; we recognize your contribution to our generation and consider you a vital link to our past. You are the reason for the Fifth Commandment." Second, it sends a message to younger adults and children that the past is important, that the gospel and ministry are not reinvented with each generation, and that we all build on those who have gone before. Third, it provides an opportunity for spiritual genealogies to be read aloud before the entire congregation, to let others know that those of advancing years can also give honor to those who went before them. Since every family in heaven and on earth derives its name from the Father, all will gain a sense of continuity and persistence of God's faithfulness, mercy, and grace.

Reengineering Attitudes and Operations

To the extent the institutional church reflects the prevailing social *ethos* and perpetuates non-Christian stereotypes regarding the elderly, there is a need for Christians to reengineer their attitudes. A change is also required in the internal operations of the church to reflect a more biblical, intergenerational life view. The following recommendations are illustrative of a whole range of potentially beneficial changes or additions to senior ministry.

Reexamining Stereotypes
A great service is rendered when members are informed of how older adults are perceived. How does leadership perceive them? How do other age groups perceive them? There are a number of good surveys that can be used for this purpose, and the National Institute of Aging or state commissions on aging are good places to request copies of the most recently designed surveys.

Establishing Christian Witness in the Community
When stereotypes and non-Christian ways of accommodating an elderly population are identified, the church then has to ask: "What should our witness to the community be?" The aforementioned information and referral, advocacy, and ombudsman services are answers to that question. These can also be made available to other churches, the Chamber of Commerce, and the local Board of Realtors so they can inform people from outside the community who want to bring an aged parent with them to the area. I know of one Miami, Florida, company that specializes

in geriatric case management, and their clients—adult children located worldwide—use the company to manage social and health care services for aged parents living in South Florida.

In the area of advocacy, a church can establish a strong community presence by saying, "We will be an advocate for any older person who has suffered injustice or is threatened with injustice." This is the message of the hope of Christ for those who are downtrodden and victimized. It takes little imagination to see what impact this would have on the posture of the church in the community.

Elders as a Task Force

A representative task force of older adults from the congregation should be convened. The first purpose is to give them a place at the table as a definable, necessary, vital group involved in the policy and decision making processes of the church. Unless I have misinterpreted Scripture, the hoary head retains the wisdom of an earlier generation and this is integral to what God wants to do in the local congregation today. God places His people in flocks and He jointly fits them one to another. It becomes the task of regular members to find out why God has placed and fitted each person in the local congregation.

I do not like the idea of age grading, and recommending that a task force of older persons be convened borders on what some may feel I advocate against. Nevertheless, age grading is all around us and we are constrained to start somewhere. Demographic distinctions are contrary to God's plan, but we should nevertheless use the wisdom of the ages to benefit the whole congregation.

The task force is free to consider a broad range of issues, similar to some issues we have already discussed, such as (1) the difference between being ministered to and ministering; (2) the role of purpose later in life, how it is detected, and how it is then carried out; (3) the concerns of older adults and their adult children as declining days set in, and how the church can minister to whole families in this regard; and (4) the opportunities for age-specific ministry that reflect what older adults consider realistic and dignifying of who they are and where they have come from. There are many other possibilities, limited only by the creativity of church leaders.

Older Ministry Leadership

Time is past due to develop a specific program for older adults and to staff it (if possible) with a pastor who is assisted by older adults whose skills and experience make them valuable contributors. For churches considering a full-time salaried pastor in this area, the evidence indicates that the ministry generates gifts and offerings in excess of what it takes to accommodate professional staffing. Some of the ministry services should generate targeted gifts much in the same way donations are made to a missions fund. Services with market value include day care, adult day health care, and ombudsman and advocacy services. These produce tangible benefits to adult children who otherwise would have to purchase them in the marketplace for their dependent parents or relatives.

Depending on the location where the adult day health care is located, it will cost from $35 to $150 a day. From 1985 to 1988, my wife (a geriatric case manager) and I designed, developed, and managed such a program in conjunction with a multispecialty physicians practice where I was administrator. Our clients averaged seventy-six years of age, and all of them had been certified by two sets of criteria as eligible for intermediate nursing home care. Our goal was to keep each person in their homes and communities without an increase of functional disability, rather than admitting them to institutional care. We provided transportation, morning and afternoon snacks, a catered noon meal, physical and occupational therapy, recreation, and instruction in health promotion and disease prevention. At the end of thirty months, not one of our participants had been admitted to a nursing home. The per-person cost of our program in the mid- to late-1980s was $11.60 a day, which, even with an inflation factor built in, is within the range of most working couples. At the time, we determined that any church of 250 adult members would be able to underwrite as a ministry the cost of a similar program within their own facilities for those members who were likely to need the care. Churches with less than 250 members could join in a consortium with other churches, using the management strategy described in the next chapter.

The minister of older adult services is best recruited from among those who have had professional management experience in older adult professions. It may be a hospital, nursing home, or retired military chaplain, a medical social worker or geriatric case manager, a professional gerontologist, or an older adult activities manager.

Whether volunteer or salaried, the minister of older adult services should be ordained publicly for his or her role and provided an opportunity to share with the congregation his or her philosophy for carrying out the ministry. One of the early tasks of the new minister will be to bring all older adult services in the church under his or her umbrella, in order to optimize coordination, minimize duplication, and otherwise establish a common vision and mission of the program.

Older Adults as Elders

Fortune 500 management consultant and leadership develop-ment expert Ralph Mattson said in *Visions of Grandeur* that the institutional church sits on the largest unused human resource in America, and since resource utilization is a matter of Christian stewardship, failure to use resources becomes a waste of God-deployed gifts to the church.[1] Waste is sin.

There are few areas of biblical theology that compare with the role elders have played in the stability of Israel as a nation and in the growth, development, and stability of the church. The elder appears to be the only leadership role brought over from the Old Testament to the New, and along with the role of the mentor, it was the mainstay of stability and continuity in the primitive church. Despite the reluctance of many denominations to recognize the value of multiple elders in the local church, the functional aspect of the elder role need not be thrown out with the title. The wisdom of ages is to be found in those of advancing years, and recognition and implementa-tion of this fact ministers as much to the older adult as it does to those who are recipients of services by elders. A lady well into her sixties returns from over twenty successful years as a missionary to Korea; she is a potential elder to the church's mission board. A retired army colonel is selected by the church board to oversee advanced leadership development and team building for younger staff members. A

The elder appears to be the only leadership role brought over from the Old Testament to the New, and along with the role of the mentor, it was the mainstay of stability and continuity in the primitive church.

retired Spanish teacher is appointed as elder to the inner-city ministry program to oversee teaching migrant workers English as a second language.

Every area of church life involving leadership has a veritable corps of "stand-alongside" elders available who can provide leadership perspective, support, and counsel to those who have been hired to fulfill a particular job. These older members are ministered to as they minister as partners-in-prayer and serve as skilled and learned servants to those in authority. The focus here is for the institutional church to minister to the elderly by providing structures and opportunity to allow them to minister to others.

Older Adults as Mentors

There are many levels of ministry provided in churches. The counseling ministry provides services for those with marital distress, parent-child conflicts, and moral and emotional problems. The clients of these services are "high maintenance/low impact" people. They need restorative counsel, and are sometimes referred to outside clinical professionals because of the seriousness of their problems. Pastors also provide counseling for people in trouble: matters of sin, spiritual unrest, and the usual evil trilogy of resentment, lack of forgiveness, and bitterness. The list goes on.

As God would have it, there are people who are ready to move on in their walk in the Lord and who have already been through the steps of discipling—learning basic Christian doctrine, living under the authority of God's word, and pursuing a healthy course of character development. They are ready to hear from God and learn the next step in their calling and purposes of God. They are the ones who will benefit from a biblically oriented mentor, a person seasoned in the experience and skills of the world, biblically literate, and willing to invest his or her life in assisting a younger, less experienced person discover God's unique calling and purposes in his or her life.

Mentors, like elders, are the personification of the continuity of Christian culture. They sense God's movement in the life of the mentoree, and then in prayerful partnership with the Lord, come alongside the mentoree to bring the Father's purposes to fruition. Some may see mentoring as a ministry *by* older adults rather than as a ministry *to* them, similar to the illustration of providing opportunities to be an elder. They would be right, except for the fact that we still have to overcome existing stereotypes and structural problems in the church. There remains the need to reengineer both attitude and organization. The church ministers to older adults first by providing for the development of a mentoring program, which is then established and staffed by older members. By virtue of its own change of perspective and operations, the church ministers to those of advancing years who are potentially the mentors amongst us!

Many older Christians whose lives have been full of increasing holiness and righteousness, are now asking the question, "Is this it?"

In a castaway society, where discarding and replacing commodities is less expensive than repair, the *ethos* of dispensability and expendability extends to older adults. The casual attitude in recent years by many over the debate on physician-assisted suicide and euthanasia supports this *ethos*. One state governor was reported to have said: "The old have an obligation to move aside [that is, die] and make room for the young." This kind of attitude could be dismissed as frivolous were it not for the fact the same governor went on to head a university think tank on social policy. The information age and the shortening half-life of knowledge also make the sociological relevance of those of a prior generation appear less important, particularly if they are slower (or see no need) to learn the jargon of twenty-first century America. Many older Christians whose lives have been full of increasing holiness and righteousness, are now asking the question, "Is this it? Has my past come to naught merely because hair dye and wigs are more important than gray hair?" This kind of question should never be asked within the church. The church performs a valuable service whenever it dispels questions of this kind. Instead, when it promotes a viable mentoring program, the person of advancing years can say, "My needs are met. This is what I have been waiting for. My seventy (or eighty or more) years now have meaning; I have been granted a new defining moment."

P A R T 3

OLDER ADULTS MINISTER IN AND OUT
FROM THE CHURCH
A PRACTICAL THEOLOGY

INTRODUCTION TO PART 3

Prelude to Proaction

Early 1999 marked a turning point in the American institutional church's perception of ministry in behalf of those of advancing years. The Strategic Summit for Senior Ministry convened invitation-only representatives from fifty of the outstanding Christian organizations, major denominations, and churches across America at a retreat center outside Chicago. The general theme of the summit, which was sponsored by the Christian Association of Primetimers, focused on the issue: How do we mobilize older Christian adults for a movement of multiplication? A broad spectrum of ministry opportunities by older Christians was discussed, and the first drafts of strategies for each of a variety of organizations were formulated. Early the following year, the summit reconvened, this time with twice the original number of representatives of organizations. Progress reports were presented, and new issue papers were reviewed.

── **A NEW PERSPECTIVE**

The critical difference between these intensive, nonstop times of roundtable discussions and strategic planning compared to most other conferences regarding the elderly was its deliberate departure from exploring how the church ministers *to* the elderly and instead focusing on how the church and parachurch organizations should instead provide opportunities and facilitate ministry *by* the elderly. Ralph Mattson's indictment of the church sitting on the largest unused pool of resources, cited earlier, finally had been heard and was now taken seriously.

Part 1 left few stones unturned in establishing how man was crafted with purpose from the beginning of time, and purpose followed him through the seasons of life as illustrated by various age-graded leadership positions among Old Testament Israelites and the New Testament primitive church. Contrary to the stereotypes of many people, purpose—as defined in Scripture—does not diminish and disappear during the believer's declining days; instead, purpose shifts in focus and continues to include the dying person who provides the occasion for others to minister to him! This too is purposeful and is a time wherein ministry skills to the dying are acquired by yet another generation of Christians.

The dying and death of one person becomes the crucible in which others can taste the Father's pain at the time of the Cross and learn from Him how to comfort others in time of need. Dying is also the final occasion for bestowing a blessing, thereby passing the baton of faith and purpose to others. Purpose prevails to the end. It is an element in the activities of a sovereign God among His people. Like a track-and-field relay team, athletes hand the baton from one to the other, each in his or her turn, but the baton—the legacy of generations—continues in perpetuity until the race is finished.

Part 2 began by continuing the purpose-oriented theme. The basic premise was that the most important ministry the church can provide for older adults is to remove barriers to the realization of purpose in each person's life. This idea may be as much a challenge for leaders as it is for older adults themselves.

To live under the comfortable shadow of inertia can be as pleasant for whole societies and organizations as it is for individuals. All of us have a deep affection for our individual comfort zones. It might be a shock for older adults to awake one Sunday morning, go to church, and hear booming from the pulpit the pronouncement that there are still many years remaining in which God wants to accomplish more through their lives. However, many older people have told me during the forty years I have been "doing" gerontology that what they have been waiting for is purpose, not potluck, but they never thought others believed it. Implicitly, they knew their best song (or at least, another good one) was yet to be sung, and they waited with bated breath for the loosening of bonds and the opportunity to do their thing, finally, in the name of the Lord!

Part 2, however, laid a trap. If you got the impression I was contradicting myself and returning to a traditional orientation by suggesting an expanded spate of services to offer, I apologize. I was careful to include only services that were reasonable and feasible from an economic standpoint. They were not capital intensive by requiring extensive facilities, equipment, personnel, or cash. Where then was the trap? The recommended services for the elderly were those that could be provided by the elderly themselves. The ministry *to* older adults becomes the occasion for ministry *by* those of advancing years to pursue their purposes in God.

The Purpose of Part 3

The Gray Zone is a field of action that may be better carried out by the elderly than by the younger, since the former have a stake in the success of ministry in behalf of their peers. Older people, however, do not jealously guard the sole right to minister; they will welcome people of all ages to join with them.

Chapter 12 deals with two elements of ministry infrastructure that often are overlooked, namely the types of leadership required in program design and management, and the elements of a consortium when two or more churches join forces to more economically and effectively provide for their older members.

Chapter 13 is an encouragement to thousands of older adults who are even now ministers without portfolios. I have sought out and found those who, without formal permission from others, demonstrate the reality of an unshakable kingdom. I cite them for their nobility and as models for thousands more.

Chapter 14 identifies ministries by older adults outside the institutional church. Some are parachurch organizations, others are proprietary or not-for-profit corporations. These require God's grace as much as those remaining under the church umbrella and also are illustrative of the variety of God's continuing calling and purposes. These take a kingdom message to the marketplace and are excellent venues for the multiplication of skills, gifts, and experience identified by the Strategic Summit for Senior Ministry.

CHAPTER TWELVE

Leadership and the Consortium

IN RECENT YEARS, ONE OF THE MORE PREVALENT DISCOVERIES AMONG MANAGEMENT CONSULTANTS, BEHAVIORAL SCIENTISTS, AND NOW RELIGIOUS LEADERS, IS THAT LEADERSHIP COMES IN MANY shapes and forms, and there is no single type of leader, independent of other types of leaders, capable of producing success for an organization. Understanding the varieties of leadership, along with knowing how to form a consortium helps to apply the practical aspects of a theology of growing old.

MOBILIZING LEADERS

There was a time when *visionary leadership*, a term coined by Burt Nanus, was defined as "a little bit of everything," capable of being called up whenever an organization had a particular need.[1] The visionary leader was coach, change agent, spokesman, and direction setter; if these credentials were not enough, he or she was also operations expert, manager, team builder, and research analyst. Of course, this model is not easily found in modern times or in the Bible, and recent research shows that only 5 percent of all senior pastors see themselves as having the gift of leadership. Only another 10 percent as having the gift of management.[2]

Historically, elders came from secular settings. They first met the standards set by Paul and Peter in the New Testament, which were largely the same standards established among Old Testament Israelites. Despite the predominance of their experience in the secular environment, elders also differed in leadership styles. They weren't visionary leaders in the sense Nanus described. Their gifts were spread over a broad spectrum of styles and talents. This is comforting, for it says God in His wisdom spreads gifts and talents across the entirety of the church and makes a place for everyone.

Types of Leadership

Leadership is a gift from God, and most varieties of leadership are found in most congregations. Ralph Mattson has identified three leadership families. Within each family are two subtypes, for a total of six types, each of which is used to manage the several ministries described in part 2.[3]

Expert Leaders

The expert leader knows how to find, generate, and organize specialized knowledge and technology. He or she comes in two types: the managing expert and the motivating expert. The managing expert works with technical or conceptual skills but is also able to manage others. He or she can design, compile information, and oversee an information and referral ministry. He or she conducts the internal assessment of factual information on older members (e.g., household, health, financial issues) and administers inventories on the perceptions of members' attitudes.

The motivating expert likewise works out of technical or conceptual know-how but is motivated to make an impact on other leaders, professionals, or an entire organization. This person accumulates information and performs an advocacy role, influencing others—a judge, police chief, and nursing home administrator—in behalf of an elderly person threatened with some injustice. A registered nurse accumulates detailed health information on older members and makes a presentation to the board of directors showing the impact on the church if it fails to sponsor its own ministry for ill members.

By his or her nature, an expert leader is required to develop any new program. He or she collects, sifts, clarifies, and collates large amounts of relevant information. Among the spiritual gifts, the expert leader will likely have the gift of wisdom, and therefore is foundational for the proper exercise of the other gifts.

Often overlooked in discussions of the gift of wisdom is that it comes with the ability to think globally—to see the big picture. Motivating leaders—those with the vision for the program—require expert leaders in order to convince others. Without the research done by the expert leader, managing and motivating leaders are deprived of the kind of information necessary to conduct cost/benefit studies when having to choose from among several program options.

Motivating Leaders

These are the visionaries, and their major strength is that they foster a sense of rightness about older adult ministry. They are divided into managing and technical motivators. The managing motivator frequently is a stand-alone kind of person who is out in front, inspiring audiences. His or her tendency, however, is to want independence and to be left alone, particularly from management types, who, nevertheless, are a boon to this kind of leader since they keep an eye on long-term goals and make sure results are achieved. The motivating leader, if we continue to tie leadership gifts to spiritual gifts, possesses what is called the gift of prophecy. He or she sees into the future and senses God's intentions for a particular place, people, and time. The motivating leader may envision a time when the church will be the main provider of services for older adults, maintaining them in the body of Christ as integral and jointly fitted members during their last days. This leader can explain the global implications of the entire older adult ministry program, not only in terms of ministry to elders but also ministry by elders. He or she likely has a good grasp of the information provided by the expert leader, on whom he or she depends, and can communicate it.

The motivating leader . . . sees into the future and senses God's intentions for a particular place, people, and time.

The technical motivator differs from the managing motivator in his or her ability to convince others to use one particular technology over another. This leader aspires to provide support services for the elderly, but, for example, makes a distinction between and encourages a successful vote in favor of less complex day care rather than more staff-intensive adult day health care.

Managing Leaders

Managing leaders work through people to get results within the constraints of times and resources. The manager sustains the progress of goals initiated by motivating leaders, who in turn rely on expert leaders. Some managers are distinguished by focusing their skills on managing people. The personnel manager can motivate the entire staff and oversee the operations of the older adult program or any of its departments, such as home renovation, geriatric architecture, or adult day care. This leader is a team builder. He or she knows how to encourage, allay anxieties, defuse antagonisms, and otherwise be a peacemaker. Without the people manager, the visionary leader would constantly be initiating new projects, establishing new goals, and otherwise exhausting his or her people. There is a remarkable balancing resource in having this kind of leader.

Other managers have talent to command technical projects. The technical manager can identify and manage the volunteers who best meet the technical requirements of the older adult program, such as computer operations, web page development, and mentoring by the Internet.

Churches with 250 or more members will have sufficient numbers of older adults to be responsible for the ministries identified in part 2. About 20 to 25 percent of the total number of members, or fifty to sixty older adults, will be the pool from which to develop an older adult program.

BUILDING A CONSORTIUM

The church's big umbrella covers different doctrinal loyalties. Despite the differences between denominations, high and low church, evangelical and Pentecostal, sect and ecclesiastical, God's grace prevails, and it is possible for differences to make no difference. Some tasks are often too large for a single congregation, and the occasion arises for churches to collaborate to achieve common goals.

The consortium is a means to achieve unity of purpose, even between churches of different doctrinal preferences. In its structure and intent, the modern-day consortium is structured in such a way as to reflect scriptural principles while accommodating doctrinal differences. I see it, therefore, as a viable model for cooperative and collaborative efforts by two or more congregations in meeting the needs of the elderly.

Leaders face a real challenge when resources cannot support program goals. This may be due to lack of transportation to ferry elderly people to a day care program, space for congregate feeding, volunteer staff committed to other activities, or the right kind of leaders. In these situations, a consortium may be in order.

Walking in Unity

Scripture supports cooperative approaches to meeting common goals. The psalmist extolled the value of cooperation in Psalm 133. There, two brothers could not afford to argue and go their separate ways; the land had to be plowed, the crop harvested, and the grapes and olives picked and pressed. The culture of Israel was built on the hope of there being many sons who cooperated in the family business. The herding of sheep was a common cooperative effort among flock owners. Few flocks were large enough to support a full complement of shepherds, so several flocks were combined and overseen by shepherds hired by their employers. Unity, the psalmist wrote, was like the healing balm of precious oil. The encouraging symbolism had oil flowing down the priest's beard, bringing the paternal blessing of fruitfulness, celebration, and God's promise of life everlasting. Jesus' high priestly prayer envisioned oneness among all believers similar to the oneness between Father and Son.

The secular marketplace during the last two decades of the twentieth century saw a major shifting of allegiances among corporations. Some have new foreign directorates, others have been swallowed and chopped up; some move whole divisions to other countries, and there are mergers and retirement of corporate identities and trademarks. Some enter into joint ventures where neither party gives up control. The loosest arrangement is the strategic alliance, and I will discuss it under the name *consortium*. The consortium pursues important goals by two or more churches, where neither can reach them alone and where both parties retain their respective place and identities in the community.

Nature of the Relationship

The relationship between two or more churches wanting to establish a consortium dedicated to older adult ministry will eventually exhibit five qualities: (1) jointly developed structure which is purpose-specific, (2) shared responsibility, (3) mutual authority, (4) mutual accountability for success, and (5) a sharing of resources and rewards.

Older adults who possess the leadership types discussed above are ideally suited to be bridge builders between churches to form a consortium. After all, they have a moral stake in the success of the consortium, since it promises to benefit friends and neighbors. At this time in their career, most of them have given up empire building, and they aren't particularly interested in accumulating more wall-mounted certificates. They no longer have to prove themselves in the marketplace, having done so years before, and they have traveled the trenches of competition, made their mark, and now want to commit themselves to new purposes free of striving for position, privilege, and promotion. These are the best persons to be granted ownership of the program, since they want to serve and mobilize their peers for the kingdom primarily, and, secondarily, for the institutional church.

Elements of Success

Six elements comprise the basis on which a successful consortium is built, and these will be familiar to older members who have spent a career in the secular marketplace and appreciate the structure these elements give to interchurch cooperation.

Having a Purpose

In Amos 3:1–3, the Lord admonished the tribes of Israel to see themselves as a single people whom He had saved from slavery in Egypt. Their continuing success in walking together was based on their willingness to be in agreement. The first requirement of a successful consortium is to have a common purpose—a program of older adult services. Expert leaders will identify the needs of the elderly, and visionary leaders will lay a basis for consensus on the priorities among several options for ministry.

Knowing the External Environment

Nehemiah knew the wall in Jerusalem had been destroyed. Instructions from God to repair it were not enough. He had to survey the specific places of weakness and deploy men to do the repair. Then he appointed laborers to do the work. The manner in which he assigned workers is similar to how we assign older persons in ministry. The workers were assigned to repair the wall adjacent to where they lived. This assured greater safety for the worker's home and family. Ownership of this kind is what we want to achieve in older adult ministry.

Assessment of the external environment is an important part of strategic planning no less than it was for biblical stewardship. Unless the problem is documented, you never know whether you have solved it. Jesus made the disciples accountable for the tasks He assigned to them as they embarked on their missionary journeys. It would have been a sad day in their Capernaum headquarters had they merely returned from Samaria without documenting that they had blessed the town, met human needs, and proclaimed the coming of the kingdom. Therefore, it is necessary to determine what kind of needs exist among the congregations forming the consortium.

Defining the Membership

Paul wisely recommended to know those who labor among you. In the movie musical *The King and I,* for Anna and the king of Siam, "getting to know you" was important for relationship and cooperation. Rather than allowing this task to be a loose and casual sort of thing, members of the consortium must have defined goals. Objectives should be (1) to gain a mutual respect for each others' values, limitations, and expectations from the consortium; (2) to understand the leadership styles of each, detect any unspoken private agendas, and put them out on the table for negotiation; (3) to seek agreement on how networking will be carried out, and work toward mutual trustworthiness; (4) to know who it is that is affected (older adults, their adult children, and nonfamily caregivers), and work toward a balanced inclusiveness; (5) to recognize and admit where the benefits of the consortium need to outweigh losses of autonomy;

When forming a consortium, experience and time are always on the side of the elderly.

204 Working the Gray Zone

204 WORKING THE GRAY ZONE

and (6) to recognize that compromise will emerge as there is feedback at each step of development, and that rules are written to accommodate compromises.

The consortium brings dissimilar Christians together. Each denomination and congregation has its own particular culture. Older adults are less likely to feel uncomfortable among strangers, since their life experiences have brought them in contact with a larger number of odd types whom they eventually came to accept. When forming a consortium, experience is always on the side of the elderly. But where difficulty of forming a common membership does exist, communication helps to lessen anxiety.

Building Communication

World-class management consultant Alvin Toffler quipped about communication, "Without it, forget it." Interaction needs to be frequent, updated, and documented. Formal communication includes official communiqués, announcement of scheduled meetings, documentation of minutes, and a review of any changes related to the services offered. Informal communication is equally important and involves personal sharing, sharing resources (inclusive of people resources), and having occasional social times.

Understanding How Work Is Done

In this consortium, you and I are going to enter a room (we call it our consortium) as leaders, and in that room we are going to discuss and decide on how we are going to get along together. We have already agreed on what our purpose is, what particular needs of the elderly are going to be addressed, who is available to help us, and that we are going to send a lot of notes back and forth, have lots of coffee breaks, and an occasional potluck dinner in order to reduce the chances of misunderstanding. But in order to get the work done, there are four other goals: shared ownership, flexibility, roles and policies, and adaptability.

Shared ownership has both positive and negative sides. Ownership involves how we go about making decisions, how we manage and work in the consortium, and who claims credit for the outcomes. All members of the consortium participate in making decisions, which result in actions—good, bad, or indifferent—

which produce outcomes for which all participants are responsible. In a consortium, stewardship and its fruits are shared things. Ownership is as much a responsibility as it is a privilege, and joint decision making occurs at each level of authority. In the development of an information and referral service, for example, there are those who gather data, others who compile it, some who enter it into a computer, and those who manage the program. Both churches come to have a stake in I&R.

Flexibility is necessary since the objectives, goals, and means of reaching them may look fine on paper, but in reality, practically everything takes unexpected turns. Flexibility should be one of the first areas where members grant themselves some slack. Mercy, patience, and understanding are key qualities of flexibility. They provide breathing room for the participants to make mistakes, change their minds, and otherwise find better ways of doing things. After all, none of us has been this way before. As we march toward mutual goals, some will get out of step, some will stumble, and others will slip off the side of the road and have to be pulled out of the ditch.

Roles, rights, and responsibilities are of two types, and understanding the difference is important to success. There are first the roles, rights, and responsibilities of each church participating in the consortium. Each church has its own closely guarded culture, and each member's familiarity with the culture makes him or her predictable to other members. Predictability contributes to an atmosphere of conviviality and belonging. Getting a dog and a cat into the same pen makes for interesting fellowship, and churches often have the same problems in "getting to know you."

Next, there are the roles, rights, and responsibilities inherent to the consortium itself. Members of each church have to come to the table agreeing that each by itself cannot have a productive older adult ministry except through a consortium relationship, and the consortium is eventually expected to develop its own culture. This is not the time to have a war of cultures, but rather to recognize that the provincialism of either church can interfere with the objectives and goals of the consortium. The consortium will have its own charter and constitution independent of (but encouraged by) the participating churches. The sponsoring organizations cannot jealously control the roles, rights, and responsibilities of the consortium. Parent organizations, while remaining independent of each other, also allow the consortium its own independence. In the consortium, all members have a consortium hat, and when getting down to the business of the consortium, they hang their church hats on the rack at the front door.

Adaptability is a close cousin of flexibility. Roles, policies, and members will change. The consortium adapts in order to sustain itself in the face of these challenges. Every organization goes through stages of development. Adaptability is problematic in the earlier stages, but as long as the participants have agreed to be flexible, they can increasingly adapt to new challenges. As services are provided, adaptability is discovered, almost in retrospect, as having occurred; this is a measure of maturity. Under these circumstances, the consortium can revise its missions without suffering disruption. For those still wondering about the difference between flexibility and adaptability, think of the difference between the process of development and the stages of development. We are flexible in the sense of putting up with learning how to live with each other; this is the challenge of process. But in the course of time, we become a different organization, moving from one stage or level of maturity to another.

Identifying and Gathering Resources

Too often, we prematurely determine the kind of facilities, equipment, and personnel we need for an older adult ministry program before we have decided on what the needs of older adults are. Only after priorities are determined and the consortium is in place should resources be determined.

The first resource is a convener who should be an older adult, recently retired from the business world, who has excelled in the secular marketplace, especially in an administrative role. This leader should (1) have interpersonal skills and be fair, respected, and legitimate in the eyes of the consortium members; (2) have good mental process skills and a good image; (3) be able to identify and prepare leaders for succession at the proper levels of ministry development; (4) maintain a balance between process and goal-oriented activities; and (5) enable the consortium members to maintain their roles.

The second resource is material needs. Based on the services to be offered—assuming an inventory of needs for services has already been completed—the time comes to catalogue needed resources such as clinical, office, and communications equipment and supplies, as well as space and accommodations. In the event a day care center is planned, local codes will specify the number of gender-specific rest rooms required based on the number of persons served, as well as barrier-free access, lighted exit signs, and visible and accessible fire extinguishers. Vehicles, vehicle maintenance, and insurance costs must be determined. Most churches comply with local codes and building regulations, but it is important to publish and post these in a public place for the benefit of client members, their spouses, adult children, and other caregivers.

Only after priorities are determined and the consortium is in place should resources be determined.

The third resource is financial. Start up costs should come from a variety of sources in order to optimize donor identification with the consortium. The more sources the better. It is better to have ten groups each donating one hundred dollars than it is to have one group donating one thousand dollars. In addition to donations, such as vehicles, advertising, facilities, equipment, and supplies, the sources are best varied: churches, adult children, volunteers, and clients.

The fourth resource is the ministry's audience consisting of (1) older adults who are served, (2) the adult children of the older adults being served, (3) the older adults who are serving, (4) the adult children of those serving, (5) the supporting congregations, and (6) the community at large. As the ministry develops in breadth of services offered and the efficiency and effectiveness when serving, it will become more visible to the larger community. Visibility is the vehicle for the consortium's witness for Christ.

CHAPTER THIRTEEN

The Unknown Ministering Majority

THE OLD ARE GETTING REVITALIZED BODIES, LIVING LONGER, DOING MORE THINGS HERETOFORE EXPECTED OF YOUNGER PEOPLE, AND MOST CERTAINLY ARE OUTPERFORMING MIDDLE-AGED COUCH POTATOES. Despite the clamor about putting the elderly to work and awakening them from slumber, there has always been an unheralded group of older Christians who have silently been at work in the nooks and crannies of life. They, too, warrant our attention, for to do otherwise focuses too much on what we do and neglects those who have been busy and present among us as models for emulation. God is active among the silent majority, many of them working in isolation of others. The similes and metaphors used in the New Testament to depict the kingdom are evidence of the manner in which these unobtrusive people work: they are like seeds that silently grow and sprout, lamps that light some small corner, salt that flavors food, or yeast that quietly penetrates the whole loaf. The kingdom just keeps on coming. During the era of Josef Stalin, the church went underground and emerged even more viable once the Iron Curtain came down. When a small band of Christians in Ethiopia went into hiding, some five thousand strong, they turned into fifty thousand and emerged from their hiding places once communism in that country was diminished. Countless older Christians are doing the kingdom thing in hidden corners, and this chapter is dedicated to them.

American Christianity has become so mixed with secular marketing, advertising, and the symbols of success, that the realities they stand for are dismissed as irrelevant. Having come through more than half a century of Christian faith, much of it devoid of modern symbolism, many believers of advancing years place less stock in outward appearances. Also, they operate with a shorter time frame and fewer resources. In a word, they have a greater sense of what it takes to please the Father in matters of ministry. They go directly for the jugular vein, paying less attention to public opinion. They are not alone in this regard.

The Scriptures also are filled with unnoticed people who carried out the mundane affairs of life and then were mentioned in an Old Testament scroll, a Gospel account, or in a letter sent to one of the early churches . . . they are unsung heroes.

The Scriptures also are filled with unnoticed people who carried out the mundane affairs of life and then were mentioned in an Old Testament scroll, a Gospel account, or in a letter sent to one of the early churches. They had little to draw the attention of others to them; they are unsung heroes. A brief mention of them serves us well and sets the tone for modern counterparts and still others who would quietly follow in their steps.

Unnoticed Bible Characters

Jesus' choice of disciples avoided people of reputation. In the eyes of man, the disciples were the least likely to accomplish the purposes of the kingdom. The same could be said of the Old Testament prophets who were said to have achieved success as prophets only when their mentors had so challenged and threatened their self-image and confidence that the only voice they heard was God's. Those were the kind of prophets Israel needed. Paul built on these traditions when he said that God does not choose the strong, noble, and wise to proclaim the kingdom; rather He chooses the weak, ignoble, and unwise, so that men will understand that it was God at work and not man.

We do not champion those of less esteem to the exclusion of those with high esteem. The standard is that if God and the gospel are to come to the forefront, nothing is allowed to stand in the way. One's education, economic, and social status are not indicators of success in matters of the kingdom. This should encourage those who know they have something to offer to please their Father.

There is another piece to this perspective. Modern marketing and the mass media put before our eyes and ears people of great renown. God's grace is sufficient for what He has determined these giants are to do in their day. Without God's grace, they work in their own strength, and one prophet stated, "Woe to them who build a fire made of their own brands, rather than accepting the brands provided by God." One spoken sentence, empowered by God's grace and sovereign purpose; one face on television; one sentence written by a contemporary author: all can be seed spread abroad to thousands of listening persons who hear, receive, and act on the Word of God. This is how the kingdom works.

Ananias

Ananias is a pivotal character in the New Testament. Unknown and unheralded, this disciple was chosen to be the first to minister to Paul following his Damascus road experience. Paul, the intellectual and cultural giant, needed to be introduced to the continuing power of the gospel by a nobody who, as far as we know, had no power of his own. All Ananias had was what God supplied him for the moment. After he did what he was told, we hear of him no more.

It is a strange thing about grace. The Lord told Paul that His grace was sufficient for Paul's needs, and the needs were also a work of God. Paul was merely an actor on a stage, doing God's will and receiving the grace to pull it off. This is how it was with Ananias and a million others like him. "Do God's will; receive God's grace to perform the will." I hope this theological gem is not lost on the reader.

Gideon

Hiding, timid, afraid of the Midianites, belonging to one of the least of the tribes and families of Israel, reluctant to believe the angel of the Lord, and then having the audacity to demand that God prove Himself through the fleece episode, Gideon is not someone we would single out for great and mighty ministry, nor would he be considered a good mentoring candidate. Oh, he's referred to many times by Sunday school teachers, since his name is in the Book, but this is after the fact. For all practical purposes, he was an inconsequential dot in the annals of mankind. It was his obedience that made a difference, resulting in a great military victory for Israel. Although the fleece served as a relatively minor means of determining God's guidance, Gideon nevertheless provides an occasion for a further understanding of a forbearing God who goes one step further to accommodate His children's weaknesses.

Simeon

Simeon was an old man, not wanting to die until he had seen the consolation of Israel—the Messiah. The Holy Spirit led him to the temple the same day Joseph and Mary brought Jesus to the temple. No one would have picked him out of even a small crowd. We often forget when we memorialize some of these people that they were of no great importance at the time. Simeon was a devout and righteous man, and he took Jesus into his arms and blessed God. Many are the people who bless God and bless little children today, but the ministry and mention of Simeon has continued to this day in churches throughout the world. Unknown in his time, this simple, devout man became the unintended patriarch of a worldwide ministry wherein parents dedicate their infants to God.

Theophilus

What kind of man is it that deserves two books, in the form of letters, to be addressed to him personally? We do not know. He was likely a Greek, and his name meant "beloved of God." Luke, in his Gospel, introduced Theophilus to the details of Jesus' life and followed that, in the Acts of the Apostles, with the events connected with the growth of the early church. The commitment of Luke to this one man has served as a model for two thousand years. Today, letter writing is a disappearing art. But we are reminded of the need for others to be dedicated to an unknown Theophilus, who awaits letters as a foundation on which to grow in Christ.

Hannah

Hannah was barren. Despite her husband's efforts to console with promises of his love, she wanted more. Oh, the disdain she must have suffered from insensitive peers who reminded her of God's judgment upon her womb. Hannah wanted, desired, and needed a male child. She wept, prayed, and committed the hoped-for fruit of her womb to the service of God. He heard; she conceived, gave birth to a son, and dedicated Samuel to the Lord. At his weaning, Hannah took him to Eli, the priest who served as mentor until Samuel graduated and became a young priest, prophet, judge, intercessor for Israel, and founder of the school of prophets. In the annals of time, "barren Hannah who prayed" stands alongside Samuel as an honored individual. In her misery, Hannah established a precedent for a ministry that has comforted many childless women for thousands of years. Parents dedicate their children to the Lord, affectionately remembering Hannah's consternation and then renewed hope and joy.

Ruth

The ministry of faithfulness and obedience characterized Ruth, first with her mother-in-law, Naomi, then with her husband, Boaz. Ruth was a foreigner of no reputation, was dark of skin, had no resources other than confidence in Naomi, and was willing to go to a strange land with stranger customs. Ruth relied on her mother-in-law for instructions on how to expedite the obligation of the kinsman-redeemer. Boaz gave her a name among the honored, and she became an ancestor to King David and Jesus. Ruth had no idea of her destiny. Ministry often works that way.

Many others could be added to this list. Ministry is purpose in the process of happening: it often holds the one who has the purpose ignorant of the long-term consequences of what he or she is doing. Only hundreds or thousands of years later do we learn of how noble otherwise obscure people turned out to be. There is a humility that must come with ministry, and those of advancing age have to understand that they walk by faith, not by sight. The farmer plows, plants, and harvests, but the yield is left up to the Lord. In faith, we do what we are supposed to do, but fruitfulness is not always measured in the here and now. The saint of advancing years may have a sense of rightness about what he or she does, and doing it for the Lord is reward enough. Ministry then becomes focused on pleasing the Father. Denis Waitley once said that the mature person doesn't need the applause of others; this person knows when he or she has done right, and then pats himself or herself on the back. This provides the kind of perspective we need. Jesus warned against seeking the reward for ministry while on earth, since receiving it now deprives one of receiving it in heaven.

Unnoticed Moderns

Legacy and destiny are strange things. People who leave legacies seldom know what history will say of them. We who come later talk about another's legacy or destiny and presumptively insist on something similar for ourselves. The demand for this is so great that others make a business of it—purveyors of easy destiny, selling it as a commodity that everyone feels they have a right to possess. We find it among countless secular publications; it has become a well-honed art form in religious circles. But we cannot pursue and achieve what it takes someone else hundreds of years later to recognize. Legacy and destiny are historical artifacts. They are created by those who place value on that which, at the time, had little exceptional value and was merely enjoyed for its own purposes or performed as a matter of necessity. I recently watched a television documentary about the ten outstanding automobiles of the twentieth century—the luxurious Dusenberg, the before-its-time Ford Mustang, the durable Mercedes Benz, the family-friendly Plymouth Voyager—all pioneering in either style or safety. Number one on the list (get this!) was Henry Ford's Model T. All Ford wanted to do was make a car affordable for America's everyman, but he initiated a worldwide revolution, and the legacy remains with each new generation of automotive designers and engineers.

Grandma's Catatonic Schizophrenic

As young graduate students, we were told by our professor, a consulting social psychologist, about a grandmother-type who came from her home in a nearby town to volunteer some time at the local state mental hospital. Every week, she took a severely disturbed person for a walk around the hospital grounds. The patient, diagnosed as a catatonic schizophrenic, had not spoken for years and had received every kind of treatment known at the time. Grandma never stopped talking about her grandchildren, bridge club, church, and husband's gardening, all the time carrying on as if her mute friend heard every word. Then one day, after about six months, Grandma reached for the doorknob to leave the ward and return home, and the patient said, "Thank you. I'll see you next week." Several months later, the patient was discharged and returned to her home, healed.

Our professor, one of most creative and renowned behavioral scientists of the day, quietly said, "There is much we do not know; why disease [exists], the how's of treatment, the mechanisms of recovery; but somewhere there is a sentiment, call it love if you will, that refuses to believe the inevitable and lives in an 'as-if world,' and this is sufficient reason for us to maintain open minds and proceed on what seems to work." I have told this story many times over the last fifty years, and hundreds never fail to applaud Grandma's unobtrusive ministry at the state mental hospital.

Roy's Waves

Roy is a very young eighty-five years. Every Sunday finds him hauling an overloaded brief case filled with notes, maps, and charts into one of the classrooms of the church he attends. For years, he has taught a course on Bible prophecies about the last days. Each year the materials are updated with insights from new authorities and new publications from Palestine and other places of the Near East added to his library. His materials are as fresh as yesterday's issue of Reuters, Associated Press, or the *Jerusalem Post*.

Roy is a walking evangelism machine. His love for God seems to be without limit. Whoever stands still long enough will hear of the Truth. But Roy has an obsession that always seems to make waves: water. He is a Senior Olympian. Four to five times a week, he is in the YMCA pool. He recently bought a new book, *Total Immersion* and its videotape version. He has been completely revising his stroke and taking a few more seconds off his lap time. "What's been good enough for thirty years is not enough for the new competition," Roy says. "Everybody is getting faster, bringing their times down. I don't know how long I can keep competing with those seventy-year-olds."

Where Roy goes, the gospel goes. Everyone hears about Jesus. God seems to honor that; early in 2000, Roy came home with six gold medals. The day following the competition was Sunday, and the class was waiting for some fresh bread by way of end days prophecy.

What is true about Roy is true about all the exceptional people described in this chapter: they were not formally trained for what they did. Some latter-day evangelist or minister had not singled them out to perform a new mission that would make an everlasting mark on society. Theirs had been a steady plodding through the trenches of everyday, sensitive to the Other Voice and obedient to its appeals in the hidden places of mankind.

TuTu's Tribe

My wife and I were invited to attend a birthday party for a family member who had married into a large group of native Hawaiians. These Hawaiians had rediscovered each other after they had relocated to the westernmost counties of Florida's panhandle. We arrived early to visit with our niece who was married to Greg, a retired air force master sergeant and one of the group's leaders. The party was in their home. The smoker was belching the thick rich smells of chicken, ribs, and steaks. Inside, bowls and platters of food were already crowding the long counters in a kitchen tailor-made for such occasions. A dozen others had already gathered by the time we arrived. Others dribbled in; the men talked, joked, and told a few war stories; the wives helped in the kitchen, took care of kids, or changed an occasional diaper; most of the kids headed for the pool. There were about two dozen, then three, and after about an hour, fifty or more people crowded, talked nosily, and enjoyed being close.

The din of noise continued, and then someone yelled, "TuTu is here, TuTu is here." As if on command, adults and teenagers stopped their chatter and began to move into the living room, lining up one behind the other. I followed to see what in the world a "tu-tu" was: she was about four feet eight inches tall, perhaps in her mid-seventies, and overweight for her height, but typical of what you'd expect if you were looking for an undersized Hawaiian queen or matriarch.

One after another went up to her, hugged her, took her hand and kissed it, expressed adoration or pleasure at her health, and showed unusual respect, reverence, love, and gentleness. Kids threw arms around her neck, or if they were too short, clung through her long skirt to her chubby legs. Three generations of friends and family lavished affection on this single ancestor who was several generations removed.

TuTu had arrived, and now it was time to give thanks for the food. There were Baptists, Methodists, Episcopalians, Roman Catholics, everything in between, and others outside the faith. TuTu prayed. Not a brief or perfunctory prayer like something recited rote from a prayer book. She had an intimate familiarity with the One she was thanking. She was abundantly thankful, and no one in that crowd had any doubt they were to be thankful, too. This was not a particularly religious group of people as professional religionists might define it, but for those few moments, TuTu led the equivalent of a small church up to the throne of God, and they seemed to appreciate the journey.

I later made my way over to meet TuTu, to find out more about this person. I had to wait in line just like everyone else; some waited all evening to see her. "These are my children," she said, "Oh, not all blood children; just my precious ones. I pray for every one of them every day. I am the last of the old generation, and they need to know it's important to live good lives and to love God. To remember where they came from, to honor family." We chatted some more. I asked how she spent her days. "Well, when I go shopping, I'll be in the line waiting to check out, and I just start asking people if they would like me to pray for them. Most of them say yes, so I do, and most say thank you, and a few get tears in their eyes. This is pretty much how I serve God." Would not every pastor just love to have a congregation filled with TuTus?

Monday's Three Js

John, Jim, and Jack have been meeting together for years on Monday evenings in a nondescript room hidden off the main path traveled by most of the church traffic. They gather to pray with each other and then for others who arrive unannounced. The Js don't allow anyone else to enter their private and intimate circle, but they are available to minister. All are now entering advancing years. Jim has had numerous illnesses, but he continues to rally and return to the group to be available to pray for all who come. Notable among their gifts is sensing with uncanny accuracy God's dealings in the lives of those who come to them. They don't call themselves prophets or even claim to have the gift of personal prophecy. For years, they have been listening to the requests of those who come, praying, giving a word of encouragement, offering a sense of the Lord's directions, and sending the people on their way.

Congregations need their own Js, who serve as silent watchmen on the wall, sharing anything necessary to keep whole congregations on the right path.

Jim has not often sent a written note to his pastor concerning what he and the other two Js sensed in their spirits God had to say to them. Sometimes, however, they sensed a special message having to do with the church's welfare, and then Jim would quietly hand the pastor a note containing a word of wisdom or warning. The pastor never failed to receive it with the sobriety it deserved, and, when warranted, shared it with the several thousand parishioners who convened the following Sunday. Congregations need their own Js, who serve as silent watchmen on the wall, sharing anything necessary to keep whole congregations on the right path.

Wayne's Toys

The woodworker shop in the basement of his daughter's home, where Wayne and his wife Margaret now lived, was not large—perhaps sixty square feet at the most. But, in that space, one would find a table, a band saw, a drill press, and pegboards on every wall holding hundreds of hand tools. Canvas covered the doorframe; this kept most of the sawdust in the shop area. Hour after hour, Wayne made toys for packing and shipping to a missionary in Kazakhstan. I remember the first time he needed a cane, then a walker, and later the arm of Margaret on one side and his daughter on the other, as they entered their church. Each week he was a little more bent over; still the toys came—sanded, wrapped, boxed, and mailed to children a world away. He was eighty-five, and eventually constant bed care and a respirator hood provided some relief. He never lost his concern for the children who played with his toys—a wagon, a truck, a wheelbarrow. Wayne died, but the children continued to play.

Wayne didn't advertise his skills. Many years earlier he had retired from his work as a stonemason, and perhaps it was the accumulation of dust from the stone and later from the toys that led to respiratory failure. Someday, I expect to meet a young man or woman from Kazakhstan who was challenged to follow God because of a little toy he or she received years before.

John and Sally's High Ropes

John retired from banking and spent time with Sally doing experience-based counseling. They had a ropes course installed in California's Sierra Mountains at a summer church camp. It was as challenging as any group wished it to be. It was a far cry from banking, but it was as close to John's heart as it could get.

John and Sally were a team working the ropes, and at the day's end, they prepared one of their famous meals complete with steaming hot sourdough biscuits. All kinds of groups came through: a family of twelve, the staff of an accounting firm, and the members of the sheriff's SWAT team. Once a team of high-risk delinquent teenagers came; they had never trusted anyone before, and this would be their first opportunity to have to trust another team member who held safety or harm in their hands.

Over thirty years handling other people's money had prepared John for dealing with their hearts. Today he travels the nation, far beyond his first retirement and years away from his last one, doing team building, experience-based counseling, and carrying a rough-and-tumble, gut-wrenching version of the gospel to those seeking reality beyond their offices.

Jane's Enemas

Keith Miller told the story of Jane who had been a registered nurse her entire adult life in his book *Habitation of Dragons*.[1] In her younger professional years, Jane had become incensed over how the hospital had turned away the poor of the city. Now in her eighties, she shared with her small group, "I've found that there is a terrible problem among the bedridden old people in this town. Many of them suffer constantly because they are constipated, and there is no one to give them the proper nursing care of an enema." Miller went on, "This dear, cheery little saint has been going around among the poor giving the very sick old men and women in our town a fantastic number of enemas for Christ's sake."

The initial financial support for Jane came from a local fiery Episcopal bishop (who later became one of the outstanding bishops in the church) whom she approached with her story. At the end of his career, influenced mightily by Jane and her simple obedience to God, the bishop was responsible for promoting a mammoth Christian medical center that ministered to all denominations.

There is an important sociological truth about Jane and a moral that emerges from that truth. Every society has the challenge of determining who will carry out the less desirable tasks. Who will pick up the garbage? Who will sweep the streets? Who will sweep the chimneys? Who will be the janitors and window washers on skyscrapers? And who will give enemas to old and decrepit people hidden away in apartments? Jane willingly took on one of society's less desirable tasks. But it moved an Episcopalian leader to build a giant medical center and serves as a model among kingdom people who hear God and feel that His voice is the only one that is important.

Granny's Violent Teenagers

Bernie is a consulting psychiatrist who travels around the country advising mental hospitals on treatment programs for violent teenagers. On a trip to a hospital in the Southeast, he was taken to a double-locked ward holding some of the most violent youth he had ever seen. The attending nurse cautioned him, "What you are about to see might at first startle you; just let it take its course." Through the ward window he watched mayhem, screaming, and aggression. It was frightening. Then through a side door, a pudgy little old grandmother with snow-white hair appeared. One and then another of the youths saw her. The screaming stopped; someone yelled to get her a chair and it was placed in the middle of the ward allowing access to any of the youth who cared. They surrounded her, stroked her soft white hair, sat at her feet, talked excitedly, and listened to every word she said. Peace was in the process of happening.

Granny became their mother, grandmother, and great-grandmother, all rolled into one. She spanned the generations; her presence awakened an archetypal residue of respect for elders learned long ago, and she elicited civil behavior from every one. Granny will never write articles for the *American Journal of Psychology* or the *Annals of Psychiatry*. She will never travel the consultant's circuit or present papers at professional meetings, but she will live *agape*. This goes deeply into the souls of disturbed youngsters who are seeking more than drugs, power, or acceptance by passing an initiation ceremony by murdering someone or gang raping an unsuspecting girl.

I manage a training program for mentors, and I am always seeking new ways to make use of their skills. I asked Bernie if he would be able to use older adults similar to Granny in the same manner on the locked ward of the facility where he worked. "I can put at least a dozen to work tomorrow; you provide the people, I'll do the training."

The City's Poor

This section concludes where chapter 1 began. Among the recorded interviews from the first national study of the noninstitutionalized elderly, *Profile of the Aging-USA*, I found the file on an eighty-seven-year-old man. The interviewer reported that he reluctantly knocked on the broken wooden door of this man's home—a disheveled old shack. After all, anyone who lived there certainly couldn't provide the kind of information needed for the study. The interviewer was welcomed in. A skillet hung from a nail near the wood-burning stove; skillet drippings had formed a pyramid of grease on the dirt floor. Roaches and ants moved along their well-traveled paths. A yellow mange-covered dog was lying on a bare-springs cot cushioned with straw. The interview began. "What is your income?" ("Oh, about five hundred a year.") "How long have you lived here?" ("Been here for twenty years.") "Do you have enough food?" ("Yep, have a garden, raise a few chickens, barter a bit.")

The answers were all leading in the wrong direction. The interviewer wrote on the interview schedule that he felt he was wasting his time. The final question: "Do you do anything for the community?" The answer: "Well, I give to the poor!"

In the mind of this octogenarian, his surroundings were not the important thing. He had clothes, shelter, and food, and these were what comprised the contentment implied by Matthew 6 and Jesus' lessons on how to reduce anxiety.

Reexamining Ministry by Older Adults

The foregoing vignettes are not atypical of what I have observed over four decades working as a gerontologist. Octogenarians like Roy, Jane, Wayne, and Grandma do not attract attention. They almost have to be caught in the act doing something good to be noticed. They don't warrant special articles in the human-interest section of the Sunday newspaper, and an annual dinner honoring them is unlikely to be hosted by church leaders. There is something too ordinary about them to capture the attention of others. And yet they are typical of the vast majority of older Christians who have lived through the most intense time of social change and technological development in the history of mankind. That reason, and the fact that they continue to serve God in unnoticed ways, makes them the most realistic model for Christians of advancing years. They have experienced the contentment that comes from practicing the biblical principle of praying and fasting in secret.

Why did Jesus use the metaphors of salt and yeast when describing those who believed and followed? No one sees the salt and yeast once they are put into the dough. These secretly permeate the whole loaf, give flavor to every bite, and make the bread light and more palatable. Salt flavors, disinfects, and preserves. To the older saints I've honored here, Jesus likely says: "You are the salt of the earth."

Jesus took the metaphor a step further in last verses of Luke 14. If the believer refuses to serve in ways determined for him by God, he is like salt that has lost its flavor and is good for nothing else than to be heaped onto a pile of manure.

Church leaders need to remember that older adults (1) no longer have to sell themselves; they jumped through those hoops long ago; (2) desire to engage in ministry to please the Father and live out their purposes in Him, not to establish a place of privilege or promotion in institutional settings; (3) cannot be judged with the same standards as other ministries, since the outcomes they seek do not require extensive infrastructure and capital costs; (4) have personal resources (discretionary time, funds, contacts, community influence) and wish to use these in direct services to others; and (5) have shown they can keep up with technological changes and use them to implement the ministries they feel God is giving them.

In addition to the leadership style distinctions that were made in chapter 12, older adults also need to be seen in terms of possessing the same varieties of spiritual and ministry gifts that are true of any other age group. Not all have the gift of serving and therefore should not be thought of as "one size fits all." Older adults demonstrate as much variety as are provided for by 1 Corinthians 12 and Romans 12. The same is true of the ministry gifts. Some may be gifted in evangelism, others in a pastoral capacity, and still others as teachers. Many will serve, and this is their gift.

A Sobering Postscript on the Ministry of Elders

Not all persons who exhibit the qualifications of elders will be formally ordained as elders by a recognized presbytery. No matter. People of elder quality will find a place of their own choosing or they will be found by others to assume an eldering role. This is a quality thing, and God is the Master Steward in behalf of the body.

The last three decades of the twentieth century witnessed an unprecedented number of persons in church and parachurch ministry falling by the wayside: ruined ministries because of immoral behavior, financial mismanagement, or fraud. Whenever I hear of situations involving fallen leaders, I inquire whether there was an overseeing elder or board of elders to whom the minister was accountable. In no situation where I inquired was there a known elder or board of accountability to whom the minister had to answer. This has been true of evangelists and teachers with national ministries, of senior pastors with internationally recognized churches, and of musicians who have sported numerous gold and platinum recordings.

Take away, deprive, or merely acquiesce in the matter of elder oversight, and failure of moral character is likely to follow. I have wondered, "Is there no person or group of people who love this minister enough to tell him the truth about the slippery slope he is approaching?" Peter's elders were the kind of men who would not hesitate to do this.

Take away, deprive, or merely acquiesce in the matter of elder oversight, and failure of moral character is likely to follow.

Here, then, lies one of the most needed areas for older adult ministry. The integrity of the body of Christ is dependent on the accountability and oversight elders can provide, especially for those who are in ministry. In larger churches, senior pastors are unlikely to mentor or elder all their ministerial staff. The demands are too great, and authority has frequently been so concentrated in a few as to prevent delegation of shepherding even to the most trusted senior statesmen in the church.

Promise Keepers' Secret Weapon

In the last decade of the century, the men's movement Promise Keepers (PK) broke onto the evangelistic scene as a force to rally thousands of men, confront them with unabashed toughness, and send them home as newly committed husbands, fathers, parishioners, and citizens. The plan was to enroll men into accountability groups where they would be discipled by pastors, more mature brothers, and older, experienced mentors.

Bobb Biehl served as consultant to Promise Keepers, bringing the mentor concept to its leadership. His book *Mentoring: Confidence in Finding a Mentor and Becoming One* became a handbook for PK.[2] Father and son team Howard and William Hendricks entered the PK arena with *As Iron Sharpens Iron: Building Character in a Mentoring Relationship*, another publication used as a PK handbook. It too emphasized that mentoring was the viable basis for assuring that the commitment made by thousands of men in emotional, fever-pitched stadium rallies would become cemented into the local community of believers in more sedate settings.[3]

In Old Testament culture, mentors were waiting for mentorees who were seeking to rise to the next step on the staircase to natural or spiritual maturity. This was part of the social trust fund that was basic to the stability and continuity of the culture. The same ethic was brought over into the New Testament church through the inextricable network of brothers and sisters of the faith who assisted in bringing believers to new levels of maturity. The secret of long-term Promise Keeper success will be found in identifying and mobilizing senior statesmen to mentor younger ones to maturity. This will occur as the responsibility for generalized growth in each congregation of the body of Christ is delegated to a wider array of persons who are not formally part of the local church hierarchy.

CHAPTER FOURTEEN

To the Uttermost Parts

MUCH OF THE HISTORY OF PARACHURCH MINISTRY IS THE TALE OF
THE INSTITUTIONAL CHURCH OR DENOMINATIONAL BOUNDARIES
BEING UNABLE TO PUT GOD'S WILL IN A BOX. BEING OUTSIDE
church walls does not disqualify one from obedience to God in
the affairs of everyday life or ministry. Many of today's
outstanding parachurch organizations first sought denominational sponsorship, but soon found they just would not fit.
Ministry can be widely varied, and this variation welcomes those
of advancing years.

Ministries respond to needs that are perceived to be unmet.
Some are patterned after other Christian ministries, secular
organizations, or companies. The Christian Association of
Primetimers (CAP), is an example of a Christian response to the
American Association of Retired Persons (AARP); it provides its
growing membership with the same things many secular organizations provide: dental and pharmacy plans, insurance, travel
services, bed and breakfast memberships, and conferences. The
Christian Association of Senior Adults publishes a newsletter,
Energizing Seniors, whose purpose is to report on news, trends,
and resources for pastors and leaders of seniors' ministries.
Focus on the Family published its premier issue of *LifeWise* in
1999 and began its Focus Over Fifty constituency group. For a
generation, Youth With a Mission has provided for short-term

missions trips for people in their sixties and seventies, and its Cross Roads Program is specifically designed to accommodate those of middle-age who seek transition to new adventure after leaving or retiring from their first careers. There are Christian-sponsored health plans offered as alternatives to commercial insurance, some with prayer chains waiting to be activated for any member calling in ill.

There seems to be no limit to what Christians are doing in the marketplace. Many are legitimate, offer an excellent service, and convey a genuine Christian testimony. Others are religious look-alikes that market to a Christian clientele with deep pockets, but in reality are unethical, hocking modern-day snake oil with Bible verses attached. Alert Christians who are sensitive to these kinds of scams have formed yet other organizations like the Evangelical Council for Financial Accountability (ECFA)—a certifying organization for not-for-profits that meet high standards of accounting practices. Many people look for the ECFA seal before making contributions to unfamiliar organizations.

The focus here is on older Christians who . . . have not sought or achieved widespread notoriety. They . . . are unsung heroes of the faith, whose lives challenge others and serve as models readily duplicated by older believers who hear a voice and decide to be responsive to God's call.

ElderQuest Ministries of Florissant, Colorado, sponsors teams of visiting senior adults who spend several days mentoring college students on their campuses, and then continue the relationship by correspondence. The Servant Opportunities Network, a subsidiary of Senior Ambassadors for Christ, is a worldwide placement service bringing together older adults possessing rich lifelong skills in the marketplace and Christian organizations that have a need for staff.

The focus here is on older Christians who have what they define as a ministry outside the institutional church. They may be not-for-profit or proprietary. Many are unheralded champions who have not sought or achieved widespread notoriety. They, like the unobtrusive ministers of the last chapter, are unsung heroes of the faith, whose lives challenge others and serve as models readily duplicated by older believers who hear a voice and decide to be responsive to God's call.

Entrepreneurs among Us

The entrepreneurial spirit does not stop when one retires from a lifelong pursuit of dreams that has been connected with profit. Some older Christians see profit as a viable outcome of providing ministry to others. Others incorporate as not-for-profit corporations, not because they are giving away the shop, but because they just use their profits in ways that qualify for the Internal Revenue Service's designation. Whether for-profit or not-for-profit, the entrepreneurial drive is alive and well. Many older Christians get a new kind of bang out of "doing well for having done good."

I anticipate that the creativity resident in the Baby Boomer generation will not diminish as it passes base one and moves toward the late fifties and early sixties of base two in the game of successful aging. These people were weaned from their teens on entrepreneurial milk, and it is in their blood to see ministry validated by God's pleasure in terms of profits.

At a recent conference of leaders of older adult programs, an unintended dividing line was drawn in the presentations of speakers and participants in terms of how they defined evidence of stewardship. The older traditionalists held more to a "profit is dirty" orientation. Among these people, support for ministry was solicited from the donated surpluses accumulated by donors who worked in the marketplace. But the intensity of commitment to doing God's work by younger leaders saw profit as evidence that the venue in which they worked was of God's doing and was consistent with many of Jesus' parables on stewardship. Among these people, profits supported them, their families, the expansion of their ministries, and provided surpluses to network with and support other ministries.

In the final analysis, the issue is not about profit vs. not-for-profit, but whether the one who ministers applies kingdom principles to the marketplace, for which there is ample biblical support.

Bed and Breakfast Businesses

One of the fastest growing industries in America today is the bed and breakfast inn. Clever married couples are converting fully paid-off homes into income-generating places for travelers.

The Wayside—A B&B Travel Club now sports over five hundred Christian-oriented B&B homes for travelers over age fifty. Lower and more controlled traffic results in less facility damage; overhead is less than in commercial motels, and staff size is maintained at a constant level across seasons. The usual service is for one or two nights, a hearty breakfast each morning, and often a free tour guide to local sights.

It is not unusual for B&Bs to charge 40 to 50 percent less than the average cost of fifty dollars per night in a commercial motel. B&B hosts who occasionally travel and become guests themselves in another B&B in the Wayside program are charged even less. This will be an incentive for more couples to convert their homes into B&Bs. With the room and breakfast come Christian hosts, Christian fellow travelers, and opportunities for a night on the town or sight seeing with new friends of similar beliefs.

The home atmosphere lends itself to contentment and relaxation and contributes to conversations that often consist of a spiritual nature. When the B&B advertises itself as a Christian-oriented accommodation, the conversation between host and guests is more likely to be in the form of fellowship with other Christians, rather than one of evangelism. In contemporary society, many non-Christians are searching for a different relevance to life than they can find on the street, and in attractive, low cost situations like Wayside, an evangelistic witness can be a natural outcome of nonthreatening conversations between sensitive hosts and seeking wayfarers.

Homes Turned into Retreats

A variation on the bed and breakfast is the home retreat center. While not a for-profit enterprise in the usual sense, fees are charged to cover the costs of room and board in a setting designed for ministry by the hosts. Nestled in the Appalachian Mountains west of Asheville, North Carolina, the inn was conceived by Jay and Sally Fesperman after Jay retired from a career as an internationally recognized management consultant. He and Sally had a commitment to couples and family stability, and the Inn became a place where groups would come for retreats of a weekend or longer.

Evangelists in the Great Outdoors

In their working years, they would steal away on occasional weekends during fishing and hunting season or perchance manage a week long trip to a favorite place for bird shooting, mule tail deer hunting, or fishing a mountain stream. These were men and women who had worked hard for thirty or forty years and used their sport as a means of relaxation and tension management. Now retired, some of these men and women use their sports for business with an evangelistic flair. There seems to be no setting equal to the out-of-doors, with the sharp wind biting one's face while waiting for a circling flock of geese, in which to share Christ with an unbelieving acquaintance or a group of fathers and sons on an outing. At the recent national shootout—a gathering of hundreds of skeet and trap shooters— the participants described the family atmosphere and the opportunities some had to share their faith as they "broke another clay."

The professional guide is a valued commodity in a fast-paced world, and others with little or no faith seeking a relaxed time of shooting, fishing, backpacking, or mountain biking have lowered their guards and temporarily set aside the social distinctions that separate people. The out-of-doors is the great leveler: the symbols of authority and power are temporarily ignored, and despite the steep fees people pay for such opportunities, a word of spiritual counsel or about hope in Christ becomes an added benefit derived from a day or week in the company of a profit-making guide.

Crafts and Witness

For years I have been a woodworker. Early in marriage, my skill was turned to furnishing our home as a matter of necessity; young married couples often lack the funds to buy all they want. Later, necessity turned to hobby, and eventually hobby turned to work by commission and for profits. I was never trained in any formal sense of the word, but my love for craft has never diminished, and I take every opportunity to attend the craft shows that are held in the spring and fall of every year.

I happened into the pottery section at one such show; Susan sat next to her wares, gorgeous plates, bowls, and oil lamps, all done in azure blue and cream colors, her trademark choice, and every piece was liberally inscribed with verses from the Bible. This was not a gathering of Christian artists and craftsmen. It was secular, and only those whose wares passed the selection criteria were welcome to exhibit and sell. We began to talk, and I asked how she decided to use Scripture in all of her pieces. What followed could have been a page from a kingdom handbook on marketplace strategy.

Susan had been throwing pots in a commercial studio in the foothills of Tennessee, and because she was a Christian, she recommended to her employer that they experiment with pieces that would attract a Christian clientele. "Put a few Bible verses on each plate," Susan said, "and it will attract a new group of customers." She and her husband had discussed this beforehand. (He was sitting in the back of the tent the day I visited her booth, and he nodded agreement when she shared her account.) Susan's boss was firm and unyielding—she refused to go along with the idea, but Susan had heard from God.

With her husband's consent and promise of cooperation, Susan quit her job, set up her own studio, and began throwing pots and plates in feverish preparation for the next craft fair. That was five years earlier, and even then, Susan and her husband (who handled the marketing and financial side of the business) were both in their early-sixties.

I bought a large serving platter adorned with segments on God's love from 1 Corinthians 13 and other segments on the gifts of the Spirit from the twelfth chapter. I also purchased a small oil lamp, and it appropriately reminded me to let my light shine before men.

All of this ended in Susan sharing her philosophy of business. "Do God's work, in God's time, where He puts you, and the profits will be sufficient for your needs and to share with others." And then she added, "You'd be amazed at how many people, both Christian and non-Christian alike, share these principles. These fairs are one of the best mission fields we could imagine."

On another of our annual visits, my wife and I came to a large tent that housed many of the show's top prizes, and a banner reading "Best of Show" drew us to a corner reserved for bronze sculptures. There were two pieces both from the same artist, who lived in small, out-of-the-way Bell Buckle, Tennessee.

The first to catch my eye and command my fixed gaze was *Dancing in the Spirit*. The delicately curved, lithe, feminine figure seemed to leap from place to place, as if lightly skipping through a forest fresh from a spring rain with sunbeams bending around giant trees. Of course, the sculpture did not move, but my mind and heart said it did, and I was moved—transfixed, having caught the artist's message of joy in the presence of God. Carolyn and I just stood there in our moment of reverie. We grabbed hands, pressed into each other, and swayed slightly as this static, unmoving bronze figure ministered to us.

As if *Dancing in the Spirit* was not enough, we turned our attention to the other piece, *Worship*. The figure was strong, muscular, and each rippling sinew glistened as light sneaked in the open corners of the tent and bounced off the figure's skin. At first, it seemed his countenance was firm, determined, and confident, but in the fullness of his strength and virility, his head was bowed, knees bent to the ground, arms extended high above his head, and the light caught what the artist meant to be tears trickling down both cheeks. The more we looked, the more the figure's strength capitulated—a weaker force yielding in worship to the Greater Force. We were mesmerized. I turned to Carolyn and said, "Dear God, I don't know if I can keep from falling to my own knees; this is almost too much for me."

The journey to that corner of the tent had captivated and brought us into the presence of Father, and we rejoiced, worshiped, and gave praise. The Father had ministered to us in that place. Before we left, we happened onto the price tags for these wonders. The artist was a well-known Christian who had dedicated his skills and who reminded us of Bezalel who crafted the tabernacle in the wilderness as described in Exodus 35–39. We were told by one of the other bystanders that the artist could command any price he wished from interested buyers. *Dancing in the Spirit* and *Worship* were priced between twenty-five hundred and four thousand dollars. Those who could not afford to purchase the artworks were nevertheless left refreshed, contemplative, enriched, and lifted up after having fellowshipped with two lifeless, inanimate bronze statuettes.

Getting Connected

Millions of older adults are signing up and signing on to the Internet, and the distance via cyberspace between granddad and the kids is measured by minutes rather than by days and a first class postal stamp or by dollars for a short phone call. The social trust fund is being revived in a new way, leaving excuses of distance and time behind. The Internet is economics-neutral. It can be used by not-for-profit and for-profit organizations alike.

In the last year of the twentieth century, one half of the American economy was built around the communications industry. A significant part of that came from the Internet and World Wide Web. The elderly are not being left out. They belong to Internet clubs whose members exchange e-mail messages of every description: health and alternative medicine, nutrition and health foods, travel, world news, sports, dating, on-line pharmacies, religion, and e-trading of stocks, mutual funds, and futures.

Some Baby Boomers were raised on first generation Apple computers and DOS systems. My younger son oversees networking across the nation between his central corporate server and several hundred systems in corporate America. Brad is a mere thirty-five years old, and cyberspace will likely be a staple tool and fun toy for him for the next fifty years. All of our grandsons, none yet six years of age, are being introduced to educational games on the computer.

Cyberspace will demand a prominent place at the table, offering religious enrichment for the masses.

If American institutional religion is more and more becoming a smorgasbord of choices for the religious, then cyberspace will demand a prominent place at the table, offering religious enrichment for the masses. For years, older Americans have been among the most responsive to appeals to "return to nature," particularly in areas such as alternative medicine and natural foods. If they cannot get counsel on these subjects from traditionally trusted physicians, they now have access to close to twenty thousand web sites hawking every imaginable form of medicine, health food, and device designed to increase the length and quality of life.

Sale of Products

At present, most of the people making money from the Internet are those who sell a service or a product through personal or group-sponsored web pages. One Christian group based in Roanoke, Virginia, provides a server on which hundreds of ministries with their own web pages are advertised to a prescreened audience of a quarter of a million churches and Christian organizations.

Small businesses are able to subscribe to the federal government's Small Business Administration's ProNet that enables no-cost listing of one's products and services to over 260,000 businesses nationwide. Each subscriber is able to hyperlink to any other subscriber's web page. Christian-owned businesses are not excluded, and every visitor to the Christian owner's web site has the opportunity to read a message backed by biblical principles.

Executive Coaching and Mentoring

Retired executives have corporate clients whom they coach at standard coaching fees, starting at about fifty dollars for thirty minutes. Retired Christian executives have learned a lesson from the Senior Corps of Retired Executives (SCORE), which is sponsored by the U.S. Department of Labor's Small Business Administration.

Mentors can accommodate six or more mentorees, irrespective of where they are located. In 1997 the Open Text Listing identified three thousand web pages dedicated to mentoring. And on-line bookseller Amazon.com identified and accessed a worldwide listing of over eighteen thousand articles, books, chapters, newsletters, and references to mentoring and mentoring consultants and organizations. One professional mentor I know provides biblically-based counsel and guidance, illustrating the direction Christians will be moving in the next several years. He mentored a medical technician in a Middle Eastern Islamic nation on how to be a better father and husband, an American embassy trade specialist in a Pacific Rim nation on how to know God's purposes in her life, and three businessmen—one in California, another in Maryland, and the third in North Carolina. The gospel travels cyberspace.

Missionary Outreach

A church can extend its missionary outreach through support teams that provide counsel to missionaries. Prayer requests are received in moments; a prayer team is mobilized; transcriptions of the prayers and the team members are sent to the missionaries; answers to prayers are reported back to the host church. One missions coordinator for a national denomination agreed that mentoring by Internet is an excellent means of providing support to missionary couples who may be experiencing marital difficulties, early symptoms of burnout, or spiritual attacks in countries where Devil worship is frequent. Perhaps they are in need of technical assistance: linguistic clarification of an unfamiliar dialect, instructions for the repair of a generator or outboard motor, information on the culture, or information about other mission groups in an area.

Information Collection

The church seeking to develop practically any new ministry can use the Internet to access thousands of web pages. The range of information available is unimaginable, readily identifiable, usually free, and easily downloaded. Also available is the National Library of Medicine with its twenty five million medical articles, as well as other libraries with extensive literature on caregiver programs, a national registry of organizations providing services for the elderly, or detail-by-detail planning for retirement, including questionnaires on how to determine retirement options.

Required Skills

Anyone who has typing skills, a computer, monitor screen, keyboard, printer, and access to a phone line modem attachment can use the Internet. Several Internet services are free and most cost less than twenty-five dollars a month for unlimited use.

More enterprising older adults will use the Internet as the medium of choice to run an ever-growing number of remunerative services: travel agencies, billing, medical record transcription, literature search, spiritual guidance, computer-assisted architectural design, arts and crafts design, wedding invitations, greeting cards, and auctioning of almost any item imaginable. The face of advertising has been changed forever and anything that can be advertised over the Internet can be sold over the Internet.

Future Spirituality

Some observers suggest that 15 to 20 percent of Christians will get their spiritual enrichment from cyberspace by the year 2010. Many do so now. Practically every Christian organization of size is publishing devotional papers or theological essays on-line. More and more churches have web pages, and travelers can check for the church of their choice for Sunday worship before heading across country. E-mail chat rooms enable real-time communication among several people at the same time—an electronic home group.

I am not concerned here with whether the Internet takes the place of live fellowship and makes congregational gatherings obsolete (since Communion cannot be served, and laying on of hands and baptisms are excluded), but many people nevertheless receive benefits they either did not have before or are now expanding or improving upon.

The most important question that can be asked (and many have already asked it and are exploring answers) is how to use the Internet for the glory of God and to make His glory known in the earth. Older Christians on their creative tiptoes will take the time to explore alternatives, look beyond the usual obstacles and institutional hindrances, and exclaim in response to the spontaneous urgings of the Holy Spirit, "That's me, and I'm going to go for it!"

Inside the Halls of Power

My introduction to civilian government officials came after my discharge from the military in 1955 when I worked for a short time for International Christian Leadership. That experience whetted my appetite, so that when we moved to the Washington, D.C., area twenty years later, many opportunities came my way to lobby for or against legislation, some of it in the statehouse in Annapolis, Maryland, or on Capitol Hill. My wife and I had the privilege of working hard to see bad legislation killed and good legislation passed. Even in the northern Maryland county where we lived, we got a big kick out of working behind the scenes one year to stack every open candidacy for the parents and teachers association of the school system with committed Christians; to our joy, every one of our candidates won. It drove most of our non-believing friends crazy, but the kids benefited, at least for another year.

Jesus implored His disciples to be shrewd like serpents and innocent as doves (Matt. 10:16). This is the challenge every man and woman must face in order to carry a kingdom message into the halls of power. Over the years, I have often reflected on the kind of Christians who could best perform a gospel function among power brokers, and I have concluded they have to be people who, first and foremost, cannot be bought, controlled, intimidated, or blackmailed by others. I have written a book about those who have an Audience of One, and like the Lord, know from whence they came, who they are, and where they are going. So singular is their focus on God and His Christ that everything else is measured against a seasoned faith that does not come from youth and exuberance, but from years of deliberate, persistent, and consistent evaluation of people, policies, and programs against the higher standard of God's Word.

The Fellowship is a model for any church wanting to penetrate the halls of power with the gospel, knowing that many of those in positions of authority and influence may never enter the institutional church. The church has to be taken to them.

I am also convinced, despite the unending demands made on energy, sanity, and morals, that taking a kingdom message into the statehouses, the county courthouse, or onto Capitol Hill requires a skill and wisdom born of years of effort. Success belongs to those of seasoned shoulders. A man or woman must be summoned to this calling by the Lord who rules over all governments and who surveys and considers the nations as but a drop in the bucket. It is a holy calling as much as any other.

Harvest Evangelism

Ed Silvoso tells of the mobilization of church members in San Jose, California, and provides an exciting model applicable to prayer evangelism by older adult ministry.[1] The chiefs of police and fire departments were asked whether people representing the city's churches could individually or in small groups adopt police officers and firefighters. These groups would regularly pray for the officers' safety and bring coffee, donuts, cookies, and pizza to them during the night shift. Permission was granted, and within a year of beginning this program, the police department reported the lowest incidence of violent attacks, and the fire chief reported the lowest number of injuries from fighting fires. The kingdom had intruded into the affairs of local government and the gospel prevailed.

Armed with record-breaking success in San Jose, Silvoso took Harvest Evangelism to California's north central valley and the twin cities of Marysville and Yuba City. Again, members from numerous churches were mobilized, and a home canvass began. First, they would knock on the door: "Hello, we're from such and such a church, and we were wondering if there was some need you have that you would like us to pray for?" Over 80 percent of homes responded in the affirmative: "Yes, pray for us." From that point on, the Holy Spirit had the occasion to woo that household, and local church members stood ready to provide more ministry if requested.

The Fellowship

The membership of the Fellowship is unknown. It was started by a retired airlines pilot who was joined by an assortment of retired business executives and professionals. Christians from various doctrinal persuasions, the members respond to requests for mentoring from chiefs of state, cabinet-level secretaries, and high-ranking military officers. Their purpose is to apply biblical principles to every secular situation. The Fellowship is a model for any church wanting to penetrate the halls of power with the gospel, knowing that many of those in positions of authority and influence may never enter the institutional church. The church has to be taken to them.

International Christian Fellowship

When one reads of the prayer breakfasts at the White House, the House of Representatives, and the Senate, as well as many small unannounced Bible study and prayer cells scattered across all of Capitol Hill, one should think of International Christian Leadership. ICL convenes international conferences of Christian heads of state and other governmental leaders from around the world, but few give little thought to how it all began.

It was started by an old man who had already completed two careers and was beginning his third. The man was Abraham

Vereide, and few in modern days have had as significant and lasting an impact on the seats of power. Whenever men and women today hear of some notable elected leader espousing Christian principles from Capitol Hill or insisting on an amendment to a piece of legislation that calls for a more moral voice, Abraham Vereide's boldness likely played a role.

Vereide was first a circuit-riding Methodist minister from the wild country of Idaho, Wyoming, and Montana. He carried a Bible under one arm and a six-shooter ready for the draw in the other. Following his time as a minister, preacher, and evangelist, Vereide became General Secretary of Goodwill Industries, and brought it into the modern era. But it was after World War II that his third career began in a most inauspicious way on the steps of the U.S. Capitol in Washington, D.C.

He had memorized the names and faces of all the elected officials; he would wait on the steps of the Capitol. A senator would approach. The perfected routine was always the same, as if it had been scripted in Father's throne room:

> "Senator [name], my name is Abraham Vereide; may I ask you a question, sir?"
> "Yes."
> "Senator, do you believe in God?"
> "Well, yes."
> "Well, sir, do you then also believe that the Bible is the Word of God?"
> "Never thought about it that way, but yes."
> "Sir, do you know what the Bible says about your position and responsibilities as an elected official of this great country?"
> "Well, no."
> "Senator, will you give me permission to spend no more than fifteen minutes each week, at your convenience, sharing what God's word says about your place here in the seat of government?"

And then came the private mentoring sessions: one elected official at a time in the quiet of an office behind closed doors; then came the prayer breakfasts and, later, the international conferences of Christian world leaders.

CONCLUSION

I have deliberately chosen to discuss older adult ministries that were not capital-intensive, not because they are more impacting than those that attract lots of financial support, but because I wanted to deprive skeptics of any excuse for not creatively applying what God has deposited in them over a lifetime of work and experience. Spiritual deposits are necessary, but so are the natural deposits of skill, talent, leadership, and creativity. Every experience is a potential crucible in which positive character qualities are honed and negative ones are stripped from the man and woman of God. The older adult, by virtue of long years and the backup of the Master Planner, is the ideal minister in both religious and secular settings, and that is the heart of *Working the Gray Zone*.

NOTES

Chapter 1

1. J. I. Packer, et al., *The Bible Almanac* (Nashville, Tenn.: Thomas Nelson Publishers, 1980), 233. Also Herbert Lockyer Sr. gen. ed., *Illustrated Bible Dictionary* (Nashville, Tenn.: Thomas Nelson Publishers, 1986), 54.

2. I. Howard Marshall, et al., eds., *New Bible Dictionary* (Downers Grove, Ill.: Inter-Varsity Press, 3rd ed., 1996), 482.

3. Paul Billheimer, *Destined for the Throne* (Fort Washington, Penn.: Christian Literature Crusade, 1975).

Chapter 2

1. W. E. Vine, Merrill F. Unger, and William White, *Vine's Complete Expository Dictionary of Old and New Testament Words* (Nashville, Tenn.: Thomas Nelson Publishers, 1985), 51–52.

2. Some examples include: Isa. 40:26, 28, 42:5; Jer. 10:12–16; Ps. 33:6, 9, 90:2, 102:25; Job 38:4ff; Neh. 9:6; John 1:1; Acts 17:24; Rom. 1:20, 25, 11:36; Col. 1:16; Heb. 1:2, 11:3; Rev. 4:11, 10:6.

3. This discussion derives in part from Marshall, *Bible Dictionary*, 239–41.

4. John Calvin, *Institutes of the Christian Religion*, trans. Henry Beveridge (Grand Rapids, Mich.: William B. Eerdmans Publishing Co., 1997), 142–43.

5. Gen. 2:18, 21–22. See also discussion by Herbert Lockyer Sr., et al., *Nelson's Illustrated Bible Dictionary* (Nashville, Tenn.: Thomas Nelson Publishers, 1986), 261–62.

6. Rom. 2:3–10, 12:17–19; Packer, *Almanac*, 544.

7. Gen. 1:28; see Lockyer, *Nelson's*, 502.

8. Charles Hodge, *Systematic Theology* (Grand Rapids, Mich.: William B. Eerdmans Publishing Co., 1997), 2:96–102.

9. Ibid., 99.

10. Ibid., 101.

11. Ibid., 170.

12. 2 Cor. 4:4; Col. 1:15. These are primarily creedal passages, expressed agressively to counter the false or inadequate notions of Paul's audiences; see Marshall, *Bible Dictionary*, 500.

13. 2 Cor. 3:18 and 1 Cor. 15:49, as in F. F. Bruce, *Paul: Apostle of the Heart Set Free* (Grand Rapids, Mich.: William B. Eerdmans Publishing Co., 1977), 122.

14. Ibid., 420–23, 460.

Chapter 3

1. For example, polygyny—one husband with two or more wives—might have been tolerated as a cultural custom, but it was not a biblically prescribed one. Also, contrary to Abraham's marriage to his half-sister, Sarah, not only is that illegal in our culture, but it was eventually determined by God to be too close for marriage. See Gen. 20:12; Lev. 18:6,9.

2. Ps. 128:1,6; Prov. 3:1–2, 13–16; Ps. 34:11. Historical examples of challenges and threats to family stability have always existed. Select parts of this discussion are from J. I. Packer, *Almanac*, 411–19.

3. 1 Sam. 24:11; 2 Kings 1:12, 6:21; Gen. 45:8.

4. Matt. 10:30; Isa. 63:15–16; Hos. 11:1–3; Matt. 6:33; Exo. 20:12; Levi. 19:3; Deut. 5:16.

5. Vine, *Expository*, 78. 1 Sam. 8:4–21; 1 Kings 19:4; Jer. 35:6; 1 Chron. 24:19; 1 Kings 15:3; Josh. 24:3.

6. Packer, *Almanac*, 413.

7. Gen. 2:18; 3:24; Prov. 31:10–31.

8. 1 Tim. 5:10; Titus 2:4–5; Charles Simpson, ed., *The Covenant and the Kingdom* (Kent, England: Sovereign World, Ltd., 1995), 181–83.

9. Packer, *Almanac*, 413.

10. Ezek. 22:7; Prov. 19:26; Matt. 15:4–9.

11. Gen. 27; 2 Sam. 13: 1 Kings 2:19–25; 2 Chron. 21:4.

12. Job 12:12; Prov. 16:31; Ps. 92:12–15; Prov. 17:6.

13. Marshall, *Bible Dictionary*, 363.

14. Acts 16:15, 31–34; 1 Cor. 16:15; Acts 18:8; 1 Cor. 1:14–16; Rom. 16:23; 1 Cor. 16:19; Rom. 16:5; Philem. 1–2; Col. 4:15; Rom. 16:14–15.

15. Acts 5:42, 20:20; Col. 3:18–4:1; Eph. 5:22–6:29; 1 Pet. 2:18–3:7; Rom. 16:5; 1 Cor. 16:19; Col. 4:15; Philem. 2.

16. Marshall, *Bible Dictionary*, 363. See also Eph. 2:19; Gal. 6:10.

17. This is consistent with Eph. 4, where *pastor* was elevated to a ministry gift within the growing church.

18. Gen. 25:8; 1 Kings 12:8; Ps. 148:12; Prov. 17:6; Jer. 31:13; 1 Pet. 5:1, 5; Mark 7:3, 5; Heb. 11:2; Rev. 4:4; Lev. 19:32; 1 Tim. 5:1; 1 Kings 12:6–15; Prov. 4:1; 5:1.

19. Prov. 1:8, 2:1; Eph. 6:1–3; Deut. 5:16. See also Simpson, *The Covenant*, 213.

20. Rom. 3:20; Gal. 3:24; 2 Cor. 6:17; Exod. 20:12.

21. Calvin, *Institutes*, Book Second, 344–46.

Chapter 4

1. Luke 15:4–10. See Kenneth E. Bailey, *Poet and Peasant* and *Through Peasant Eyes* (Grand Rapids, Mich.: William B. Eerdmans Publishing Co., 1976), 142–56. Bailey's cogent analysis answers the frequent question, "Why would the shepherd leave the ninety nine and go after the one?" He didn't; he left them with the other shepherds who cooperated in herding the larger flock of sheep! And when the lone shepherd returned at night, lamb in tow, the other shepherds joined in rejoicing because "that which was lost has been found."

2. Exod. 18; Ruth 1–3; 2 Kings 3; 1 Sam. 19:18–20; 2 Kings 2:15, 4:38, 6:1.

3. Charles Oakes, *Mentoring for an Audience of One*, (Columbus, Ga.: Christian Life Publications, 1998), 5.

4. Marshall, *Bible Dictionary*, 305–6.

5. Num. 19:12, 21:2, 22:15, 25:7; Josh. 20:4; 1 Sam. 8:4ff; 2 Sam. 5:3; 2 Kings 8:1, 3; 1 Kings 20:71, 21:8; 2 Kings 10:1, 19:2, 23:1; Eze. 8:1; 14:1; 20:1.

6. Exod. 20:12. Marshall, *Bible Dictionary*, 18.

7. 1 Tim. 5:2; 1 Pet. 5:5; see also Lockyer, *Nelson's*, 18.

8. Exod. 19:7; Judg. 21:16; the most thorough recent study of elders and eldership is to be found in Alexander Strauch, *Biblical Eldership: An Urgent Call to Restore Biblical Church Leadership* (Littleton, Colo.: Lewis and Roth Publishers, 1995), from which portions of this discussion derive.

9. Philo, Hypothetica 7:13; Luke 2:46; John 9:22, 12:42, 16:20; Matt. 23:34; Mark 13:9; Acts 22:19, 26:11; Luke 13:14; Acts 13:15; Luke 4:20.

10. Marshall, *Bible Dictionary*, 954.

11. Strauch, *Eldership*, 125.

12. Ibid.

13. Matt. 23:8; 1 Pet. 5:1; 2 John 1; 3 John 1; 1 Cor. 11:23; 15:1, 3; 2 Thess. 2:15; 3:6; 2 Tim. 2:2; Acts 14:23; Titus 1:5; Acts 6:6; 11:30; 1 Tim. 4:14; 5:22; 2 Tim. 1:6.

Chapter 5

1. Gen. 25:1–11, 27:27–29, 48:8–22, 49:1–33.

2. Deut. 33; Josh. 22:6–7; Luke 24:50; Gen. 1:22–23; see also Lockyer, *Nelson's*, 185–86.

3. Deut. 11:26; Prov. 10:22; 28:20; Isa. 19:24; Deut. 33, 11:27.

4. Ps. 24:5, 133:3; 2 Sam. 7:29; Ps. 3:8.

5. Ps. 133:3; Vine, *Expository*, 18–19.

6. Gary Smalley and John Trent, *The Blessing* (New York: Pocket Books, 1990), 36–37.

7. Luke 1:64, 2:28, 24:51; James 3:9; Heb. 6:7; 12:17; 2 Cor. 9:5; Rom. 15:29; Eph. 1:3; Marshall, *Bible Dictionary*, 143; Vine, *Expository*, 69–70.

8. Lev. 16:21, 22; Gen. 48:14; Num. 27:18–23.

9. Luke 4:40; Acts 28:8; Mark 16:17, 18; Mark 10:16. This discussion in part derives from Patricia Beall Gruits, *Understanding God and His Covenants* (Detroit, Mich.: Rhema Incorporated Publishers, 1985), 206–10.

10. Strauch, *Eldership*, 78.

11. 1 Tim. 1:18; 4:14; 1 Thess. 5:19. A complete discussion of this is found in Bill Hamon, *Prophets and Personal Prophecy—God's Prophetic Voice Today* (Shippensburg, Penn.: Destiny Image Publishers, 1987).

12. Henri J. M. Nouwen, *The Return of the Prodigal Son* (New York: Doubleday, 1994).

13. V. Raymond Edmund, *The Disciplines of Life* (Wheaton, Ill.: Victor Book Division of SP Publications, 1948), 45–53.

14. Rom. 5:3–5; 1 Pet. 1:6–7; James 1:2–4.

15. James A. Michener, *The Source* (New York: Random House Publishers, Balentine Books, 1965).

Chapter 6

1. Prov. 16:31, 20:29; Ps. 92:12–15; Job 12:12; Ps. 91:16.

2. Deut. 4:40, 5:33; Prov. 3:1, 2, 10:27; Eph. 6:2, 3.

3. For further discussion on the distinction between *thelema* and *boulema* and the hermeneutics of guidance, see Dan McCartney and Charles Clayton, *Let the Reader Understand: A Guide to Interpreting and Applying the Bible* (Wheaton, Ill.: Victor Books, SP Publications, Inc., 1994), 252–54.

4. 2 Kings 2:15; 4:38; 6:1. For a historical discussion on this, see Hamon, *Prophets*.

5. George Matheson, *Thoughts in Life's Journeys* (London: James Clarke and Co., 1907), 266–67.

Chapter 7

1. Paul Billheimer, *Don't Waste Your Sorrows* (Fort Washington, Penn.: Christian Literature Crusade, 1977), 8.

2. Ibid., 9.

3. Marshall, *Bible Dictionary*, 265–67.

4. See also Vine, *Expository*, 56.

5. Bruce, *Paul*, 67.

6. Ibid., 309–10. See also 1 Cor. 15:15f.

7. See Robert L. Thomas, consulting editor to the Introductions to the Individual Books of the New Testament, *New American Standard Bible*, *The Open Bible Edition* (Nashville, Tenn.: The Lockman Foundation, 1976), 1112.

8. Billheimer, *Sorrows*, 10–11.

9. Calvin, *Institutes*, vol. 2, 25–30, 31–35.

10. Ibid., 25.

11. Ibid.

12. Donald McCullough, *The Trivialization of God* (Colorado Springs, Colo.: NavPress Publishing Group, 1995).

13. Herbert Schlossberg, *Idols for Destruction—The Conflict of Christian Faith and American Culture* (Wheaton, Ill.: Crossway Books Division of Good News Publishers, 1990).

14. Calvin, *Institutes*, 26.

15. Ibid., 28.

16. Ibid.

17. Ibid., 29.

18. Ibid., 35.

19. Ibid.

Chapter 8

1. Peter L. Berger, *The Noise of Solemn Assemblies: Christian Commitment and the Religious Establishment in America* (Garden City, New York: Doubleday, 1961), 40f; see also Jeffrey K. Hadden, *The Gathering Storm in the Churches* (Garden City, New York: Doubleday, 1969), 221.

2. George Barna, *The Second Coming of the Church* (Nashville, Tenn.: Word Publishing, 1998), 5–7.

3. Schlossberg, *Idols*, 235–41.

4. Gal. 5:19–21; James 1:6, 8–9; see also Helmut Schoeck, *Envy* (Indianapolis, Ind.: Liberty Press, 1966, 1970, 1987), 316–17.

5. Will Durant, *The Story of Civilization: The Renaissance* (New York: Simon and Schuster, 1953), 5:607–8.

Introduction to Part 2
1. Schlossberg, *Idols*, 139.
2. C. S. Lewis, *God in the Dock* (Grand Rapids, Mich.: William B. Eerdmans Publishing Co., 1970), 96.
3. Charles Oakes, *Foundations of Practical Gerontology*, 2nd ed. (Columbia, South Carolina: University of South Carolina Press, 1967), 1973.
4. John Rowe and Robert Kahn, *Successful Aging* (New York: Pantheon, 1998).

Chapter 9
1. Edmund Sinnott, *Biology of the Spirit* (New York: The Viking Press, 1955).
2. Ray Beeson and Ranelda Mack Hunsicker, *The Hidden Price of Greatness* (Wheaton, Ill.: Tyndale House Publishers, Inc., 1991).
3. Edmund, *Disciplines,*
4. Anders Nygren, *Agape and Eros* trans. Philip S. Watson (Philadelphia, Penn.: The Westminister Press, 1953).

Chapter 10
1. I define "discipline" broadly to mean any experience which tries and tests us in the context of Hebrews 12.
2. Tim Stafford, *As Our Years Increase—Loving, Caring, Preparing: A Guide* (Grand Rapids, Mich.: Pyranee Books, Zondervan Publishing House, 1989).
3. Arthur H. Becker, *Ministry with Older Persons* (Minneapolis, Minn.: Augsburg Publishing House, 1986), 22–28.
4. Ibid., 198–204.
5. Barna, *Second Coming*, 29–39.
6. Walter M. Abbott, ed., "Excerpts from the Documents of Vatican II," *Ethical and Religious Directives for Catholic Health Care Services* (Washington, D.C.: American Press, 1955).
7. Becker, *Ministry*, 105.

Chapter 11
1. Ralph Mattson, *Visions of Grandeur* (Chicago, Ill.: Praxis/Moody, 1994), 163.

Chapter 12
1. Burt Nanus, *Visionary Leadership* (San Francisco, Calif.: Jossey-Bass Publishers, 1992).
2. Barna, *Second Coming*, 114–18.
3. Mattson, *Visions*, 66–93.

Chapter 13
1. Keith Miller, *Habitation of Dragons* (Waco, Texas: Word Books, 1970), 91–94.
2. Bobb Biehl, *Mentoring: Confidence in Finding a Mentor and Becoming One* (Nashville, Tenn.: Broadman and Holman Publishers, 1996).
3. Howard Hendricks and William Hendricks, *As Iron Sharpens Iron: Building Character in a Mentoring Relationship* (Chicago, Ill.: Moody Press, 1995).

Chapter 14
1. Ed Silvoso, *That None Should Perish* (Ventura, Calif.: Regal Books Division of Gospel Light, 1994).

BIBLIOGRAPHY

Abbott, Walter M., ed. *Ethical and Religious Directives for Catholic Health Care Services*. Washington, D.C.: American Press, 1955.

Bailey, Kenneth E. *Poet and Peasant*. Grand Rapids, Mich.: William B. Eerdmans Publishing, 1976.

————. *Through Peasant Eyes*. Grand Rapids, Mich.: William B. Eerdmans Publishing, 1976.

Barna, Geroge. *The Second Coming of the Church*. Nashville, Tenn.: Word Publishing, 1998.

Becker, Arthur H. *Ministry with Older Persons*. Minneapolis, Minn.: Augsburg Publishing House, 1986.

Beeson, Ray and Ranelda Mack Hunsicker. *The Hidden Price of Greatness*. Wheaton, Ill.: Tyndale House Publishers, Inc., 1991.

Berger, Peter L. *The Noise of Solemn Assemblies: Chrisian Commitment and the Religious Establishment in America*. Garden City, New York: Doubleday, 1961.

Biegel, David E. and Arthur Blum, eds. *Aging and Caregiving*. Newbury Park, Calif.: Sage Publications, 1990.

Biehl, Bobb. *Mentoring: Confidence in Finding a Mentor and Becoming One*. Nashville, Tenn.: Broadman and Holman Publishers, 1996.

Billheimer, Paul E. *Destined for the Throne*. Fort Washington, Penn.: Christian Literature Crusade, 1975.

————. *Don't Waste Your Sorrows*. Fort Washington, Penn.: Christian Literature Crusade, 1977.

Bruce, F. F. *Paul: Apostle of the Heart Set Free*. Grand Rapids, Mich.: William B. Eerdmans Publishing Company, 1977.

Calvin, John. *Institutes of the Christian Religion*. Translated by Henry Beveridge. Grand Rapids, Mich.: William B. Eerdmans Publishing Company, 1989.

Durant, Will. *The Story of Civilization: The Renaissance*. New York: Simon and Schuster, 1953.

Dychtwald, Ken. *Age Wave*. Los Angeles, Calif.: Jeremy P. Tarcher, Inc., 1989.

————. *Wellness and Health Promotion for the Elderly*. Rockville, Md.: Aspen Publishers, Inc., 1986.

Edmund, V. Raymond, *Disciplines of Life*. Wheaton, Ill.: SP Publications, Inc. 1948.

Enns, Paul. *The Moody Handbook of Theology*. Chicago, Ill.: Moody Press, 1989.

Evashwick, Connie J. and Lawrence J. Weiss, eds. *Managing the Continuum of Care*. Rockville, Md.: Aspen Publishers, 1987.

Fries, James F. *Aging Well*. Reading, Mass.: Addison-Wesley Publishing Company, Inc., 1989.

Gallo, Joseph, William Riechel, and Lillian Anderson, eds. *Handbook of Geriatric Assessment*. Rockville, Md.: Aspen Publication, 1988.

Gilford, Dorothy M., ed. *The Aging Population in the Twenty-first Century*. Washington, D.C.: National Academy Press, 1989.

249

Gruits, Patricia Beall. *Understanding God and His Covenants*. Detroit, Mich.: Rhema Incorporated Publishers, 1985.

Hadden, Jeffrey K. *The Gathering Storm in the Churches*. Garden City, New York: Doubleday, 1969.

Hamon, Bill. *Prophets and Personal Prophecy—God's Prophetic Voice Today*. Shippensburg, Penn.: Destiny Image Publishers, 1987.

Hendricks, Howard and William Hendricks. *As Iron Sharpens Iron: Building Character in a Mentoring Relationship*. Chicago, Ill.: Moody Press, 1995.

Hodge, Charles. *Systematic Theology*. Grand Rapids, Mich.: William B. Eerdmans Publishing Company, Reprinted 1997.

Institute of Medicine. *Care of the Elderly Patient*. Washington, D.C.: National Academy Press, 1989.

Institute of Medicine. *The Second 50 Years—Promoting Health and Preventing Disability*. Washington, D.C.: National Academy Press, 1990.

Kane, Rosalie A. and Robert L. Kane. *Long-Term Care*. New York: Springer Publishing Company, 1987.

Krout, John A., ed. *Providing Community-Based Services to the Rural Elderly*. Thousand Oaks, Calif.: Sage Publications, 1994.

Lewis, C. S. *God in the Dock*. Grand Rapids, Mich.: William B. Eerdmans Publishing, 1970.

Lockyer, Herbert, Jr. *Illustrated Bible Dictionary*. Nashville, Tenn.: Thomas Nelson Publishers, 1986.

Lockyer, Herbert, Sr. *Nelson's Illustrated Bible Dictionary*. Nashville, Tenn.: Thomas Nelson Publishers, 1986.

Marshall, I. Howard. *New Bible Dictionary*. Downers Grove, Ill.: InterVarsity Press, 1996.

Matheson, George. *Thoughts in Life's Journeys*. London: James Clarke and Co., 1907.

Mattson, Ralph. *Visions of Grandeur*. Chicago, Ill.: Praxis/Moody, 1994.

McCartney, Dan and Charles Clayton. *Let the Reader Understand: A Guide to Interpreting and Applying the Bible*. Wheaton, Ill.: Victor Books, SP Publications, Inc., 1994.

McCullough, Donald W. *The Trivialization of God*. Colorado Springs, Colo.: NavPress Publishing Group, 1995.

Michener, James A. *The Source*. New York: Random House Publishers, 1965.

Miller, Judith Ann. *Community-Based Long-term Care*. Newbury Park, Calif.: Sage Publications, 1991.

Miller, Keith. *Habitation of Dragons*. Waco, Tex.: Word Books, 1970.

Nanus, Burt. *Visionary Leadership*. SanFrancisco, Calif.: Jossey-Bass Publishers, 1992.

National League for Nursing. *Indices of Quality in Long-Term Care Research and Practice*. New York: 1989.

National League for Nursing. *Strategies for Long-Term Care*. New York: 1988.

Nouwen, Henri J. *The Return of the Prodigal Son*. New York: Doubleday, 1994.

Nygren, Anders. *Agape and Eros* trans. by Philip S. Watson. Philadelphia, Penn.: The Westminster Press, 1953.

Oakes, Charles. *Foundations of Practical Gerontology*, 2nd ed. Columbia, S.C.: University of South Carolina Press, 1967.

————. *Mentoring for an Audience of One*. Columbus, Ga.: Christian Life Publications, 1998.

Packer, J. I. *The Bible Almanac*. Nashville, Tenn.: Thomas Nelson Publishers, 1980.

Parkes, Colin Murray. *Bereavement*. New York, N.Y.: International Universities Press, Inc., 1972.

Persily, Nancy Alfred, ed. *Eldercare*. Chicago, Ill.: American Hospital Publishing, Inc., 1991.

Pocinki, Karen McCrory, ed. *Resource Directory for Older People*. Bethesda, Md.: National Institute on Aging, 1989.

Prevention Magazine Health Books, eds. *Future Youth*. Emmaus, Penn.: Rodale Press, 1987.

Ramm, Bernard. *Protestant Biblical Interpretation*. Third Revised Edition. Grand Rapids, Mich.: Baker Book House, 1970.

Rowe, John and Robert Kahn. *Successful Aging*. New York: Pantheon, 1998.

Sanders, J. Oswald. *Your Best Years*. Chicago, Ill.: Moody Press, 1982.

Schlossberg, Herbert. *Idols for Destruction*. Wheaton, Ill.: Crossway Books, 1990.

Shelton, Phyllis. *Long-term Care Planning Guide*. Nashville, Tenn.: Shelton Marketing Services, Inc., 2000.

Shock, Nathan W., et al., eds. *Normal Human Aging: The Baltimore Longitudinal Study of Aging*. Bethesda, Md.: National Institutes of Health, 1984.

Silvoso, Ed. *That None Should Perish*. Ventura, Calif.: Regal Books Division of Gospel Light, 1994.

Simpson, Charles. *The Covenant and the Kingdom*. Kent, England: Sovereign World, Ltd., 1995.

Sinnott, Edmund. *Biology of the Spirit*. New York: The Viking Press, 1955.

Smalley, Gary and John Trent. *The Blessing*. New York: Pocket Books, 1990.

Springer, Dianne and Timothy H. Brubaker. *Family Caregivers and Dependent Elderly*. Newbury Park, Calif.: Sage Publications, 1984.

Stafford, Tim. *As Our Years Increase—Loving, Caring, Preparing: A Guide*. Grand Rapids, Mich.: Zondervan Publishing House, 1989.

Strauch, Alexander. *Biblical Eldership*. Littleton, Colo.: Lewis and Roth Publishers, 1995.

Thomas, Robert L., ed. *New American Standard Bible, The Open Bible Edition*. Nashville, Tenn.: The Lockman Foundation, 1976.

Vine, W. E., Merrill F. Unger, and William White. *Vine's Complete Expository Dictionary of Old and New Testament Words*. Nashville, Tenn.: Thomas Nelson Publlishers, 1985.

FURTHER READING

Arn, Winn and Charles Arn, *Catch the Age Wave*. Grand Rapids, Mich.: Baker Book House, 1993.

Carlson, Dosia. *Engaging in Ministry with Older Adults*. Bethesda, Md.: The Alban Institute, 1997.

Chinen, Allan B. *In the Ever After: Fairy Tales and the Second Half of Life*. Wilmette, Ill.: Chiron Publications, 1989.

Clements, William M., ed. *Ministry with the Aging: Designs, Challenges, Foundations*. New York, N.Y. Harper and Row Publishers, 1981.

Cole, Thomas R. *The Journey of Life: A Cultural History of Aging in America*. New York, N.Y.: Cambridge University Press, 1992.

Cole, Thomas R. and Mary C. Winkler, eds. *The Oxford Book of Aging: Reflections on the Journey of Life*. New York, N.Y.: Oxford University Press, 1994.

Fecher, Vincent John, *Religion and Aging*. San Antonio, Tex.: Trinity University Press, 1982.

Fischer, Kathleen. *Autumn Gospel: Women in the Second Half of Life*. Mahwah, N.J.: Paulist Press, 1995.

Fischer, Kathleen R. *Winter Grace: Spirituality for the Later Years*. Mahwah, N.J.: Paulist Press, 1985.

Fischer, Kathleen. *Winter Grace: Spirituality and Aging*. Nashville, Tenn.: Upper Room Books, 1998.

Gentzler, Richard H. Jr. and Donald F. Glingan. *Aging: God's Challenge to Church and Synagogue*. Nashville, Tenn.: Discipleship Resources, 1996.

Halverson, Delia. *Leading Adult Learners: Handbook for All Christian Groups*. Nashville, Tenn.: Abingdon Press, 1995.

Hiltner, Seward, ed. *Toward a Theology of Aging*. New York, N.Y.: Human Sciences Press, 1975.

Hunter, Carlita. *Gray Hair and I Don't Care: Leading Activities with Older Adults*. Harrisburg, N.C.: Hunter House Productions, 1990.

Kimble, Melvin A. and Susan H. McFadden, et al, Eds. *Aging, Spirituality, and Religion: A Handbook*. Minneapolis, Minn.: Fortress Press, 1995.

Koenig, Harold G. *Aging and God: Spiritual Pathways to Mental Health in Midlife and Later Years*. Binghampton, N.Y.: The Haworth Press, Inc., 1994.

Koenig, Harold G. and Andrew J. Weaver. *Counseling Troubled Older Adults: A Handbook for Pastors & Religious Caregivers*. Nashville, Tenn.: Abingdon Press, 1997.

LeFevre, Carol and Perry LeFevre, Eds. *Aging and the Human Spirit: A Reader in Religion and Gerontology*. Chicago, Ill.: Exploration Press, 1981.

Levin, Jeffrey S. *Religion in Aging and Health*. Thousand Oaks, Calif.: Sage Pub. Co., 1993.

Lustbader, Wendy. *Counting on Kindness: The Dilemmas of Dependency*. New York, N.Y.: Free Press, 1993.

Morgan, Richard L. *Autumn Wisdom: A Book of Readings*. Nashville, Tenn: Upper Room Books, nd.

Morgan, Richard L. I *Never Found That Rocking Chair: God's Call at Retirement*. Nashville, Tenn: Upper Room Books, nd.

Morgan, Richard L. *No Wrinkles on the Soul: A Book of Readings for Older Adults*. Nashville, Tenn.: Upper Room Books, nd.

Morris, Virginia. *How to Care for Aging Parents: A Complete Guide*. New York, N.Y.: Workman Publishing. 1994.

National Clergy Leadership Project to Prepare for An Aging Society. *Incline Your Ear and Apply Your Mind to Knowledge: A Congregational Resources Book*. Washington, D.C.: National Interfaith Coalition on Aging, National Council on Aging, 1995.

Nouwen, Henri J. M. and Walter J. Gaffney. *Aging*. Garden City, N.Y.: Doubleday, 1974.

Paul, Susanne S. and James A. Paul. *Humanity Comes of Age: The New Context for Ministry with the Elderly*. Geneva, Switzerland: WCC Publications, 1994.

Ryan, Roy H. and Richard H. Gentzler. *Guiding Adult Ministries*, "Guidelines for Leading Your Congregation 1997–2000 Series." Nashville, Tenn.: Abingdon Press, 1996.

Sapp, Stephen. *Full of Years*. Nashville, Tenn.: Abingdon Press, 1987.

Seeber, James J. *Spiritual Maturity in Later Years*. Binghampton, N.Y.: Haworth Press, 1990.

Seymour, Robert. *Aging Without Apology*. Valley Forge, Pa.: Judson Press, 1995.

Shaw, D. B. *Spiritual Biography in Early America*. Princeton, N.J.: Princeton University Press, 1968.

Simmons, Henry. *Pastoral Responses to Older Adults and Their Families: An Annotated Bibliography*. Westport, Conn.: Greenwood Press, 1992.

Swenson, Harriet Kerr. *Visible and Vital: A Handbook for the Aging Congregation*. Mahwah, N.J.: Paulist Press, 1994.

Taylor, Blaine. *The Church's Ministry with Older Adults*. Nashville, Tenn.: Abingdon Press, 1984.

Thibaut, Jane Marie. *A Deepening Love Affair: The Gift of God in Later Life*. Nashville, Tenn.: Upper Room Books, nd.

Thomas, Eugene and Susan A. Eisenhandler, Eds. *Aging and the Religious Dimension*. Westport, Conn.: Auburn House, 1994.

Tibbits, Clark, Ed. *Handbook of Social Gerontology: Societal Aspects of Aging*. Binghampton, N.Y.: Haworth Press, 1994.

Tobin, Sheldon S., James W. Ellor, and Susan Anderson-Ray. *Enabling the Elderly: Religious Institutions within the Community Service System*. Albany N.Y., SUNY Press, 1986.

Wulff, David. *Psychology of Religion: Classic and Contemporary Views*. New York, N.Y.: John Wiley and Sons, 1991.

ABOUT THE AUTHOR

Author, academician, management consultant, gerontologist, and entrepreneur, Charles Oakes spent forty years in the secular marketplace and fifty-five years studying the Bible for its relevance to the affairs of everyday life. Dr. Oakes received graduate training at the University of California, Berkeley, and Stanford and Emory Universities. He has been on the teaching and research faculties of the University of Tennessee College of Medicine and Duke University Medical Center. This book represents an integration of his training as a behavioral scientist and management consultant to arrive at a practical application of biblical gerontology, and derives from many years of having designed and developed programs benefiting over 45,000 older adults nationally. He is the recipient of the coveted Ross Laboratories Award for Excellence in Community-Based Long Term Care. More information is available from www.perfecting-purpose.com.

Carolyn, his wife, is trained as a medical social worker and geriatric case manager and has been a constant companion and colleague in business and professional pursuits and in guiding their two sons, Mark and Brad, who also have successful business careers.